Get Fresh!

get fresh!

How to cook a kumquat and other useful tips

for more than 100 fruits and vegetables

Madeleine Greey

Macmillan Canada
Toronto

Colour photographs of the squash and hot peppers that appear within this book are reprinted with permission by Melissa's/World Variety Produce and Faye Clack Marketing and Communications.

First published in Canada in 1999 by Macmillan Canada, an imprint of CDG Books Canada

Copyright © 1999 Madeleine Greey 1999

Canadian Cataloguing in Publication Data
Greey, Madeleine, 1957–
    Get Fresh! : how to cook a kumquat and other useful tips for more than 100 fruits and vegetables
Includes index.

ISBN 0-7715-7601-3
1. Cookery (Fruit). 2. Cookery (Vegetables).
3 Fruits. 4. Vegetables.
1. Title.
TX811.G743 1999   641.64   C98-932513-X

This book is available at special discounts for bulk purchases by your group or organization for sales promotions, premiums, fundraising and seminars. For details, contact: CDG Books Canada Inc., 99 Yorkville Avenue, Suite 400, Toronto ON, M5R 3K5.

We acknowledge the financial support of the Government of Canada through the Book Publishing Industry Development Program for our publishing activities.

2 3 4 5 6 TRI 03 02 01 00

Cover and interior design:
Counterpunch/Peter Ross
Cover illustration: Laurie Lafrance
Back-cover photograph: Donald Nausbaum

Macmillan Canada
An imprint of CDG Books Canada Inc.

Printed in Canada

To the best purple dog in the whole wide world.

Acknowledgements

Embarking on a book can be both exhilarating, and absolutely terrifying. It is one thing to talk about an idea, but quite another thing to *do* it. First, thanks goes to my agent, Karen O'Reilly, for believing in this project and swiftly placing me in the arms of Macmillan Canada, where I have received guidance and encouragement from my editor, Nicole de Montbrun.

Yet, were it not for the dedication of my cousin, Lorraine Greey, *Get Fresh!* would never have moved beyond an idea and into the tough reality of research, writing and creative cooking. Graceful persistence, wise insight and generous humour are just some of Lorraine's gifts. Debbie Diament, my recipe tester, has provided meticulous, professional testing, balanced by invaluable insights on taste, presentation and technique. Thanks to Debbie's persistence, the *Get Fresh!* recipe schedule stayed on track.

Many friends kindly offered up their kitchens, time and taste buds for this project. Thanks is due to Yanina Jezek, Julia Lee, Melanie Lovering and Susan Pedwell. I also want to pay tribute to the outstanding palate of my neighbour and friend, Nora Brooks. Also, thanks goes to my mentor, colleague and friend, Cynthia David, who has helped my food-writing career more than anyone else. The Canadian Produce Marketing Association, Foodland Ontario, Faye Clack Marketing & Communications Inc. and a host of other fresh produce associations have generously provided much needed information and research.

But as any mother-who-works-out-of-a-home-office knows, the people who have made the biggest sacrifice are my family. My husband, Don Nausbaum is my number one taste tester. He has braved more disasters than masterpieces, yet still keeps a smile on his face. His steadfast support and love have filled my sails. My daughter Krystal is a huge fan of broccoli and blueberries, while my son Nicholas has seemingly sworn off fresh produce for life. I love them to bits.

Many, many others have helped bring *Get Fresh!* to life. You know who you are. Rest assured that the next time we meet, I'll nudge you again to eat more fruits and vegetables.

Contents

Introduction

I believe that most people want to eat more fruits and vegetables – but don't know how. Of course, most of us know how to munch on an apple or peel a potato . . . but when we try to move beyond the familiar and into the unknown, we get confused and give up.

The problem with fruits and vegetables is that they don't come with a set of instructions, like so many other foods do today. We've become so accustomed to checking the panel on the side of a box or can that when we're face-to-face with a fruit or vegetable we've never met before, we get a little shy.

That's why I say "get fresh!" Take a chance and pick up a stranger in the produce section. Once you're home, you can look it up in this book and get to know each other a lot better.

Humour aside, I promise you this: *Get Fresh!* will give you the confidence to go into a store and buy a fruit or vegetable that you've never bought before. If you read about it first, then you'll know how to buy the freshest, ripest one. Or, you can take a leap of faith and buy something you know nothing about. Once you're home, *Get Fresh!* will tell you what to do with it. Whether it's getting your best mileage in the storage bin, finding out what parts of a vegetable to trim, or learning new tricks with cabbage – all are covered in this book.

But getting fresh is more than just good tasting food. Fresh fruits and vegetables offer vital protection against heart disease and cancer. They are bursting with vitamins, minerals, fibre and phytochemicals that help safeguard your health. All this important information can be found in these pages.

So go ahead, take a walk on the wild side and *Get Fresh!* more often.

Fruits

Apples

When our ancestors said "an apple a day keeps the doctor away" they knew what they were talking about! But little did they know then that the doctors they were talking about were actually heart surgeons and oncologists. Modern research has revealed that the pectin in apples lowers cholesterol and the quercetin (a flavonoid) protects against cancer. It's quite a mouthful.

Looks like/Tastes like

There are 7,000 different kinds of apples, and the apple tree is the most heavily cultivated fruit tree in the world. Here's how to tell the difference between a Mutsu and an Empire.

The **McIntosh** reigns supreme as one of the most popular apples. It originated in Ontario and was discovered by John McIntosh in 1811 in Dundela in what is now Ontario. This apple has a deep red colour on a green background. The white flesh is tart to sweet. It's right for eating and cooking, but don't bake it whole.

Look for five distinctive bumps at the base and a deep red colour, and you've found a **Red Delicious**. It's slightly elongated, has crisp, white, sweet flesh, and is best eaten whole or tossed in a salad.

The **Granny Smith** was first grown in Australia and is now the darling of the California apple crop. It's large and bright green, with sweet-tart, crisp flesh that makes it per-fect for eating out of hand, and for putting in pies and applesauce.

The **Empire** is a newer variety, with a dark red blush skin and cream-coloured flesh. Do everything with it except use it for baking. **Idared** arrives at Christmas with bright red skin and greenish-yellow patches. The tart-to-sweet flesh is white and firm, making it a good apple for a salad, eating fresh, or put-ting in a pie.

The **Mutsu** is another newcomer. It's a cross between a Golden Delicious and a Japanese apple. The greenish-yellow skin has an orange blush. The tart-to-sweet flesh is white and firm, making it a good apple for eating fresh or in a salad, or putting in a pie.

The **Golden Delicious,** like its cousin Red, has five distinctive bumps and an elongated shape. The skin and flesh are yellow. The tart-to-sweet flesh keeps its shape while cooking, so it is a good, all-purpose apple.

The **Spartan** has dark red skin with white, crisp, sweet-tart flesh. Eat it fresh, try it in a Waldorf salad or put it in a pie.

The **Cortland** is one apple that doesn't turn brown after it has been cut, and it's per-fect for everything except baking whole. Look for a red blush skin with white, crisp flesh and a mildly sweet flavour.

If you want to make a pie, turn to **North-ern Spy**. Its firm, yellowish flesh is perfect for baking. This red-striped apple is also fine in applesauce or baked whole, but most peo-ple don't like to eat it fresh.

Other apples to watch out for are **Royal Gala**, **Rome Beauty**, **Jonathan** and **Fuji**, to name just a few!

Select it

To buy the best apple, look for those that are firm and hard with tight skins. You don't want an apple that has a broken or blemished skin. If you are picking apples right from the tree, here's a tip: turn the apple upside down while it's still attached to the tree. If the apple snaps off the stem easily, it's ready and ripe. If it doesn't, leave it on the tree.

Store it right

Apples love it cold. In fact, if they aren't kept cold, they'll become overripe and mealy in as little as 2 or 3 days. So store your apples in a plastic bag in the fridge. They'll keep for up to 6 weeks. As they ripen, all fruits emit ethylene gas, which speeds up the process. Apples (and bananas) give off large amounts that can affect the ripening process of other fruits that are kept in close proximity. Thus, always store apples in a separate plastic bag in your fridge and, if possible, keep apples and other fruit in separate crispers. If you have a large amount, store them in a cool, dark, well-ventilated place such as a fruit cellar or garage. Apples don't freeze well, which doesn't matter because they're available fresh year-round. It's also easy to dry your own apples. Cortland apples stay whiter than other varieties, but all apples can be dried. Core, peel and slice them into thin rings. Place in a cool oven (150°F/66°C) with the door ajar for 30 minutes. Turn off the oven, close the door and leave the apples to dry overnight. In the morning, store them in an airtight container.

Prep it right

Apples need thorough washing and scrubbing, especially if you are eating them unpeeled and fresh. Since many apples are treated with pesticides or are lightly waxed, it makes sense either to peel them or buy organically grown fruit. (Remember, the peel is full of many nutrients and fibre.) You can eat an apple out of hand – everything is edible except the core and seeds. Or you can peel an apple and core it. Apple corers are inexpensive tools and handy to have, especially if you are baking with apples. To prevent apples from browning, brush with lemon or lime juice or drop the slices into acidulated water (3 tablespoons/45 mL of lemon juice to 1 quart/1L of water).

Tips

Apple butter is simply cooked-down applesauce with lots of spices. It contains no butter and is low in fat.

Add apples instead of sugar when cooking. For instance, a few apples added to cranberry sauce reduces the amount of sweetener required. Ditto with rhubarb and other tart fruits.

Culinary destinations

Glaze your next pork tenderloin with a combination of homemade applesauce, mustard, vinegar and curry powder. Try grating some apples into a meatloaf or meatballs. Add apples to a pilaf, put them in poultry stuffing or add them to a stir-fry. Apples even work in a salsa – try them combined with pears, lime juice, garlic, green onion and fresh coriander. The next time you make a cheese melt, slip some apple slices under the cheese before you broil it. Marinate apple rings in some Italian dressing and grill briefly on the barbecue. When it comes to desserts, the sky's the limit, whether it's baked apples stuffed with dried fruit (see recipe), apple cobbler or apple fritters.

To your health
The best thing in an apple is its fibre, and about one third of that fibre is found in the skin. For instance, one small apple contains 2.8 mg of fibre. Once peeled, it contains 1.9 mg. Apples are low in calories, too (only 80 calories in a medium apple). There's almost no sodium in an apple but it does contain some potassium, which is good news to those with high blood pressure. Apples contain other nutrients in small or trace amounts: vitamins A and C, calcium, iron, thiamin and boron.

Apples are an excellent source of pectin, a soluble fibre that lowers blood cholesterol – especially LDL or "bad" cholesterol. Apples also help relieve both constipation and diarrhea. There's an abundance of flavonoids in apples, particularly quercetin, which may help regulate blood cholesterol and prevent diabetes-related eye damage. A Finnish study revealed in 1997 that quercetin in apples can protect against many common types of cancer, including breast and lung. Apples have been a traditional remedy for arthritis, rheumatism and gout, and scientists believe that quercetin's antioxidant powers may have something to do with that. The boron in apples is also attracting interest among researchers, who are tentatively calling it a phytoestrogen, possibly able to relieve menopause symptoms and protect against calcium loss. And apples are often called "nature's toothbrush" as they increase saliva flow and reduce the build-up of cavity-causing bacteria.

Quick ways
If you've never tried sangria with white wine, now's the time. In a pitcher combine one bottle of dry, white wine from Portugal or Spain (such as Vino Verde) with 2 ounces (56 mL) Southern Comfort, 2 peeled and chopped McIntosh or Empire apples and ¼ cup (60 mL) of sugar. Chill 1 hour and serve.

Apricots

One of the first tender fruits to appear in summer, apricots are a fruit-lover's dream come true – they're high in nutrients and low in calories. While Nature teases us with only a few weeks of fresh local apricots, dried apricots can fill the long gap in between seasons.

Looks like/Tastes like

Apricots have a velvety, bright orange skin, with a rose or peach blush. Smaller than a peach, they are roughly the same size as plums, averaging about an ounce (28 g) in weight.

Select it

New apricot varieties have been designed to travel better from farm to store. But buyer beware. Apricots do not ripen further once picked: they will get softer, but not sweeter. Avoid rock-hard fruits or any tinged with green. Apricot varieties range in colour from yellow to bright orange, but the colour or blush does not necessarily affect flavour. If you can smell a little fragrance, you're on the right track. The flesh should yield to gentle pressure and the fruit should have a smooth, velvety skin without spots or bruises.

Store it right

Store apricots at room temperature away from direct sunlight until they are soft. Ripe fruit should be stored uncovered in the fridge and will last up to a week.

The easiest way to freeze apricots is the dry-pack method. Peel and slice 4 cups (1 L) of apricots and arrange on a baking sheet. Mix ¼ teaspoon (1 mL) of ascorbic acid powder and ¼ cup of white sugar in a small bowl. Sprinkle this mixture evenly over the sliced fruit. Freeze until solid. (It takes a few hours.) Transfer the fruit to a freezer bag as soon as it's solid, to prevent freezer burn. Keep frozen up to 6 months.

Prep it right

Don't wash apricots until you are ready to eat them. To remove the pit, slice around the seam (along the length of the fruit), twist the top half over the lower half to separate and lift out the pit. To remove the skin, blanch apricots in boiling water for 1 minute, remove with a slotted spoon and transfer to a bowl of ice water. Once cool, the skin should slip off the apricot with the aid of a sharp knife.

Culinary companions

Apricots are compatible with a surprising range of flavours. They work with rosemary, thyme and mint, and with sweet spices such as cinnamon, cloves, ginger and cardamom. Try serving apricots with Cointreau or Grand Marnier. Nuts such as walnuts, pistachios and almonds also taste terrific with apricots. Many cheeses complement the taste of fresh apricots, particularly brie, Camembert, Roquefort, sweet Gorgonzola and aged cheddar.

Culinary destinations

Slice apricots over a bowl of cereal or yogurt. Make a fresh apricot salsa to serve with grilled fish or chicken. Skewer peeled apricot halves in between marinated lamb cubes and sliced onions to make a nouvelle kebab. Toss diced apricots into rice, barley or bulgur pilafs. Try them in stuffings, with couscous dishes or in a glaze for baked ham.

To your health

There are only 48 calories in three fresh apricots. Ounce for ounce, you get more nutrition when you choose dried apricots over fresh. But dried apricots contain more calories than fresh ones do.

Fresh apricots are an excellent source of beta carotene. Three apricots supply 26 per cent of the Recommended Daily Intake (RDI). The deeper the colour of the apricot, the more beta carotene it contains. Apricots are also a source of vitamins C and E, potassium and dietary fibre.

The beta carotene and vitamin C in apricots are two antioxidant vitamins that may help prevent cancer and heart disease. Apricots (especially dried) are high in potassium, which helps normalize blood pressure and heart function. The boron found in apricots may help prevent osteoporosis by helping post-menopausal women retain estrogen, facilitating calcium absorption. Those allergic to apricots are often also allergic to almonds, cherries, peaches and plums.

Quick ways

It's easy to poach apricots in the microwave. Simply cut 6 apricots in half and remove the pits. Place in a microwave-safe bowl and cover with water or orange juice spiked with Grand Marnier or Cointreau. Add some whole cloves, cinnamon stick, cardamom and a little brown sugar if you like. Cook covered, on high, for 4 to 5 minutes, turning halfway through. Remove with a slotted spoon and slip off the skins. Serve warm or chilled with the sauce.

Trivia

That apple in the Garden of Eden could have really been an apricot after all. Apricots have been around since biblical times, originating in China thousands of years ago.

Bananas

Ask any fresh produce manager what moves off the shelves faster than the speed of light and the answer will make you go bananas! That's right. The average Canadian eats two bananas a week, or about 29 pounds (13 kg) a year.

Looks like/Tastes like

The biggest-selling banana is the common, yellow **Cavendish,** also known as the dessert banana. There are more than 300 varieties of bananas grown around the world. Many of these lesser-known varieties are now called boutique bananas – they look great in a fruit bowl, are perfectly packaged for children and can be cooked just like regular bananas.

Baby bananas (also known as **Ladyfinger, Mysore, Ninos, dwarf** and **Chicaditas**) are smaller than a Cavendish and considerably sweeter, with a denser texture.

Lemon bananas (also known as **burro bananas**) are small, chunky bananas imported from Mexico. They have a faint, lemon flavour.

Likewise, **apple bananas** (also known as **Manzanos**) taste a bit like apples or strawberries. They're not as sweet as regular bananas, are about half the size and have golden flesh.

Red bananas (also known as **red Cubans** or **Colorados**) turn a purplish red when ripe. They have sweet, creamy flesh often

tinged with orange or pink and sometimes flecked with fine black dots.

Select it

You'll find bananas sold at all different stages of ripeness – green, yellow, brown-flecked and even black. Buy according to when you want to eat them and how you like them. All the bananas in a bunch will ripen at the same time. If you see bananas being sold at different stages of ripeness, separate big bunches into small bunches and take home a variety so you can have perfect bananas all week long. Look for plump, evenly coloured bananas and avoid those with a greyish caste – they've been chilled accidentally and won't ripen properly.

Store it right

Always store unripe bananas at room temperature away from heat or direct sun. Never store unripe bananas in the fridge – cold temperatures interrupt the ripening cycle and ruin the fruit. To speed up ripening, place bananas with an apple in a brown paper bag.

Once ripe, bananas can be stored in the fridge. Although the skins will turn dark, the fruit won't be affected and will keep nicely for about 3 days.

Bananas freeze well. Store ripe, firm bananas in the freezer. Peel, pierce on a wooden skewer and wrap in plastic. Kids love this frozen treat (especially if it has been dipped in chocolate). Mashed ripe banana can be stored in an airtight, freezer-safe container.

When bananas are overripe, don't throw them out – freeze them instead. Peel them and wrap in plastic, or leave them unpeeled and pack in a freezer bag.

Prep it right

Just peel a banana and it's ready to go! A potato masher is handy when mashing bananas. However, you can use the blender or food processor to achieve the same results.

Culinary destinations

While bananas are most commonly eaten out of hand, they have excellent cooking potential, too. Bananas are delicious in quick breads, muffins, cakes, puddings and pancakes. Add them raw and sliced to a peanut butter sandwich or on top of cereal. Green bananas can be braised, boiled, steamed and fried in savoury dishes just like plantains. Try them with rum, chocolate, cashews, oranges and other culinary companions.

To your health

If you could only eat one fruit, make it a banana – your body will thank you. One medium banana contains 105 calories, and 0.5 g fat and is low in sodium. Bananas are high in potassium, an excellent source of vitamin B^6, and a source of vitamin C, magnesium and folate.

Bananas are popular with athletes. They are considered the ultimate "recharge food" because almost 100 per cent of a banana's calories come from carbohydrates. Many athletes will reach for a banana because potassium helps to control body fluid and also regulates the heartbeat and blood pressure.

But bananas aren't just for athletes. They're easy to digest, making them the food of choice for infants and the elderly. Loaded with pectin, bananas are a natural cure for diarrhea, plus they help replace lost potassium caused by diarrhea or vomiting. Potassium-rich bananas may also offer protection from strokes and heart disease. And many women swear by bananas to relieve pre-menstrual stress because of their high vitamin B^6 content.

Quick ways

Baked bananas are easy to make, offering intense flavour with little work. Simply place unpeeled, firm-ripe bananas on a baking sheet covered with foil or parchment paper and bake at 325°F (160°C) for an hour. Or place them on the grill until completely blackened. Spoon the hot, creamy baked flesh on top of ice cream, yogurt, fresh farmer's cheese or marscarpone, sprinkle with some chopped peanuts and enjoy!

Tip

As they ripen, all fruits give off ethylene gas, which speeds up the process. Like the apple, the banana produces an exceptionally large amount. For this reason, think of the banana when you want to get another fruit to ripen faster. Put a banana in a brown paper bag with a green tomato or hard avocado and you'll see results.

Blackberries

Much confusion surrounds the blackberry. People confuse it with black raspberries, or they get their loganberries mixed up with their boysenberries! It's time to clear up the blackberry air and get the scoop on these luscious summertime orbs.

Other names

Blackberries are often called dewberries, which are actually another species that grows in Europe.

Looks like/Tastes like

Blackberries look like big black raspberries but here's how you can tell them apart. Look at the interior of the berry. If it has a white core, it's a blackberry. If the core is hollow, it's a raspberry. When ripe blackberries are picked, the green hull comes off, but the edible white core stays intact. Blackberries also have a firmer texture than raspberries.

There are many different varieties of the blackberry. Two of the most common cultivated varieties are loganberries and boysenberries. Ironically, **loganberries** are the oldest cultivated variety even though they aren't even black! They are dark red and quite tart, best paired with sweeter berries or used in preserves. **Boysenberries** have a deep maroon colour and their tart, aromatic flavour make them a favourite in pies. Despite the name, the **evergreen** is actually black and glossy – but it's quite mild and not very tart. Try sprucing it up with lemon juice and sugar. Other varieties include **Cherokee**, **Marion** and **Ollalie**.

Select it

Look for uniform colour and a gloss or sheen. The little sacs (druplets) should be big and plump, and large in relation to the white inner core. Avoid any boxes that are stained, indicating crushed berries. Watch for signs of mould (little white dots) – it can spread like the plague and ruin a box of berries in no time.

Store it right

Pick through the box before you store it and remove any damaged, crushed or mouldy berries. Store them unwashed, in a single layer, loosely covered with a paper towel under plastic wrap. Blackberries last for only 1 to 3 days in the fridge.

Blackberries freeze well, and last up to 6 months. Wash the berries and dry them thoroughly with paper towels. Spread them out in a single layer on a baking sheet and flash-freeze until frozen solid (about 1 hour). Transfer to a freezer bag. Berries do not need to be defrosted before using.

Prep it right

Wash blackberries gently and quickly, and never soak them in water. Or use a flower mister and spray berries lightly. Blot dry with paper towels.

Eat your blackberries out of hand, or pour fresh cream, whipping cream, crème fraîche or yogurt over them. Try them on ice cream or use them to make your own ice cream. Garnish a lemon or lime sorbet with blackberries. Blackberries, especially tart ones, are perfect for preserves, be they jams, jellies, compotes or chutneys.

Culinary companions

Cinnamon, nutmeg, allspice, cloves or ginger work with blackberries. Complementary fruits include cranberries, pink grapefruit and apples. Mint, fresh coriander and lime are all good partners for blackberries, too.

Culinary destinations

Purée blackberries to put in a vinaigrette, marinade or to make a sweet dessert coulis. Blackberries make a nice cold soup, especially when paired with melon and mint. Think of blackberries in crepes, sweet omelettes or pancakes. Try them with fresh farmer's cheese or marscarpone.

To your health

Among all the berries, blackberries are tops for fibre. A 1-cup (250-mL) serving has 7 g of fibre, supplying about one quarter of your daily fibre needs. A 1-cup (250-mL) serving of blackberries is high in vitamin C, supplying 32 mg or half your daily needs. Blackberries are also high in folate and are a source of potassium, as well as small amounts of iron and calcium.

Blackberries contain high concentrations of anthocyanins, deep-coloured pigments belonging to the flavonoid family. Anthocyanins have been shown in studies to have numerous health benefits, such as preventing cancer and heart disease, controlling diabetes, improving circulation, reducing eye strain and even combatting the loss of memory and motor skills associated with aging. Blackberries contain another valuable, cancer-fighting substance called ellagic acid. Heat does not destroy this acid, so a mouthful of blackberry jam or pie is as beneficial as a mouthful of fresh berries.

Blackberries contain salicylates, which can cause an allergic reaction in people who are sensitive to aspirin.

Trivia

The loganberry is named for Judge J.H. Logan, the original breeder of the plant developed in California in 1881.

Blueberries

The indigo hues of a just-sliced piece of blueberry pie are a sight to behold. And when the edges of a neighbouring scoop of vanilla ice cream turn a pastel violet, it becomes an edible piece of art. Long live blueberries!

Looks like/Tastes like

These small, round, bead-sized berries have a smooth skin and deep blue colour. The juicy interior tastes sweet and tart.

"Wild" or "low bush" blueberries are native to North America and are smaller than so-called cultivated, or high-bush blueberries. Actually, both types are cultivated, but it wasn't until 1920 in New Jersey when the high-bush variety was introduced. High-bush plants produce bigger, firmer berries. Some people prefer the larger ones, which are more succulent. But the wild, smaller berries tend to have a more intense flavour and are better suited for baking than their high-bush cousins.

Select it

Look for firm, dry, plump berries that are free of leaves and stems. Blueberries should have a powdery look on the surface, called a "bloom," which indicates freshness. The older the blueberry the more faded the bloom. Search out blueberries that are uniformly blue in colour. If they are reddish or have a reddish tinge, pass them up – they're not ripe and won't ripen any further. Overripe berries appear dull and watery.

Store it right

Blueberries have the best fridge-life of all berries. Stored unwashed and loosely covered, they can last up to 2 weeks. Blueberries stored for too long look wrinkled due to dehydration.

Blueberries freeze well. The secret to proper freezing of blueberries, like all berries, is to make sure they are completely dry before freezing. Spread in a single layer on a baking sheet in the freezer until solid. Transfer to a freezer bag or container and the berries will last up to 6 months.

Prep it right

To wash or not to wash, this is the question among blueberry lovers. The anti-washers maintain that washing removes a blueberry's protective bloom – but if you plan to eat them right away, that doesn't matter. Never soak berries in water, for they soak up water like a sponge and lose their flavour. Give a quick and gentle wash under running water or spray thoroughly with a flower mister, drain and then blot dry with paper towels. Another cleaning option is to roll blueberries gently in a clean, lightly dampened tea towel to remove surface dust and dirt.

Culinary companions

Cinnamon, ginger, mint and black pepper all work with blueberries. Lemon and orange juices are complementary, as is Cointreau. Maple syrup and even molasses add an interesting component to blueberries, too.

Culinary destinations

Move over blueberry pie and make room for a blueberry and melon salsa, corn and blueberry relish, blueberry vinaigrette, blueberry marmalade, blueberry and spinach salad, blueberry and peach crisp, blueberry-banana bread or blueberry smoothies... the possibilities are endless.

To your health

Some fruits and vegetables aren't that high in vitamins and minerals, but contain fibre or phytochemicals that contribute to health. Blueberries are a case in point. These blue orbs contain vitamins C and A, but in relatively small amounts. Low in calories, blueberries have only 40 calories in a ½ cup (125 mL) serving.

When it comes to fibre and phytochemicals, this berry stands out. Blueberries are loaded with pectin, a soluble fibre that can help relieve diarrhea. As well, blueberries, especially wild, low-bush blueberries, have high concentrations of anthocyanins, a deep-coloured pigment belonging to the flavonoid family. Anthocyanins have been shown in studies to have numerous health benefits, such as prevention of cancer and heart disease, controlling diabetes, improving circulation, reducing eye strain and even combatting loss of memory and motor skills associated with aging. Finally, blueberries, like cranberries, are beneficial in treating and preventing urinary tract infections. In 1998, Rutgers University scientists reported in the *New England Journal of Medicine* that blueberries and cranberries contain chemical compounds called condensed tannins that were found to prevent bacteria from attaching to cells in the urinary tract and causing infection, expecially in women.

Cactus Pears

The taste of cactus pears hasn't really caught on in Canada, but it's one of the world's most widely grown and popular fruits. With more than 300 varieties and lots of different names, cactus pears are as common to the rest of the world as apples are to us!

Other names

This fruit comes under many an alias. The most popular name – other than cactus pear – is prickly pear. But Spanish speakers call it "tuna" and it's "sabra" in Hebrew. Other names include Barbary fig, Indian fig and Indian pear.

Looks like/Tastes like

Cactus pears really look like the offspring of a cactus. They have leathery, firm skin dotted by a regular pattern of spine follicles (the spines are mechanically removed before the fruit is shipped to stores). A cactus pear is between 3 and 4 inches long and egg-shaped. The colours of the skin and flesh vary dramatically. Depending on the variety, you'll come across cactus pears with a green, yellow, orange, pink or crimson skin. The flesh may be green, yellow or red, and is soft and spongy. Cactus pear contains many black seeds, which are edible. It tastes like watermelon, with hints of pomegranate, strawberries or cherries. The flavour is sweet, with no acidity.

Select it

Look for cactus pears that are tender but not squishy. They are ripe when they are slightly tender. The best specimens are deeply coloured, not faded. Avoid cactus pears with mouldy spots – chances are the interior is mushy and unpalatable.

Tip

When buying cactus pears, it's wise to use a paper bag to protect your hands when handling the fruit from any sharp spines. They can irritate the skin. Although the spines are removed mechanically before being shipped, a few always elude the machines. Chances are they will elude your eyes, too, since they are nearly invisible.

Store it right

Ripen firm fruit at room temperature. But be careful: as soon as they ripen, they can deteriorate quickly if not refrigerated immediately. Ripe cactus pears, in a plastic bag, will last up to week in the refrigerator. Cactus pear purée freezes well. Store it in a freezer bag or freezer-safe container for up to 6 months.

Prep it right

Due to the risk of spines, cactus pears are best handled with thick rubber gloves. Alternately, you can use tongs or impale the fruit on a fork while peeling. To peel, first cut off a thin slice at each end of the pear. Then make four, lengthwise, skin-deep incisions. Use your gloved fingers or a knife or fork to peel back the skin and the underskin to reveal the fruit. The flesh can be sliced, cubed or puréed. Once puréed, pass it through a sieve to remove seeds and strings.

Cactus pear can be eaten raw or cooked. Try it straight, enhanced by a squirt of lemon or lime juice. Or put it in fruit salads, beverages, desserts and preserves. It also teams up well with grilled poultry and fish, whether in a cooked sauce or as a raw garnish. Deglaze a pan with cactus pear purée, white wine and a little sugar to create a sumptuous sauce for chicken breasts or pork medallions.

Culinary companions

Cactus pear complements many other fruits, especially citrus. Orange, grapefruit, lemon and lime juice are all great with cactus pear. Also, try it with banana, kiwi, melons or berries. Sweeten it with honey or brown sugar, or perk up the taste with almond extract or vanilla. Use Latin American seasonings (red pepper flakes, onion, garlic, fresh coriander and lime juice) and you can't go wrong. Cactus pear also has a special affinity with rum, gin or vodka.

Culinary destinations

Make it into a salsa to accompany grilled fish or poultry. Try it in preserves. Cactus pears can make a brilliant ruby-coloured jelly. But most of all, think of it as a beverage fruit. Try it in smoothies, milkshakes and even cocktails.

To your health

Cactus pear is low in calories. There are 40 calories in a 100 g serving. It's a good source of fibre, especially if you eat the seeds. Cactus pear is also a source of vitamin C, calcium and potassium.

Mexican Indians and early Spanish settlers drank cactus pear juice to bring down a fever.

Quick ways

Take two, peeled cactus pears, purée, then remove the seeds and strings by passing the purée through a sieve. Add the juice of one lemon, and sugar to taste. Add carbonated mineral water to create a nonalcoholic cactus pear spritzer, or spike it with an ounce or two of vodka.

Trivia

In Israel, the word "sabra" has a double meaning. While it directly translates to "cactus pear," it is also used to describe the Israeli temperament: prickly on the outside and sweet on the inside.

Cherries

Life is a bowl of cherries when these tender, juicy, sweet morsels of summer come into season. And if you're really feeling young and reckless, go outside and see how far you can spit the pit!

Looks like/Tastes like

There are an estimated 1,000 different varieties of cherries. They fall under two species, sweet and sour. (In Ontario, they don't like to call them sour, but Red Tart.)

The two main types of sweet cherries are defined by colour: either dark-red to purple or yellow. **Bing** is considered "king" by most sweet cherry connoisseurs. It is large, meaty, sweet and firm with a rich, crimson-purple colour that verges on black at peak ripeness. **Lambert** is a smaller, heart-shaped red cherry closely resembling Bing in taste and texture. Others include **Van**, **Chapman**, **Larian** and **Black Republican**. Among yellow cherries, **Rainier** is the best known – it sometimes has a pinkish tinge to its skin and is quite sweet. **Montmorency** is the most common variety of sour cherry grown.

Select it

When buying sweet cherries, look for plump, firm cherries with green stems. Avoid sticky cherries, for they are overripe and leaking their juice. Good colour is important. A sweet cherry should have a deep red or yellow colour.

Store it right

Pick through your cherries and discard crushed ones before their juice spoils the fruit around them. Refrigerate as soon as possible. Chilling not only preserves cherries, but also improves their flavour. Store on a plate or in a bowl lined with paper towel. Cover loosely.

Prep it right

Rinse in cool water and drain on paper towels. Cherries look best with the stem still attached. You can purchase a cherry-pitter gadget (olive pitters do the same job), which makes removing the pit easier and cuts down on waste, too. Or cut a cherry in half and pry the pit out with the tip of a knife.

Sweet cherries can be eaten out of hand, sprinkled into pancakes, scattered over breakfast cereal, tossed into muffin recipes or even made into a sweet, cold soup. Try them in pies, glazes, fruit salads, sauces for grilled meats and jams. You can also poach cherries briefly in water, fruit juice or wine until just heated through (1 to 3 minutes). Sour cherries are too tart to eat on their own, so use them in pies, jams, sauces or pancakes. Pair them up with sweeter fruits such as peaches or apricots and make a crisp or cobbler. Try them in a chutney or salsa.

Culinary companions

Besides the obvious – ice cream, whipping cream and yogurt – cherries go well with fresh ginger, lemon juice and chutney-like ingredients (vinegar, raisins, ground coriander, curry powder, cinnamon, cloves, nutmeg and black pepper). Try them with soft, unripened cheeses or a splash of balsamic vinegar. Almond extract and orange zest are other good companions.

Culinary destinations
Put some pitted sweet cherries in a blender and whirl with some yogurt or silken tofu and you've got a breakfast shake. Poach some cherries with orange juice, fresh ginger and balsamic vinegar, and serve over chicken breasts. Substitute sweet cherries for strawberries on shortcake or angel food. Try some sweet cherries in a sweet omelette or crepe, pair them with a soft, unripened cheese for a classy finish to a meal or sprinkle them on vanilla ice cream.

To your health
One cup (250 mL) of sweet cherries contains 140 calories while sour cherries contain 126 calories. Both are a source of vitamins A and C and potassium. Sour cherries contain more beta carotene than their sweet cousins.

An American study found cherry juice to be a potent antibacterial agent in the fight against tooth decay. The study showed that cherry juice could block up to 89 per cent of the enzyme activity leading to plaque formation.

Cherries are rich in pectin, a soluble fibre that has cholesterol-lowering powers. Anthocyanins are found in cherries; these flavonoids are linked to prevention of cancer and heart disease. Cherries, especially their juice, have long been considered a folk remedy for gout. Unfortunately, many people are allergic to cherries and develop hives or a tingling and itching feeling around the mouth. Those allergic to cherries are often also allergic to almonds, apricots, peaches and plums, which all belong to the same family. Introduce these fruits slowly and carefully to babies over 12 months old.

Trivia
The small and very sour **Maraschino** cherry originated in Yugoslavia. Modern-day processors often use a sweet yellow cherry called **Royal Ann**. The cherry is transformed into the familiar red or green fruit after being pitted and bleached by the addition of syrup, bitter almond oil and food colouring.

Ontario Red Tart Cherries
Something very special and very sour happens in Ontario every summer. Ontario Red Tart cherries are pie cherries that grow in the Niagara Peninsula and in southwest and central Ontario. The season commences in July but you won't find them for sale in the produce section . . . you have to order them through your supermarket produce manager. Ontario Red Tart cherries are sold (sweetened, chilled and already pitted) in 10-pound (5-kg) pails. Use them immediately or freeze them in quantities of 2 to 4 cups (500 mL to 1L). These cherries are highly perishable and only last 4 days in the fridge. Eat or freeze right away.

Cranberries

While these hollow red orbs are too tart to eat out of hand, their sharp, distinct flavour can inspire creativity in the kitchen. Don't confine these berries to cranberrry sauce at Thanksgiving. Try cranberries in baking, preserves and even savoury dishes throughout the year.

Other names

The Pilgrims called them crane berries, but we're not sure why. Some say it's because cranes feed on these berries, but others say it's because the arched blossoms of the cranberry plant resemble a crane's silhouette. Another popular alias is bog ruby because cranberries grow in swamps. Less commonly, the cranberry is called a cow berry.

Looks like/Tastes like

The cranberry is a shiny, hollow red berry that's larger than a blueberry but smaller than a cherry. There are four major varieties that vary a little in size and colour, but generally speaking they all taste the same. The colour ranges from pink to deep, lacquer red. It's a hard, durable berry. The inner flesh is white and contains small, brown seeds.

Select it

Most cranberries are sold in 12-ounce (340-g) plastic bags, which limits your ability to select the finest berries. Peer through the bag and look for plump, firm, dry berries with good, clear colour. Avoid shrivelled specimens. If you spot cranberries sold loose, give them the bounce test: if a few don't bounce when you throw them on a hard surface, dont buy them.

When you're buying dried cranberries, look in bulk and health food stores. They're sometimes called "craisins" and they're so sweet that you can eat them out of hand. Or use them like raisins in baked goods.

Store it right

Cranberries store well. Fresh cranberries will keep from 4 to 6 weeks in a plastic bag in your refrigerator crisper. Frozen cranberries will keep for up to a year in the freezer. Simply pour them into a freezer bag and freeze. No need to defrost before using them.

Prep it right

Before using cranberries, discard any that are soft, discoloured or withered. Pluck off stems and rinse quickly in a sink full of water. Drain.

You can chop cranberries in a food processor fitted with a metal blade. Cranberries are never eaten raw, but are very easy to cook. Steam or boil whole cranberries until they pop. If you cook them longer, they'll turn to mush and become bitter.

Quick ways

Cranberry sauce is a cinch to make from scratch. Add 1 cup (250 mL) of sugar to 1 cup (250 mL) of water and bring to a boil in a saucepan. Add one 12-ounce (340-g) package of fresh or frozen cranberries (3 cups/750 mL) to the water and bring it back to a boil. Gently boil for about 7 to 10 minutes or until the cranberries pop. Cover and cool completely at room temperature, then refrigerate. You can reduce the sugar content by adding apples, pears, peaches or berries to the sauce and cutting back on the added sugar. They will naturally sweeten things up.

Tips

To prevent cranberry sauce from boiling over, add 1 teaspoon (5 mL) of vegetable oil to the mix.

A ¼ teaspoon (1 mL) of baking soda added to cranberries while cooking neutralizes some of the fruit's natural acidity, resulting in less required sugar.

Culinary destinations

Glaze your next chicken with ginger, orange juice and cranberry sauce, or put some cranberries in couscous with fresh mint. Make a wild rice pilaf with cranberries and pecans, or try some cranberries in rice pudding. While cranberries are great in jellies and sauce, consider cranberry and jalapeño salsa or cranberry and red wine relish. Tuck some cranberries into your next batch of bran muffins. Shortbread cookies become a gourmet event when they contain cranberries, thyme and rosemary.

To your health

One cup (250 mL) of raw cranberries contains 46 calories, is high in dietary fibre (4 g) and is a source of vitamin C. Most commercial cranberry products (such as juice and sauce) contain a lot of sugar and are high in calories.

In 1994, a Harvard study published in the *Journal of the American Medical Association* confirmed what many of us have been saying all along: drinking cranberry juice can help cure or prevent urinary tract infections. Research now confirms that chemical compounds called condensed tannins (found in both cranberries and blueberries) prevent bacteria from attaching to cells in the urinary tract and causing infection, especially in women. Cranberries also contain ellagic acid, a cancer-fighting phytochemical that doesn't break down when cooked.

Currants

Whenever I think of currants, I think of jelly bags stained blood-red by a mass of crushed, cooked currants on their way to becoming glistening, ruby-coloured jelly. When I was young, my mother and grandmother used to steam up the windows and fill the house with a glorious, sweet berry smell as they went about their jelly-making. The adults ate the jelly alongside roast chicken and we children slathered it on cream cheese sandwiches.

Other names

Black, red and white currants are sometimes confused with grape currants, but the two types are not related. The former is a berry, the latter a grape. The confusion arises from the fact that currant berries grow like grapes in bunches or clusters, but on bushes, not vines. In some parts of Europe, red and white currants are called gooseberry currants.

Looks like/Tastes like

In Ontario, the most common currant is the **black currant**. It is slightly larger than red and white currants and has a purplish-black skin. Black currants actually belong to a different species than the more closely related red and white currants. Black currants have a distinct fragrance and robust flavour. The French make crème de cassis liqueur from this berry and it's a popular juicing berry in Ontario.

Red currants look like shiny, red rubies and last longer than black currants. **White currants** are the sweetest of the bunch. They are translucent, varying in colour from cream to off-white to a buttery yellow. The **Jostaberry** is a hybrid of the gooseberry and blackcurrant. It looks like a black currant, but has a slightly different flavour.

Select it

Check your box of currants carefully before buying it. Look for juice stains on the bottom, which indicates split or squashed currants. Fresh currants should have a gleaming colour and firm, taut skin. They should be firmly attached to the cluster stems, not falling off.

Store it right

Store currants in the fridge, loosely covered with a paper towel or vented plastic wrap. They are easy to freeze. Remove the stem, wash and dry thoroughly, and then place on a baking sheet and freeze until solid. Transfer to a freezer bag and freeze up to a year.

Prep it right

To make the chore of stemming easier, slip a fork under the currants and pull.

You can eat currants raw, but they are sour and require some sweetening – team them up with other berries or sweet fruits for best results. Currants are best known as a preserving fruit; they star in jellies and jams. Black currants are popular in juices and syrups. All currants make a stunning garnish.

Culinary companions
Black, red and white currants go well with sugar and honey, citrus juice or zest, tarragon or thyme, apples and oranges, and vanilla.

Culinary destinations
Treat currants like other berries: they go into pies, flans, cheesecake, fools and puddings. Currants are famous in Austrian tortes, British summer pudding and Scandinavian cold soups. Their tart taste make currants a perfect foil for rich meats, be they duck, goose, pork or game. Try them in a turkey stuffing or as a sauce on venison. You can toss currants into a salad or use a purée instead of vinegar in a salad dressing. Or enjoy a simple dessert course with brie, apples and currants.

To your health
Black currants have more to offer nutritionally than their red and white cousins. One cup (250 mL) of black currants contains 202 mg of vitamin C, which is more than three times the Recommended Daily Intake (RDI). In comparison, red and white currants contain 45 mg of vitamin C per cup (250 mL), which still makes them an excellent source, but just one quarter of the astounding amount of vitamin C found in black currants. Likewise, black currants contain more iron, calcium and potassium than red and white, although all three are a source of these important minerals.

Long before vitamins were discovered, Europeans turned to black currants to relieve sore throats – not surprisingly, given the fact that these berries are loaded with vitamin C. Moreover, both red and black currants contain anthocyanins, with black currants containing as much as 16 times more than red, making them an excellent source on par with wild blueberries. Anthocyanins have been shown in studies to have numerous health benefits, such as preventing cancer and heart disease, controlling diabetes, improving circulation, reducing eye strain and even combatting the loss of memory and motor skills associated with aging.

All three are all high in pectin, which makes currants perfect for preserves but also vital to your health. Pectin is a soluble fibre that can lower blood cholesterol. It can also relieve and prevent diarrhea.

Quick ways
This berry sauce tastes fine on roast turkey, pork tenderloin or grilled chicken: Take 2 cups (500 mL) each of raspberries and black currants. Mix with ½ cup (125 mL) of water and 1 ½ cups (375 mL) of sugar. Add 1 teaspoon (5 mL) each of fresh tarragon and thyme. Bring to a boil and simmer lightly until soft. Serve warm.

Feijoa

Ask anyone what a feijoa tastes like and you're bound to hear a different answer from every person you ask – if they've heard of it. While this fruit is often referred to as pineapple guava, many say that it tastes nothing like a pineapple. But most agree that it has a pungent taste with a eucalyptus-menthol twist. Then there are the other flavours it evokes: lemon, strawberry, grape, quince, even banana. Taste it for yourself!

Other names

Pineapple guava, Brazilian guava and guavasteen are other popular and confusing names for a fruit that is not a true guava. The name is pronounced several different ways to further confuse matters: "fay-YO-ah," "fay-JOE-ah" and, in New Zealand, "fee-JOE."

Looks like/Tastes like

Feijoas are egg-shaped and small, only about 3 inches (8 cm) long. The thin, slightly bumpy skin can be anywhere from olive to lime green. Often, it has a white, powdery bloom. Inside, the flesh is white, tan or pale yellow with black, edible seeds in a central cavity (which is also edible) and gelatinous in texture. A ripe feijoa is a mixture of sweet and tart flavours. It's also aromatic and juicy. The texture is slightly granular, not unlike a pear.

Select it

Follow your nose when shopping for feijoa. When the fruit is ripe, you'll detect a full bouquet of floral fruitiness. Choose fruit that is free of cracks, blemishes and soft spots. A feijoa is ripe when the flesh is no longer firm and gives like a ripe tomato or plum. The skin has turned dark green and the perfume is fragrant.

Store it right

You can store firm, unripe feijoa at room temperature until it is ripe. Speed up ripening by placing it in a paper bag with a banana or apple. Once ripe, the fruit can last for a few days in a plastic bag in the refrigerator. You can freeze puréed feijoa for up to 6 months.

Prep it right

Everything about a feijoa is edible, although not to everyone's taste. The skin can be bitter and many people don't like to eat the seeds. You can eat a feijoa out of hand, or slice it in half lengthwise and scoop out the flesh with a spoon. Feijoa can also be peeled and sliced into wedges. Cut feijoa will discolour so squirt a little lemon or lime juice over the slices to prevent browning.

Add feijoa slices to cereal, yogurt, pancakes and even sweet omelettes. Try small amounts in a fruit salad – its flavour can overwhelm the other fruits. Feijoa can be puréed to make a variety of sauces. Cooking options include poaching, baking or sautéeing.

Culinary companions

Feijoa works well with citrus – orange, lime and lemon. It also shares an affinity with fresh ginger, mint and nutmeg. Try sweetening it with maple syrup or brown sugar. Complementary fruits include plums, pears, bananas, strawberries and papaya. Nutty additions include walnuts and hazelnuts. It also works with avocado and shrimp.

Culinary destinations

Puréed feijoa makes an exotic soufflé or mousse. In New Zealand, feijoa goes into an assortment of preserves, from fruit butter to marmalade. Try it in a crisp or crumble, or make it into a sweet topping for angel food. You can slice the fruit in half, dot it with butter and bake it in the oven – baste it with maple syrup and garnish with chopped walnuts.

To your health

One feijoa contains 24 calories and is a source of vitamin C and folate.

Trivia

As the name indicates, feijoa is native to South America and is found in Argentina, Uruguay, Brazil and Paraguay. It was introduced to Europeans by the Spanish. Today, New Zealand is the biggest grower. Californian producers are hopeful that feijoa will become as popular as that other New Zealand import – the kiwi.

Figs

One of the world's oldest fruits, the fig is mentioned in the Bible more times than any other fruit. Despite its vintage, this fruit – in its fresh form – is a bit of an unknown in North America. It simply doesn't travel well. While people have been eating fresh figs for a millennium or two in the Mediterranean countries, it wasn't until California started growing figs and shipping them by air that the rest of us discovered the joys of fresh figs.

Looks like/Tastes like

A fresh fig is a little smaller than an apricot and shaped like a tear-drop: a bulbous base with a long, pointed stem end. Figs vary in colour when ripe, from bright green to red to purple to black. The flesh can be golden, ruby-red or violet, with white protrusions of firmer flesh. Most figs are filled with many seeds (as many as 1,500) but every so often you might come across a seedless one that has escaped fertilization.

Black Mission (a.k.a. **common**) figs are the best known. The skin is greyish to purplish black, turning jet black when ripe. **Calimyrna** (a.k.a. **Smyrna**) is a large, amber-coloured fig with golden flesh. It has crisp, small seeds and a nutty flavour, and is considered the best-tasting fresh fig. **Brown Turkey** has brownish-purple skin and red flesh. **Kadota** is a greenish-yellow fig that ripens to a pale yellow with purple flesh.

Select it

Look for fresh figs that yield slightly to pressure but are not mushy. The fruit should have rich colour with no signs of mould or bruises. Pick one up and smell it – a fresh fig should have a mild fig fragrance and not smell sour. A fig is ripe when it yields slightly to pressure and has a delicious fragrance. Black Mission figs taste sweetest when just slightly shrivelled.

Store it right

Fresh figs spoil quickly and bruise easily – that's why 90 per cent of the world's harvest is dried. Eat your fresh figs as soon as possible. If you can't eat them immediately, store them in a paper bag or, better still, in a shallow bowl lined with paper towel in the fridge. Figs don't like humidity. Plastic bags are the kiss of death for a fresh fig.

Prep it right

A fig's skin is edible, as are the seeds. To prepare a fresh fig, all you need to do is remove the hard portion of the stem end. Calimyrna figs are thick skinned and some people prefer to peel them.

A fresh fig can be eaten out of hand or cut into wedges. You can glaze it with melted jam, honey and herbs, or a wine and sugar syrup then bake at 300°F (150°C) until tender (about 15 to 20 minutes) or you can skewer fresh figs and grill them. Fresh figs perk up any run-of-the-mill fruit salad and instantly make a green salad gourmet.

Culinary companions
Fresh figs and cheese are a match made in heaven, especially with Mediterranean-type cheeses such as feta, goat cheese, provolone, ricotta or mascarpone. Cream is another winner: try whipped, fresh, Devonshire or ice cream on your figs. Complementary nuts include walnuts, pecans and almonds. Prosciutto, Black Forest and Smithfield ham combine well with fresh figs, as do lemon and orange juices. Anisette and Cointreau are two liqueurs that taste fine with figs.

Culinary destinations
Toss together fresh figs, arugula and goat cheese and drizzle with an orange juice vinaigrette. Or wrap some fresh figs with prosciutto and serve as an appetizer. Grill fresh figs and serve drizzled with honey and chopped walnuts. Or toss some fresh figs into the pan juices of a roast chicken, lamb or pork loin during the last 15 minutes of cooking.

To your health
Fresh figs are high in fibre and are a source of potassium and magnesium. There are 74 calories in two medium-sized fresh figs. Dried figs are more nutrient-dense, offering twice as much fibre, potassium, iron and calcium as fresh figs. But dried figs contain almost twice as many calories, mostly in the form of carbohydrates.

Figs are loaded with fibre: there are 3.3 g of fibre in two fresh figs. Some of this fibre is soluble, in the form of pectin, which helps to lower cholesterol. Figs also contain insoluble fibre, which works as a natural laxative. However, if you eat too many figs, this fibre may contribute to diarrhea. Early tests show that figs may have some cancer-fighting properties, and Japanese researchers showed that fig extract can help shrink tumours. Figs may trigger migraine headaches in some people.

Quick ways
Sauté some arugula in olive oil until barely wilted. Set aside. Spread some goat cheese on a pizza crust and sprinkle wedges of fresh fig and freshly grated Parmigiano-Reggiano on top. Bake in a 375°F (190°C) oven until golden brown. Arrange arugula on top of the hot pizza and serve.

Tip
When baking or roasting whole fresh figs, puncture the skin a few times with the tip of a knife before cooking to avoid a sticky explosion.

Gooseberries

These berries with the funny name and translucent skin are a mystery to most North Americans . . . yet gooseberries are a domestic crop. They make a very short appearance during the summer, at roadside stalls, pick-your-own operations and specialty stores. In England, they're so popular that gooseberry is a slang term for an unwanted third person at a lover's meeting. But in this part of the world, gooseberries are truly exotic and a mystery to all but the berry-knowledgeable consumer.

Other names
Only the French could name a berry by the food it tastes best with. *Groseille à maquereau* means gooseberry, but translates literally as gooseberries and mackerel. The German name for gooseberry is *Stachelbeere*, which literally means prickly berry, an appropriate moniker for this thorny berry.

Looks like/Tastes like
There are many varieties of the gooseberry, which results in great confusion. The most common variety in North America is celery green, shaped like a grape with white veins and red stems. But gooseberries can be amber, pink, red or purple depending on the variety and stage of ripeness. Plus, some are round, others oval; some have smooth skins, others are fuzzy. The celery green variety ripens to a red colour. Unripe, it is tart and acidic – perfect for cooking and preserve-making, but not so great for eating. When ripe, it is sweet enough to eat out of hand.

Select it
Look for firm gooseberries that are clear and bright in colour. Most vendors sell unripe gooseberries (for cooking purposes). Since the fruit won't ripen further after it's been picked, don't expect that gooseberry to turn sweet and ripe.

Store it right
Gooseberries last longer than most berries and are not as fragile. Keep them dry and lightly covered in the fridge. Don't cover with plastic, which traps humidity. When properly stored, gooseberries may keep up to a week or more. Freeze whole on a baking sheet until solid. Transfer to a freezer bag and freeze up to 6 months.

Prep it right
As the British say, "top and tail" your gooseberries. In other words, pinch or snap off the stem and blossom ends before eating or cooking.

Pop ripe gooseberries in your mouth – but sugar is absolutely necessary when cooking unripe gooseberries. Gooseberries can be poached with wine (try a dessert wine) and sugar, cooked in pan juices to make sumptuous sauces or transformed into jams, marmalades, jellies and pies.

Culinary companions
Besides sugar, gooseberries blend well with cream, whipping cream, ice cream and crème fraîche. Compatible spices include nutmeg, allspice and cinnamon. Especially fine fruit companions are apples, pears and raisins.

Culinary destinations
Do as the French do: serve gooseberry sauce (cooked gooseberry juice and sugar) on mackerel fillets. Apple pie tastes that much better when gooseberries are included. Substitute gooseberries for tomatoes in the Italian dish osso buco (braised veal shanks).

To your health
One cup (250 ml) of gooseberries contains 66 calories, and is an excellent source of fibre and vitamin C. Gooseberries are also a source of potassium.

The high levels of pectin in gooseberries not only make them great for preserves, but also make them good for your health. Pectin, a soluble fibre, can help reduce cholesterol and prevent heart disease. Moreover, gooseberries contain ellagic acid, a natural cancer-fighting substance also found in blackberries, cranberries, raspberries and strawberries. Fortunately, ellagic acid doesn't break down when cooked, so gooseberry jams, jellies and pies all contain this important phytochemical.

Quick ways
Make a gooseberry fool by lightly sautéeing gooseberries in butter and a few spoonfuls of sugar until soft and mushy (20 to 25 minutes). Mash the gooseberries with a fork, place in individual parfait glasses and top with a dollop of freshly whipped cream. Chill for an hour and serve.

Grapefruit

Fresh, juicy grapefruit offers up a taste of sun-shine amid the dark, cold days of winter. I know quite a few people who are so enam-oured of this citrus fruit that they order it by the boxful from Florida. They always say they'll share some with me . . . then poof! There never seems to be enough left.

Looks like/Tastes like

There are three main types of grapefruits: white (a.k.a. yellow), pink and red. Two of the most popular white grapefruits are **Marsh Seedless** and **Duncan**. Keep your eyes out for the **Triumph** – it tastes like a mixture of orange and grapefruit. The **Ruby Red** is the most widely grown grape-fruit in Florida and in 1934 became the first citrus fruit to receive a patent. The taste tells you why: it has tender, melting flesh with a pleasant aftertaste. The **Star Ruby** just keeps blushing. This newer, seedless variety, introduced in 1959, is three times redder than the Ruby Red.

Select it

To get the juiciest grapefruit, remember this motto: the heavier, the better. Check out the skin, too. If it looks smooth, glossy and thin, it's a winner. If it is coarse and thick, toss it back into the bin. Search for firm (but not hard) grapefruits that are slightly flattened at the ends. Avoid coneheads.

Store it right

If you plan to eat your grapefruit soon, store it at room temperature. These fruit are at their juiciest when slightly warm. In fact, it's a good idea to bring refrigerated grape-fruit to room temperature before juicing or eating. If you don't plan to eat grapefruit right away, put them in a plastic bag in the crisper. They'll last for up to 6 weeks in the fridge compared to a few days at room tem-perature.

Prep it right

Cut a grapefruit in half crosswise, section with a serrated knife (running it between the flesh and the membranes) and serve it "on the shell." Or provide a serrated spoon for the task. Some people like it sweet, drizzled with maple syrup or honey. You can also eat it like an orange, cut into wedges with the peel left on. For salads and entrées, it makes sense to peel the entire grapefruit. You can do it by hand, but prettier results are achieved with a knife. First, cut a thin slice from the top and the bottom, then slice off the peel and pith in a circular motion, like an apple. Open up the sections with your fingers or use a knife to remove the mem-branes from each section. Or, instead of sectioning it, slice the peeled grapefruit crosswise into pinwheels. Remove the seeds before serving.

Culinary companions

Grapefruit are delicious with sugar (brown, demerara or white), honey, maple syrup, ground or fresh ginger, nutmeg, cinnamon, anise, sesame seeds, fresh mint and almond extract.

To your health

Half a grapefruit contains 37 calories and is an excellent source of vitamin C, containing 45 mg or 75 per cent of the Recommended Daily Intake (RDI). Grapefruit is also a source of potassium and folate. Pink and red grapefruit contain small amounts of vitamin A, with 32 RE (retinal equivalent; the unit of measurement for vitamin A) in half a grapefruit. White grapefruit contains little vitamin A.

Grapefruit is teeming with pectin, a type of soluble fibre that helps to lower cholesterol. Just half a grapefruit contains 6 g of dietary fibre but if you spoon out your grapefruit or section it without the membranes, it contains only 2 g. So to get the most out of your grapefruit, eat the walls! By the way, grapefruit juice contains no fibre at all.

Tips

In order for a fruit to be labelled seedless it can contain no more than five seeds. That's why you'll find the occasional seed in a seedless variety.

Grapefruit juice should not be taken with certain medications. Ask your pharmacist for more details.

Grapes

People have been eating grapes for thousands upon thousands of years. It's one of our oldest fruits. While grapes aren't on the Top Ten List for nutrients, they do contain many important phytochemicals that protect your health. Besides, they're so delicious . . . especially if you're lying down.

Looks like/Tastes like

There are an estimated 10,000 varieties of grapes, but only two dozen or so are cultivated as the table grape – the rest are used in wine, juice, jellies, and so on. There are three main types of table grapes: white, red and blue.

White grapes are generally sweeter and juicier, with thinner skins than red or blue grapes. The best known and most popular white grape is the **Thompson**. It's the number one table grape and the main raisin grape. Others include **Niagara**, **Calmeria** and **Italia**. **Emperor** is the second most popular table grape. It's a red grape that stores well and has a mild flavour. **Cardinal, Flame Seedless, Queen** and **Red Globe** are other red varieties to look for. **Concord**, which is grown in Ontario and the United States, is a blue grape with a heady sweet aroma and a thick skin that separates readily from the flesh. It makes a sweet, luscious jelly. **Black Beauty** is the only seedless blue grape and **Champagne**, while sold as a table grape, is also the grape used to make dried currants.

Select it

Since grapes don't ripen further after picking, choose them carefully. Look for plump grapes that are firmly attached to green and flexible stems. (Emperor grapes are the exception. Look for brown, woody stems on these popular red grapes.) Ripe green grapes should have a pale yellow hue. Red or blue grapes should have deep colouration with no sign of green. Look on a grape's surface for a shiny, white, powdery bloom (more visible on darker coloured grapes). It's an important sign of freshness. Avoid wrinkled or sticky grapes.

Store it right

Keep grapes in the fridge, unwashed and loosely stored in a perforated plastic bag for up to a week. Rinse well before serving. For best flavour, serve at room temperature.

Grapes are easy to freeze. Wash, blot dry with paper towels, stem and arrange in a single layer on a baking sheet. Freeze until solid, then pack in freezer bags to last up to a year. No need to defrost before using.

Tip

Kids love the novelty of frozen grapes, but don't serve them to children under three. Serve fresh grapes to children under three cut in half lengthwise to avoid choking hazards.

Prep it right

To peel a grape, dip it briefly in boiling water, drain and remove the loosened skin. Remove seeds with a toothpick.

Tip

Frosted grape clusters are an easy-to-make and attractive edible garnish. First, snip clusters with three to five grapes each. Dip the clusters into egg white that has been beaten until frothy. Then dip each cluster into granulated or coarse sugar. Air-dry on a rack before using.

Culinary destinations

Try poaching fish or chicken in white wine and stock, then adding a little cream, fresh herbs and grape halves during the last minutes of cooking. Goat cheese and grapes make a sweet and savoury stuffing for phyllo pastry triangles. Blue grapes are great in a crumble or crisp: toss them with a little cornstarch and apricot jam, cover with your favourite topping and bake until golden. Toss some grapes in a turmeric rice salad with diced chicken and fresh coriander. Think of grapes the next time you deglaze sautéed chicken or fish: deglaze the cooking pan with wine, then add fresh or frozen grapes and stir to make a quick and tasty sauce. Serve grapes with pâté, foie gras or chicken livers. Toss some grapes and mushrooms into your next poultry stuffing.

To your health

There are 113 calories in 1 cup (250 mL) of red or green grapes and 61 calories in the same amount of blue grapes. This low-calorie fruit is a source of vitamin C, potassium, thiamin and vitamin B^6. Grapes contain trace amounts of the mineral boron.

Although grapes fall short in nutrients, they score big time in phytochemicals. Grapes contain two important flavonoids: anthocyanins and quercetin. Anthocyanins are present in blue and red grapes and have been shown in studies to have numerous health benefits, such as preventing cancer and heart disease, controlling diabetes, improving circulation, reducing eye strain and even combatting the loss of memory and motor skills associated with aging. Quercetin may help regulate blood cholesterol and prevent diabetes-related eye damage. Red grapes contain lutein, a carotenoid that can help prevent macular degeneration, a common age-related cause of vision loss. Other phytochemicals found in grapes include the cancer-fighting ellagic acid and resveratrol found in blue grapes and shown to prevent heart disease. The boron found in grapes may help menopausal women retain healthy levels of estrogen and absorb calcium.

Unfortunately, grapes rank high in tests for pesticide residues. Wash well and remove skins. Or shop organic. Some grapes are treated with sulphur dioxide to extend shelf life; however, this chemical can trigger asthma in susceptible people.

Quick ways

Brush a store-bought sponge cake with 2 tablespoons (30 mL) of orange juice and then spread with mascarpone cheese mixed with a little orange zest and sugar. Top with blue grapes that have been halved and seeded. Brush the grapes with a little bit of marmalade that has been melted on the stove top for a glaze. Chill, then serve.

Guava

When you want a real taste of the tropics, splurge and buy a guava.

Other names
Guavas are known as *guayaba* in Spanish, and in French as *goyave*.

Looks like/Tastes like
The guava comes in 150 varieties, making identification difficult. It can be as small as an egg or as large as a pear, with a greenish-white, yellow or red skin, which might be smooth or pitted. Sometimes it is shaped like an apple and other times like a pear. The flesh of a guava might be white, yellow, shocking pink or red.

However, only a few varieties are imported to North America, or grown in Florida. The most common is **Beaumont**, a large commercial variety. It looks like a pale yellow lemon with a smooth skin, and it has pink flesh. Other varieties are called **lemon** or **strawberry** guavas. But watch out for pineapple guava – this is not a true guava, but a feijoa (see page 21).

The skin, flesh and seeds of the guava are all edible, but whether you want to eat them or not is a matter of taste. Most people just eat the sweet-tasting flesh. Guavas hint of honey, melon, strawberry, pineapple, banana and cloves, depending on your taste buds.

Tip
Guavas contain a lot of seeds. Although the seeds are edible and a good source of fibre, many people find them too gritty to enjoy. In some varieties, the seeds are concentrated in a jelly-like pulp in the middle and are easy to scoop out. But there are also guavas with seeds spread throughout. Purée the flesh and seeds of these guavas, and then strain.

Select it
Choose a guava that is firm to touch and has no bruises, soft spots or pits. You don't want to buy a shrivelled specimen. It's ripe when it yields to gentle pressure and has a floral scent. Guavas tend to smell musky when unripe.

Store it right
Guavas ripen very quickly, which makes them a difficult fruit to export effectively. Store them at room temperature until ripe. Once ripe, they keep in the refrigerator only a few days. Because of the fruit's strong smell, you may want to wrap it up carefully before storing in the fridge. The pulp freezes well.

Prep it right
Cut a guava in half crosswise and spoon out the flesh. You can also peel and slice a firm guava. To strain out the seeds, spoon the

flesh into a sieve and push it through with the back of a spoon.

Eat a guava out of hand, slice it up like an apple or toss pieces into a fruit salad. You can also bake, sauté or grill guava. Guavas are rich in pectin, making them perfect for jellies, jams and chutneys. Guava purée makes a nice marinade, sauce, glaze or addition to a smoothie.

Culinary companions
A spritz of fresh lemon, lime or orange juice perks up the flavours of a guava. Orange liqueurs such as Cointreau or Grand Marnier also marry well, as do rum and sherry. Creamy additions include whipping cream, crème fraîche or yogurt. Guavas combine well with strong cheeses as well as nuts such as pecans and almonds.

Culinary destinations
Guava and grilled foods are a good match. Try a guava salsa with lime juice, red onions, fresh coriander and hot peppers with grilled swordfish or tuna. Or boil down guava purée with sugar, lime juice and rum to make a barbecue glaze for poultry or pork. Make guava custard, ice cream, fools or mousses. Liven up a cheese course with slices of guava.

To your health
Guavas are exceptionally rich in vitamin C and fibre. One 3-ounce (90-g) fruit contains a formidable 165 mg of vitamin C, which supplies two and a half times the Recommended Daily Intake (RDI). Guavas are also high in dietary fibre, with 4.8 g in a single fruit. Guavas also contain vitamins A and E, plus potassium and folate.

Guavas are rich in pectin, a type of soluble fibre that has been shown in studies to reduce cholesterol. Ripe guavas are a traditional remedy for constipation.

Kiwi

Not so long ago, a kiwi garnish was the definition of chic in gourmet circles. Today, kiwis are as common as bananas. Don't let this fruit's ubiquity trick you into ignoring it. Kiwis are one of the tastiest and most nutritious fruits you'll find.

Other names

Kiwi used to be called a Chinese gooseberry until it was renamed after New Zealand's native bird – the flightless, hairy, brown kiwi. (The new name gave sales a huge boost.) Now it's not only grown in New Zealand, but it's a major crop in California, too. You'll also see it called kiwifruit.

Looks like/Tastes like

A kiwi's fuzzy brown, egg- or oval-shaped exterior camouflages a brilliant interior. Beneath that skin lies a bright green flesh, with a radius of tiny brown seeds encircling a cream-coloured core. The flesh has a smooth, melon-like texture with a slight crunch, thanks to all those poppyseed-like edible seeds. The tangy, tart and sweet flavour tastes like a combination of strawberries, pineapple and melon.

The most common variety has green flesh, but there's also a red variety. Another species – not widely cultivated – is called the **hardy kiwi**. It has a smooth, opaque green skin and is about the size of a grape.

Select it

Look for clean, plump, fragrant kiwis. Avoid mushy, shrivelled or hard-as-rock fruit. You'll want to take one home that is firm (unripe), or just ripe (yielding to slight pressure like a peach).

Store it right

Store unripe kiwi at room temperature out of direct sunlight. To speed up ripening, store the fruit in a paper bag at room temperature with an apple or banana. Once ripe, kiwis will keep in a plastic bag in the refrigerator for a couple of weeks. Kiwi purée freezes well and keeps for 4 months.

Prep it right

Kiwi is all edible and washing helps remove the fuzz. You can eat it out of hand, but most people trim off the stem and blossom end, and then peel it. It's easy to dig into kiwi with a spoon: simply cut the fruit in half crosswise and scoop out the flesh. Use a sharp knife or vegetable peeler to peel kiwi (like you would peel an apple), then slice crosswise for the best visual effect. You can also cut a kiwi in half lengthwise and then into quarters to eat like orange wedges. Peeled kiwi is easy to purée in a blender or food processor, but use a light touch. Over-processing causes the seeds to break up and turn the purée brown. Kiwi slices do not brown when exposed to air, making them the perfect garnish and a practical cut fruit for desserts.

Culinary companions

Kiwi goes with lemon, lime or orange juice. In the dairy department, it pairs with whipping cream, yogurt and cream cheese. It can stand up to Mexican seasonings (lime, fresh coriander and hot chilies) and Indian (curry powder, ginger and onions). Kiwi works with walnuts and poppyseeds. Kiwi purée or coulis generally needs a little sweetening: try sugar, maple syrup, honey or a liqueur.

Culinary destinations

Try kiwi chunks slipped between beef or fish chunks on a kebab. Or toss some kiwi into a stir-fry with sweet peppers and onions during the last minute or two of cooking. Make a kiwi sauce for cheesecake, meringue, pound cake or angel cake. Try kiwi slices on breakfast cereal, in a peanut butter sandwich or on a bagel with cream cheese.

To your health

When it comes to vitamin C and potassium, few fruits can outdo a kiwi. A 3-½-ounce (100-g) serving of kiwi (one large kiwi) contains 98 mg of vitamin C, which is one and a half times the Recommended Daily Intake (RDI). Ounce for ounce, it is higher in vitamin C than most fruits. In the meantime, the same amount of kiwi contains 315 mg of potassium. Kiwis are high in folate and a source of fibre, magnesium and vitamin E.

The potassium, fibre and vitamin E found in kiwis make them a heart-healthy food that may lower cholesterol and help regulate blood pressure. Kiwis contain antioxidant vitamins C and E, which may boost the immune system and offer protection against cancer.

Quick ways

Light Kiwi Sorbet: peel and lightly purée four kiwis in a blender or food processor. Blend in 1 cup (250 mL) of vanilla-flavoured yogurt. Freeze in shallow, airtight freezer container overnight. An hour before serving, chill 4 parfait glasses. To serve, break up the frozen kiwi-yogurt mixture into chunks and whirl in the blender or food processor until fluffy and light. Spoon into chilled parfait glasses and sprinkle with shaved chocolate.

Trivia

There are about 1,400 seeds in a single kiwi. Be sure to eat all of them! Most of a kiwi's fibre, vitamins and minerals are found in the seeds.

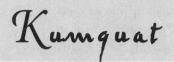
Kumquat

The kumquat is the pygmy of the citrus family. It's a cute mini-fruit that wears its taste inside out. You can gobble it all up in one mouthful, peel, seeds and all. Strange as it seems to eat the peel, you wouldn't want to miss its sweet and spicy flavours. Once you hit the interior, the kumquat delivers with a mouth-puckering explosion of flavor.

Other names

Kumquat (KUHM-kwaht) is the Cantonese name, meaning golden orange. In ancient Chinese texts, kumquats are referred to by another name that means "give guest gift." Not surprisingly, this ornamental plant is still a popular gift among the Chinese, especially at Chinese New Year.

Looks like/Tastes like

Kumquats look like miniature oranges. They are ¾ to 1 inch (2 to 2.5 cm) in diameter and from 1 to 2 inches (2.5 to 5 cm) long. The thin rind can be pebbly or smooth, and it encases three to five segments of fruit that is less juicy than other citrus fruits. Kumquats vary in colour. They may be orange, yellowish-orange or reddish-orange.

Kumquats are indigenous to China but they now grow in many parts of the world. There are several different varieties, most notably the oblong **Nagami** and the round **Meiwa**. Nagami is the most popular kumquat grown in Florida, yet most people consider the Meiwa to be sweeter.

Select it

Look for firm kumquats with no blemishes. Avoid soft or mushy fruit. Kumquats with leaves still attached (which make great centrepieces) won't last as long.

Store it right

Because of their thin skin, kumquats don't last as long as oranges. You can keep them in a fruit bowl at room temperature for up to 6 days but for longer storage, keep them wrapped in plastic in the refrigerator. They should last 3 to 4 weeks, refrigerated.

Prep it right

Be sure to wash and dry kumquats well since you will be eating the skin. They can be eaten raw or cooked. A quick 20-second blanch in boiling water, followed by a plunge in ice water, helps plump up and tenderize kumquats.

Eat them out of hand (the whole fruit is edible) or use them in place of oranges in sweet or savoury dishes. Toss them into salads, tuck them into fruit pies, preserve them in marmalades, jellies and jams, or cook them in a sauce to accompany chicken, duck, turkey, beef, pork or lamb. Try using kumquats the next time you make sweet and sour ribs or other Chinese preparations.

Tip
*It's a good idea to remove the bitter seeds
when cooking with kumquats.*

To your health

Kumquats are low in calories: a 3-½-ounce
(100-g) serving contains only 63 calories.
They are an excellent source of vitamin C
supplying almost two thirds of the Recommended Daily Intake (RDI) in just one serving. High in fibre, kumquats also contain
folate, riboflavin and thiamin.

Kumquats, like their citrus cousins, are
full of phytochemicals that protect your
health. They are loaded with antioxidants
and flavonoids, which may help prevent cancer and heart disease. And since you eat the
peel, you'll get a hefty dose of citrus oil,
which has been shown in tests to have strong
anti-tumour powers.

Quick ways

Blanch 10 kumquats in boiling water for 15
seconds and then drop into ice water to cool.
Slice the cooled kumquats into quarters.
Sauté some garlic, ginger and green onions
in canola oil until fragrant. Blend half of the
kumquats, plus all of the sautéed garlic, ginger and green onions, until smooth with 2
tablespoons (30 mL) canola oil and 1 teaspoon (5 mL) each of sesame oil, soy sauce
and sugar. Serve this dressing on a salad of
arugula leaves, quartered kumquats and
black olives.

Trivia

Kumquat hybrids include the lemonquat,
limequat, orangequat and citrangequat.

Lemons and Limes

Funny thing about lemons. If you've got a car, a lemon is the last thing you want. But if you're in the kitchen, there are times when nothing, absolutely nothing, beats a fresh squirt of lemon juice.

Looks like/Tastes like

LEMON **Eureka** and **Lisbon** are the two most common varieties of lemon. You can tell them apart by their necks: **Eureka** lemons have a short neck at the stem end while **Lisbons** don't, but they taper to a pointed nipple at the blossom end. If you like your lemons seedless, choose Lisbon. It has a smoother skin than the somewhat pitted Eureka. Both varieties have medium-thick skins and are very juicy. **Meyer** lemons are a cross between a lemon and a mandarin. They have gold-coloured, sweet juice that is abundant and tangy. **Ponderosa** is a lemon-citron hybrid that is highly acidic and difficult to peel.

LIME The most common strain of lime is the **Tahiti**, which comes in two varieties, **Persian**, which is egg-sized, oval and grown in Florida, and **Bearss**, which is seedless, larger than a Persian and grown in California. Both turn greenish-yellow when they are mature but are best for flavour when green.

Key limes are round little limes, native to the Florida Keys and Cuba, Mexico and West Indies. They are so small you can get up to 16 key limes to a pound (500 g). Although these special limes have bracingly acerbic juice and an aromatic flavour, they do contain more seeds than most other varieties. The skin is more yellow than green.

Select it

When choosing lemons, look for small to medium-size fruit – they have a thinner skin and are juicier than the large ones. Choose plump and brightly coloured fruit that are heavy for their size. Avoid lemons tinted with green – they'll be too tart and have less flavour.

When choosing limes, look for glossy, plump ones with a thin skin and deep green colour. Stay away from mature, yellow limes, which lack the true tartness of a lime. You may see limes with small brown areas on the skin called "scald" – it won't affect flavour or succulence. Avoid limes with a hard, tough, dry skin. Stock up on limes in the summer when they're cheaper than lemons.

Since many conventional citrus fruits are sprayed with fungicides and pesticides and then covered with a thin layer of wax, it makes sense to buy organic when you want to make zest or preserve lemons and limes.

Store it right

Limes need immediate refrigeration, while lemons can last at room temperature for up to 2 weeks. But it's preferable to store both in a perforated plastic bag in the refrigerator crisper for ultimate last-ability. You can freeze the juices of either fruit in ice cube trays, and then transfer the frozen cubes to a freezer bag. Defrosted lemon or lime cubes are extremely handy to have on hand and taste much better than bottled juice. Take advantage of peak season prices and freeze up some juice – and try tossing a few of these tart frozen cubes into beverages.

Prep it right

If you can squeeze, you've got limes and lemons down pat. But cash in on more juice by prepping the fruit first. Try piercing it with a sharp knife and cooking it at high in the microwave oven for 30 seconds. Or place the fruit in hot water for 2 minutes. Once warm, roll the lemon or lime under your palm on a hard surface until it feels soft inside.

When you juice a lemon or lime by hand, wrap the cut piece in cheesecloth first to trap the seeds while juicing. Or pass the juice through a small sieve.

When squeezing a wedge of lemon or lime, pierce it with a fork first to stop it from spraying. You can purchase a manual or automated citrus hand press, which usually comes equipped with a sieve. A hand-held citrus reamer is handy, but the juice will still need sieving to remove seeds.

Zest is the other important culinary feature of a lemon or lime. (Zest refers to the top layer of rind on a citrus fruit and it is also used as a verb, such as "zest the entire lemon"). Zest has more intense flavour than juice because of the heavy oil concentration found in the skin. It's important to remove only the top, coloured layer of rind from a citrus fruit and not the bitter, white pith that lies beneath. You can use a sharp knife, a gadget designed for the job called a "zester" or the finest holes on a hand grater. Zest can

be frozen or dried for later use and there's no need to defrost or rehydrate it before using. If you use a grater, brush it with a dry basting brush once you've finished grating to remove the zest wedged tightly in the holes of the grater.

The juice and zest of lemon and lime are used as flavouring agents in thousands of savoury and sweet preparations, from Caesar salad dressing to lemon chicken to lemon meringue pie. Just a squeeze of lemon or lime juice can perk up steamed vegetables, salads, seafood – even scrambled eggs. But be careful, for when lemon or lime juice is added to dairy products, especially as they are cooking, it causes curdling. Lemon or lime juice can substitute for vinegar in most cases, to produce a more delicate sour taste. Mix 1 tablespoon (15 mL) of fresh lemon juice in 1 cup of milk (250 mL), stir and let stand for 5 to 10 minutes to make instant buttermilk. Squeeze some juice on sliced apples, avocados, mushrooms, bananas or pears to stop them from browning. Lemons and limes are an excellent addition to marinades, because their acidity helps to tenderize and flavour the meat. One medium lemon yields 3 tablespoons (45 mL) of juice and 2 to 3 teaspoons (10 to 15 mL) of zest.

Culinary destinations

Lime juice is integral to many Latin American and Southeast Asian cuisines. It's found in salsas, on seafood and even wedged inside beer bottles. Most of the salads and soups of Thailand and Vietnam are served garnished with a wedge of lime, and in Cuba chicken broth is seasoned with lime juice. Throughout most of Europe, the Middle East and North America, the lemon reigns. In Morocco, lemons are preserved to be used in stews and couscous dishes. The British love their lemon curd, children all over adore lemonade and most marmalades rely on lemons for their punch and flavour.

To your health

Lemons and limes have one outstanding nutritional feature: they are loaded with vitamin C. A single lemon (47 g) contains 21 mg of vitamin C and one lime (38 g) has 11 mg. Ounce for ounce, lemons have 35 per cent more vitamin C than limes, but limes are still a good source of vitamin C. Both these citrus fruits are low in calories.

Although lemons and limes lack a broad spectrum of nutrients, they are rich in phytochemicals such as flavonoids and terpenes. Flavonoids boost the antioxidant activity of vitamin C, and may help to ward off cancer and retard the effects of aging. Terpenes help control the production of cholesterol.

There's another valuable cholesterol-fighting ingredient in lemons and limes, but we don't tend to eat it. The bitter white pith of lemons and limes is loaded with pectin, a soluble fibre that helps reduce cholesterol. (Moroccan-style preserved lemons are a good source.)

Many people turn to lemons when they have a cold, since vitamin C has been shown in studies to reduce the severity of a cold. A tablespoon (15 mL) of lemon juice in hot water with honey helps to relieve a sore throat.

On the negative side, lemons and limes contain psoralens, which make the skin and hair more sensitive to sun. Squeezing or zesting many limes or lemons will make your hands more prone to sunburn that day. Lemon peel also contains limonene, an oil that can cause skin irritation in susceptible people.

Tips

When cooking with lemon or lime juice, avoid plastic containers or wrap. The acid from the juice picks up undesired flavours from the plastic.

Trying to cut back on salt in your diet? Try lemons instead. They add flavour and punch without the sodium.

Mandarin Oranges

Each year after Halloween, I start sniffing around my supermarket for a good crate of mandarin oranges. Before the produce manager starts breathing down my neck, I've usually unearthed the contents of half a dozen crates to find the best pack of mandarins.

Looks like/Tastes like

Clementine mandarins, also known as **Algerian tangerines,** have a deep orange skin that is smooth, glossy and slightly puffy. The flesh is sweet, like apricot nectar, and the texture is delicate. Easy to peel, a clementine has thin membranes covering the sections. Sadly, a seedless variety has yet to be developed.

Satsuma mandarins come in more than 100 varieties in Japan. In North America, the most popular variety is the **Owari**, a zippery-skinned mandarin that is seedless and not as acidic as the clementine. It's considered one of the best mandarins around.

Although tangerines and mandarins are often used interchangeably, mandarin is the proper botanical name and tangerines are a mandarin subgroup. **Dancy, Robinson** and **Honey** are the three best-known varieties of tangerine, the latter considered the sweetest. Tangerines are somewhat squat, with flattened tops and bottoms. They have a deep red-orange rind that fits loosely.

Tangors are a cross between an orange and a mandarin. The best known is the Temple (a.k.a. **Royal Mandarin**) and looks like an overgrown mandarin with red-orange skin. It's sweet, slightly spicy and very juicy. Unfortunately, it is also seedy and hard to peel. The **Murcott** is another tangor and has a thin peel and reddish-orange flesh that tastes faintly of mango.

The **tangelo** is a cross between a mandarin and a pummelo, and **minneola** is the most popular variety. It looks like a large orange with a distinctive knob – some call it a neck – at the stem end. Minneolas have a tart, honey-sweet flavour, few seeds and a deep, orange-red skin.

Ugli fruit is a mandarin-hybrid that is marketed in North America as Unique – a much more appealing name. This Jamaican native can weigh up to 2 pounds (1 kg) and resembles its cousin the grapefruit – but uglier. It has a thick, bumpy orange-green rind that hides a sweet juicy flesh with few seeds. Find out where your ugli fruit was grown. They are sweeter when raised in the tropics (particularly the West Indies or Asia) than in the subtropics (such as Florida and California). Ugli fruit is easy to peel, the segments separate easily and the yellow-orange flesh tastes like a cross between an orange and a mandarin.

Select it

Look for glossy skins, free of bruises and soft spots. Orange colouring is not always an indicator – some delicious mandarins have russet skin. Although mandarins will feel soft and puffy compared to a tight, compact orange, be sure to select one that feels heavy for its size. This way you'll avoid a dry and pithy mandarin and be rewarded with a succulent, juicy one.

Store it right

Mandarins have a shorter shelf-life than oranges and last longer if stored in perforated plastic bags in your refrigerator crisper. However, they taste better at room temperature. When you buy a crate, store the bulk in the fridge.

Culinary destinations

Toss some mandarin segments into a pasta salad with broccoli, black olives and green onions and top with a mandarin juice vinaigrette. A beef stew or slowly simmered steak is enhanced by a big handful of mandarin segments added for the last five minutes of cooking. Try stir-frying mandarin sections with pork, green peppers and pineapple. For brunch, serve a sweet mandarin and cream cheese omelette dusted with icing sugar.

Tip

The Chinese use dried mandarin peel in many stir-fries, as well as in steamed and braised dishes. It tastes especially fine when combined with ginger and beef. You can dry your own peel. Just make sure it's trimmed of all the white pith. Place it on a cake rack in a sunny, well-ventilated spot. Once it's completely dry, store in an airtight container. The flavour improves with age. To use, first reconstitute in warm water for 20 minutes or until soft. Or rehydrate the peel in cooking sherry, which then becomes flavoured, too.

To your health

One medium mandarin orange contains 36 calories and 25 mg of vitamin C, which is 41 per cent of the Recommended Daily Intake (RDI). While mandarins are an excellent source of vitamin C, they contain 43 per cent less than oranges. Mandarins are a source of folate, but once again, oranges contain more – up to 60 per cent more of this important B vitamin. However, mandarins do contain slightly more thiamin than oranges. There are 1.9 g of dietary fibre in a single mandarin.

Unlike other oranges, mandarins generally aren't juiced – people just pop the sections into their mouths. Eating whole mandarins is a good practice because you get lots of fibre. Pectin is a soluble fibre found in mandarins that helps reduce cholesterol, especially the "bad" or LDL cholesterol. Moreover, the vitamin C in mandarins is a powerful antioxidant in the body, helping to fight heart disease by preventing the oxidization of LDL cholesterol, which can lead to the formation of plaque in vital arteries.

Trivia

Mandarins have been cultivated in China for several thousands of years. They were originally called "chinas" before the name was changed to mandarins.

Mango

I discovered mangoes while living in Taiwan. As soon as the season commenced, I was overcome with mango madness, and ate them from dawn to dusk, juice dripping down my chin, eyes half closed in ecstasy. My Chinese friends were appalled. They warned that mangoes were a "yin" food and that over-consumption would deeply endanger my yin-yang balance. But I had no choice. I kissed my yin-yang goodbye and kept on eating mangoes.

Other names

Samarbehisht is the Persian word for mango and it means fruit from heaven.

Looks like/Tastes like

Mangoes range in size from a few ounces to several pounds. The shape is usually oblong or kidney, but it can be round or oval. Mangoes have a thin, leathery, green or yellow skin that may have patches of orange, yellow, red – even purple. A large flat pit hides within the flesh, which can be fibrous. A mango has a complex, sweet, tart flavour that tastes like a kaleidoscope of tropical fruits in a single mouthful.

There are hundreds of varieties of mangoes cultivated throughout the world's tropics. The **Alphonso** mango from India is considered the finest mango among connoisseurs. It's small (about 4 inches/10 cm long) and kidney-shaped with a hook at one end. The peel is yellow with a slight orange blush when ripe. An Alphonso's brilliant orange flesh is fibre-free, boasting a voluptuous, rich, deep flavour. The **Haden** from Mexico is a larger fruit, plump and oval with patches of orange, red and yellow on a green background. The **Francis** (from Haiti) and **Manilla** (from the Philippines) are both yellow-skinned and kidney or S-shaped. The **Keitt** (from the United States) is unique in that it's one of the largest, meatiest mangoes you can buy and it stays green, even when it's ripe.

Select it

Mangoes, like bananas, will ripen after picking, so it's safe to buy them unripe. When buying an unripe mango, make sure it has an unblemished, taut skin. A red blush does not always indicate sweetness. Asian stores often carry small, unripe, green mangoes for cooking. When ripe, a mango should yield to slight pressure and have an intense, flowery smell. Avoid shrivelled mangoes or ones covered with lots of black dots (a sign of over-ripeness). Stay away from mangoes with a fermented, turpentine smell.

Store it right

Store firm, unripe mangoes at room temperature, or speed up the ripening process by wrapping them up in newspaper or in a closed paper bag with a banana. Once ripe, eat as soon as possible. A ripe mango can be stored in the fridge in a plastic bag for up to a week, but for best results, bring it to room temperature before serving. Cold temperatures mute a mango's flavour. You can freeze mango purée in a freezer bag, container or even in ice cube trays (emptied into a freezer bag once frozen). Flash-freeze mango slices on a baking sheet in the freezer until solid, then store in a freezer bag for up to a year.

Prep it right

To eat mangoes out of hand, try this trick: cut a mango's "cheeks" away from the pit, slicing lengthwise, to create two, near-halves. With a sharp knife, make a cross-hatch pattern in the flesh without cutting through to the skin. Press the fruit inside out, inverting it from a concave shape to a convex one. A pattern of cubes will pop out, making it easy to eat as is. Or slice off the cubes by slipping a knife under the flesh just above the skin.

To peel a mango, score the skin into four lengthwise portions and peel it away like a banana. Slice the mango where you scored it, running the knife under the flesh to free it from the pit. If the mango is firm enough, try peeling with a sharp knife or vegetable peeler. If you have a satiny-smooth, custard-like mango that is very ripe, try cutting the halves away from the pit, then scooping out the flesh with a spoon.

Culinary destinations

Try mangoes instead of other fruits in such traditional desserts as crisps, pies, flans, sorbet or shortcake. Mangoes make a great chutney. Consider a mango chutney with apricots and ancho chilies, or a mango and roasted yellow pepper salsa with fresh coriander and lime juice.

To your health

Mangoes are one of the most nutritional fruits you can sink your teeth into. An excel-

lent source of beta carotene, mangoes have more of this preformed vitamin A than apricots or cantaloupe. One (207 g) mango supplies 80 per cent of the Recommended Daily Intake (RDI) for vitamin A. Mangoes are also an excellent source or vitamin C, supplying 57 mg in one mango or 95 per cent of the RDI. There are 135 calories in a mango, and it's high in vitamins E and B^6 and in dietary fibre. Mangoes are also a source of potassium, folate, thiamin, riboflavin and niacin.

Mangoes are loaded with cancer-fighting antioxidants and carotenoids, which may help prevent cancer and reduce the accumulation of plaque in arteries, preventing heart disease.

Two kinds of allergic reactions are associated with mangoes. One is caused by the sap that oozes from the mango skin and contains a chemical that produces a rash on contact, not unlike poison ivy. People who experience this rash can still eat mangoes, but should wear gloves when peeling a mango. Another type of allergic reaction is more serious and dangerous, resulting from an allergen in the mango flesh that can cause hives and swollen lips and tongue. People with this type of allergic reaction should avoid mangoes entirely.

Melons

For many people, buying a melon is a leap of faith. It's like purchasing an expensive, wrapped present that is as likely to be a dud as a winner. Many people shy away from buying melons, simply because they can't stand to play the ripe-fruit-lottery. But there are ways to increase your odds, so you can enjoy this delicious fruit.

Looks like/Tastes like

Melons along with squashes and cucumbers belong to the gourd family. The three most common types of melon are watermelon, cantaloupe and honeydew.

Watermelon differs from all other melons because its seeds are scattered throughout the solid flesh. (All the other melons resemble squash with a hollow, central cavity containing the seeds.) The largest of all melons, watermelons are no smaller than 5 pounds (2 kg) and can weigh up to a hulking 50 pounds (23 kg). They come in more than 50 varieties, and they can be round or oval or elongated. The flesh is most commonly red, but yellow varieties are increasingly available due to their sweet reputation. Seedless varieties can be found in red or yellow watermelons. A ripe watermelon should have a symmetrical shape with a dull surface. The ground spot (or place where the watermelon rests on the ground while growing) should be yellowish or creamy in colour. Cut watermelon should have vivid colour.

Cantaloupes are technically muskmelons, the most popular melons in North America. True cantaloupes (cultivated in Europe) have a tougher, scalier exterior segmented by deep grooves. The most nutritious of all melons, cantaloupes are round, with a netted exterior and juicy orange interior. Ripe cantaloupes have a golden (never green) colour under the netting and small cracks near the stem. The flesh at the stem and blossom end should be slightly indented and yield a bit to pressure. Look for a sweet, spicy aroma and a melon that is heavy in the hand, indicating lots of scrumptious juice.

Honeydew is considered the sweetest of all melons. This round melon weighs from 3 to 5 pounds (1.25 to 2 kg) and when ripe has a creamy yellow rind. (If you see green in the rind, it is underripe). Most commonly the flesh is pale green, but there is an orange honeydew with salmon-pink-coloured flesh that tastes like cantaloupe.

Because **Crenshaw** (or **Cranshaw**) melons are considered one of the most delicious melons in the world, with a sweet and slightly spicy flesh, they are worth seeking out. These round melons with a pointed stem weigh in between 4 and 7 pounds (1.8 to 3 kg) and have a smooth, dark-green rind that turns golden yellow when ripe. The pale, salmon-pink flesh is intensely aromatic. Besides having deep wrinkles that gather at the stem end, **Casaba** melons are similar in size and shape to the smooth-skinned

Crenshaw. Ripe casabas are golden yellow without a strong aroma. The flesh is creamy white, tinged with pale yellow and sweet, but not intensely flavourful.

Persian melons look like very large cantaloupes (from 6 to 7 pounds/2.75 to 3 kg). Choose them as you would a cantaloupe.

Santa Claus melons, so named because they ripen at Christmas, are shaped like watermelons but their skin is a mottled pattern of dark green and yellow. Look for bright yellow colouring in ripe Santas to reap a juicy, crisp flesh that is not quite as sweet as other melons.

Pepino melons have a unique, satiny smooth skin unlike the common melon rind. They are oval-shaped, like eggplants. The yellow skin has striking purple stripes. The flesh should yield slightly when ripe and very little green should be seen in the skin. It's the finest-textured melon with a taste that borders somewhere in between cantaloupes, cucumbers and pears.

Kiwano melon (a.k.a. horned melon) is unlike no other. You can't really munch on a slice of it, like cantaloupe or watermelon. Instead you have to spoon it out of its outrageous shell, a bright yellow carapace with stubby horns scattered over the surface. This melon originates from Africa but is now grown in New Zealand and California, too. It's a small oval fruit, no longer than 5 inches (12.4 cm) and the jelly-like, olive green pulp is sweet and sour and contains edible seeds similar to a cucumber's.

Select it

Melons do not ripen once picked. What you see is what you get. Use this four-step guide each time you shop and you're guaranteed to bring home a winner:

Step 1: Look at it. Is the colour right? Except for watermelons, you want to see as little green as possible. Now check the stem ends. They should yield slightly and look sunken. Check for bruises and soft spots and avoid any shrivelled or lifeless looking melons.

Step 2: Smell it. Most melons have a sweet, pleasant smell, with the exception of honeydew, which is odourless.

Step 3: Hold it. The heavier the better, meaning lots of juicy flesh.

Step 4: Shake it lightly. Nothing should rattle. If it does, turn to another melon. When a melon's seeds start kicking around the interior that melon is overripe.

Store it right

Most melons – except watermelons – benefit from a day's storage at room temperature to soften (not ripen) the flesh. Once cut, any melon should be wrapped tightly with plastic wrap and stored in the fridge, where it will last no more than a few days. Watermelons should go into the fridge whole or cut.

Prep it right

Melons are a breeze. All melons, with the exception of watermelon, should be cut in half and the seeds scooped out. All a watermelon needs is slicing.

Melon is most commonly eaten raw. Cut it by the slice, scoop it out in balls or cube it. Melon can be puréed and served in cold soups or made into refreshing drinks. You can also poach melon in syrup or grill it on the barbecue. One pound (500 g) of melon yields 1 cup (250 mL) of cubed melon.

Tip
Don't throw out that watermelon rind – it makes a savoury pickle.

Culinary destinations

Try a sliver of watermelon wrapped in smoked chicken or turkey, a wedge of honeydew wrapped in smoked salmon or corned beef, or a slice or cantaloupe wrapped in prosciutto or Black Forest ham. Make a melon salsa with chopped red onion, chili peppers, lemon juice and fresh coriander or a cantaloupe and currant chutney. Purée some watermelon and mix it into a vinaigrette. Melons work well in salads: try cantaloupe with avocado slices and spinach or watermelon with baby salad greens, feta cheese and onions. Kids warm up to melon brushed with melted butter, rolled in cinnamon sugar and then grilled. And adults like a little watermelon in their margaritas. You can dry the seeds of any melon, toss them in a little oil and seasonings, then bake until toasted to make a great snack.

To your health

Melons are 90 per cent water and are consequently low in calories. There are only 80 calories in half a cantaloupe, 50 calories in a wedge of honeydew and 110 calories in a 1-inch (2.5 cm) slice of watermelon. Cantaloupes are the nutritional star among melons, offering an excellent source of beta carotene and vitamin C. A 3-½-ounce (100-g) serving of cantaloupe provides 42 mg of vitamin C (two thirds your daily needs), and 322 RE of vitamin A or 32 per cent of the Recommended Daily Intake (RDI). Cantaloupes are also a source of potassium, folate, fibre, vitamin B^6 and magnesium. Honeydew is high in vitamin C and a source of potassium and thiamin. Watermelon is a source of vitamin C, potassium, thiamin and vitamin B^6. Persian melons contain as much beta carotene as cantaloupes.

Cantaloupes, like garlic, onion and ginger, perform an anti-clotting and thinning action on the blood, and may help to prevent heart disease and stroke. The potassium in melons is also good for the heart, helping to regulate blood pressure. Plus, some types of melon are high in pectin, a soluble fibre that helps control blood cholesterol levels. Epidemiological studies reveal that diets high in melon guard against cancer and foods high in beta carotene (such as all orange-fleshed melons) help lower rates of lung cancer.

Nectarines

Nectarines get no respect. People are always referring to them as fuzzless peaches or a cross between a peach and a plum. But nectarines have been a card-carrying, distinct fruit for more than 2,000 years.

Looks like/Tastes like

There are more than 150 varieties of nectarines but the differences are subtle. They all look basically the same; however, newer varieties are larger, redder and firmer than older nectarine varieties. Look out for the relatively new white nectarines – they have white flesh and a creamy-white skin with a pink-red blush.

Select it

Nectarines, along with peaches and plums, don't ripen further once picked. A nectarine will get softer and juicier after it's been harvested, but it won't get any sweeter. To find a ripe nectarine, look for fruit that give slightly to fingertip pressure, especially along the seam. Never buy a rock-hard nectarine. Check out a nectarine's colour, too. The amount of red or pink blush on a nectarine varies from variety to variety, so don't go by blush when scouting for a ripe nectarine. Instead, examine a nectarine carefully and make sure it has no signs of green, especially around the stem end. Even the slightest green tinge on a nectarine indicates that it's unripe and consequently untasty.

Store it right

You can store a firm nectarine at room temperature, out of direct sunlight, for a day or two and it will get softer (but not sweeter). If you've bought a basket of nectarines, take them out and store in a single layer. Fully ripe nectarines should be stored in the fridge, uncovered, where they'll keep for up to a week.

The easiest way to freeze nectarines is the dry-pack method. Peel and slice 4 cups (1 L) of nectarines and arrange on a baking sheet. Mix ¼ teaspoon (1 mL) of ascorbic acid powder and ¼ cup white sugar in a small bowl. Sprinkle this mixture evenly over the sliced fruit. Freeze until solid (it takes a few hours). Transfer the fruit to a freezer bag as soon as it is solid to prevent freezer burn. Keep them frozen up to 6 months.

Prep it right

Just wash a nectarine and eat it. To peel a nectarine, blanch it in boiling water for 30 to 60 seconds. Remove with a slotted spoon and plunge into a bowl of ice water. Once the fruit is cool, the skin should slip off easily with a sharp knife. If not, repeat the process.

Peeled or sliced nectarines brown easily. Prevent this by brushing with fresh lemon or lime juice. Or sprinkle nectarine slices with a pinch of ascorbic acid (vitamin C powder), or dip them briefly into acidulated water (3 tablespoons/45 mL of lemon juice to 1 quart/1 L of water).

Use nectarines and peaches interchangeably in recipes. Nectarines are not as juicy as peaches, and can stand up to a sauté or stir-fry better than a peach. Try poaching, broiling, grilling and baking nectarines.

Culinary destinations

Whirl up a cold nectarine gazpacho in the food processor with sweet bell peppers, hot peppers, garlic, vinegar and fresh coriander. Try stuffing a baked and glazed nectarine with goat cheese and fresh basil. Put some nectarines, peaches and plums on a skewer and brush with butter, honey, lime juice and chutney, and then grill until golden. Nectarines and blueberries together make a great smoothie. Plus nectarines can masquerade as peaches in a fuzzy navel cocktail with orange juice and peach schnapps.

To your health

Nectarines and peaches are quite similar in their nutritional make-up, except that nectarines have slightly more vitamin A and E. There are 66 calories in a (136 g) nectarine. It's a source of vitamins A and E, as well as potassium and fibre.

The beta carotene in nectarines acts as an antioxidant. Studies show that people who eat foods rich in carotenes have a lower risk of heart disease, stroke, cataracts and lung cancer. Nectarines are also rich in flavonoids, another phytochemical with antioxidant properties. Fat-free, sodium-free and a source of potassium, nectarines are a heart-healthy food.

Quick ways

Mix a bottle of dry Portuguese or Spanish sparkling white wine with two peeled and sliced nectarines, a handful of blueberries, a ½ cup (125 mL) of sugar and some fresh mint. Chill for one hour. Serve as is, or with ice and sparkling water.

Trivia

The nectarine was named after the Greek god Nekter, and its juice was later called nectar, the drink of the gods.

Oranges

After bananas and apples, oranges are the most popular fruit in North America. And thank goodness! Researchers are revealing more new health benefits associated with this golden orb all the time.

Looks like/Tastes like

Oranges fall under three main types: juicing, eating and sour oranges.

JUICING **Valencia** oranges have been dubbed the King of Juice Oranges and most people agree that they are the finest in the world. Grown in Florida, Valencia oranges comprise over half the total American crop. This orange is delectably sweet, has few or no seeds and, depending on the variety, has smooth or somewhat pebbly skin. The **Hamlin** is another seedless juicing orange. It's the earliest to mature, has a thin skin, and is seedless and quite small. The **Pineapple** looks like the Hamlin; even though it is full of seeds, it is very flavourful. **Jaffa** oranges are imported from Israel and are even sweeter than Valencia. Like the Hamlin, they are small with only 10 segments each and a slightly rough rind.

EATING The **California navel** orange is considered the best eating and table orange. Easily recognizable by its belly-button scar at the blossom end, navels have a lot going for them: they're easy to peel, seedless and richly flavoured. Once a novelty, **blood** oranges are now becoming mainstream. Popular in the Mediterranean, these oranges taste like they've been dipped in raspberry juice. They are small to medium-sized, with smooth or pitted skin that is sometimes tinged with red. Blood oranges are seedless, or close to seedless. Look for **Moro**, a California-grown variety that has a rich, burgundy flesh and a deep red blush on the rind. Other varieties include the sour **Sanguinelli** and the **Tarocco**, which resembles a tangelo with flesh that is more orange then red.

SOUR Among sour oranges, the **Seville** is the best known. This Spanish orange has a golden-orange rind and flesh. It's medium-sized with a pebbly, almost bumpy, rind and about 10 large segments. Although the pulp is tender, this orange is too sour to eat out of hand. It's the signature orange for marmalade-making, but consider it also in marinades, or in place of lemon juice for a tart, orange flavour.

Select it

In the United States, the ripeness of an orange is protected. Growers are not permitted to pick oranges until fully ripe, so ripeness is rarely an issue when buying oranges. But you still want to choose carefully. Look for oranges that feel firm and heavy for their size. Avoid any with deep bruises, soft spots or mould. If an orange feels spongy or is shrivelled, pass it up. The colour of an orange's rind has no bearing on interior quality. In fact, many orange varieties are green when fully ripe and some Florida varieties can be lightly russet. Actually, some green oranges are dipped in orange vegetable dye. (However, this must be stamped on the box.) Some oranges are lightly waxed. If you are purchasing oranges to make zest or marmalade, it is wise to buy organically grown fruit.

Tip
One mouldy orange can ruin the lot very quickly. Exercise caution when buying one of those big, economical bags of oranges.

Store it right

Although you can store oranges at room temperature, they'll last only a few days. That's too bad, because oranges are juicier and tastier at room temperature. Try storing most of your oranges in a plastic bag in the fridge and keep just a few in your fruit bowl at a time.

Orange zest freezes beautifully, and doesn't need to be defrosted before using. Orange shells left over from squeezing can also be frozen and used later as dessert cups.

Tip
The Seville orange season is brief and untimely. These oranges are often at their peak around the busy Christmas season. However, you can freeze them and defrost later to make marmalade. Simply freeze whole in freezer bags.

Prep it right

Navel oranges are the easiest to eat as the peel comes off very easily with your fingers.

To peel other oranges, cut off a thin slice from the top, then make lengthwise incisions from top to base, cutting just to the flesh, and then peel. To segment an orange for a salad or dessert, peel (as described above) or pare off the peel as you would an apple. Trim away any white pith. Break the orange in half and hold one half in your hand with the flat side of the orange half facing the inside of your palm. Take a small, serrated knife and free each segment by cutting down against the membrane on either side. Or simply peel each segment.

Slicing orange pinwheels is less messy and tedious than creating segments. Peel the orange, remove any membrane and then slice the orange crosswise to create pretty, round pinwheels.

To make orange zest, see page 37 (lemons).

Tip
Warm oranges yield more juice than cold. Before juicing, store oranges at room temperature for a day or microwave oranges at high for 1 minute. Roll the orange around your countertop with the palm of your hand before juicing to produce more juice.

Culinary destinations

Pull out the blender and make an orange, banana, strawberry and yogurt smoothie. Or segment an orange, grapefruit, mandarin and blood orange, sprinkle with sugar to taste and finish with a little orange liqueur. Just a squeeze of orange juice keeps cut or peeled apples, pears and bananas from browning. Substitute orange juice for lemon juice in a hollandaise sauce, mayonnaise or vinaigrette (Seville works particularly well). Orange juice makes a good marinade, especially for fish, and can also be used instead of water to cook rice, barley or couscous. Orange zest is the secret ingredient in many cookies, cakes, scones and quick breads. Try some oranges mashed with turnip and carrots – it even works in soups with squash or sweet potatoes.

To your health

One California navel orange (140 g) contains only 64 calories. It's a source of fibre, containing 3.3 g, more than the amount found in one serving of whole wheat bread or a banana. Most importantly, oranges are an excellent source of vitamin C, with 80 mg in one navel orange, fulfilling more than a day's needs. Oranges are also high in folate and a source of thiamin, potassium and calcium.

Oranges are full of powerful antioxidants (vitamin C and flavonoids), which protect cells from damage by free radicals and reduce the risk of cancer. In fact, the National Cancer Institute of America attributes the year-round availability of citrus to a marked drop of stomach cancer in the United States in the past two decades. Oranges have also been shown to lower cholesterol, not only due to the pectin found in oranges, but due to the presence of terpenes, a phytochemical that limits the production of cholesterol. Moreover, the vitamin C in oranges prevents the oxidization of LDL or "bad" cholesterol, which can lead to the formation of plaque in arteries. It also forms collagen, the substance that builds healthy teeth, skin and bones. Vitamin C may also boost immunity and combat viral infections, lessening the severity of colds and flu and it helps the body absorb the iron in foods better, thus preventing anemia and fatigue. Folate is plentiful in oranges and, when consumed by women planning to become pregnant or already pregnant, reduces the risk of birth defects such as spina bifida.

Quick ways

Mix equal parts of fresh orange juice and yogurt together. Spike it with a little bourbon if desired, and then sweeten with sugar or honey to taste. Freeze in ice cube trays. Just before serving, crush the cubes in the blender or food processor. Serve in chilled parfait glasses, garnished with strawberries, raspberries or blueberries.

Papaya

I fell in love with papaya one morning on an island called Koh Samui in Thailand. It was love at first bite . . . sweet, floral flavours and a satiny, rich texture that simply melted in my mouth. Nothing beats a plate of tropical fruit for breakfast, and when it stars a perfect papaya, you know life is treating you right.

Other names

Papaya (puh-PIE-yuh) is sometimes called pawpaw or papaw, especially in the Caribbean.

Looks like/Tastes like

There are many varieties of papaya growing in tropical and subtropical regions around the world and as a result it has evolved into many shapes and colours. Small papayas are usually pear- or avocado-shaped, but can be round or elongated – even oval-shaped. They range from ½ pound to 20 pounds (250 g to 10 kg) with thin green, orange, rose or yellow skin. Inside a papaya's oblong cavity are black shiny seeds with a gelatinous covering, resembling beluga caviar. The flesh has a mild flavour, growing more intense if the fruit has been at least half-ripened on the tree. The texture is soft, silky and dense, similar to a melon or fibre-less mango. It has a delicately floral taste that's somewhat musky and lacks any acid notes.

Solo, an Hawaiian variety, is perhaps best known. It's a small, manageable papaya that – as its name implies – can be eaten by one person, unlike some of its mammoth cousins. The solo ranges from ½ pound to 2 pounds (250 g to 1 kg) in size. The skin is greenish-yellow, ripening to golden yellow, and the flesh is bright golden or pinkish. Other varieties hail from Mexico, Asia, Puerto Rico and other Caribbean countries. The sizes range from 1 to 10 pounds (500 g to 5 kg).

Select it

Look for a smooth, unshrivelled skin. Superficial blemishes are not a problem. Papayas are easily bruised so handle them gently. You can buy an unripe, firm papaya and let it ripen at home. To buy one that's ripe, look for a richly coloured papaya with as little green as possible. A ripe papaya should give slightly when pressed gently between the palms. It should not be soft or mushy at the stem end.

Store it right

Store an unripe papaya at room temperature. A green papaya will ripen in 3 to 5 days. Speed up the process by storing it in a brown paper bag with an apple or banana. Store ripe papayas in the fridge, in a plastic bag, where it will keep for up to a week.

Prep it right

Papayas are easy to work with. Cut in half, lengthwise, scoop out the seeds and scoop

*Bananas
(Cavendish Bananas
and Finger Bananas)*

Cactus Pears

Guava

Granadilla, or Passion Fruit, vary in shape and colour

Kiwi

Kumquats

Mangoes

Papaya

Persimmons

Pomegranate

Pummelo

*Star Fruit
(also known
as Carambola)*

Ugli Fruit

out the flesh. Alternately, you can peel a papaya with a vegetable peeler. It is easier, and less messy, to peel quarters or wedges, than to peel a whole papaya. The seeds are edible with a peppery taste not unlike nasturtium or watercress.

You can cook a green, unripe papaya that is as hard as a rock like you would a squash – bake it or steam it. It makes a delicious addition to Caribbean-style curries. Raw green papaya is also perfect for many pickles, chutneys and relishes. Ripe papaya can also be cooked. You can poach, sauté, stir-fry, bake, roast or grill it. Ripe raw papaya is a great addition to fruit salads, especially tropical ones with pineapple or kiwi.

Culinary companions

Be sure to serve ripe papaya with lime. Just one good squirt will bring an ordinary papaya into the realm of sublime. It also tastes fine with just a light dusting of cayenne pepper. Papaya makes a good salsa, and is compatible with such southwest flavours as hot peppers, fresh coriander, red onion and vinegar. Other good seasonings include fresh or crystallized ginger, orange zest, nutmeg, cinnamon, mace, cardamom and curry powder.

Culinary destinations

Green papaya salad is a popular Thai dish that is sweet, sour, salty and spicy all at the same time. Try papaya grilled with chicken or fish, or add it to kebabs. Wrap a wedge of ripe papaya with prosciutto for a delicious appetizer, or toss chunks of ripe papaya in a spinach salad with smoked turkey. Half a papaya makes a wonderful "salad bowl" heaped with shrimp or chicken salad. Or stuff the cavity of a green papaya with rice and ground meat, and bake it like squash. Papaya makes a good smoothie or milk-shake; try it in the blender with yogurt, silken tofu or buttermilk with a little lime juice or honey.

Tip
Don't throw out the seeds. You can dry them and use them like peppercorns. Or you can put them raw in the blender and add to a vinaigrette.

To your health

Move over oranges . . . papaya is an excellent source of vitamin C. One small papaya (150 g) contains 93 mg of vitamin C, which is 150 per cent of the Recommended Daily Intake (RDI). A small papaya contains only 60 calories, is high in folate and is a source of fibre and potassium.

Papaya is a traditional remedy for indigestion. Try it to soothe an upset or acid stomach. Papaya may also help prevent cancer, due to the antioxidant powers of the vitamin C. Turn to papaya to ease constipation and regulate high blood pressure, too. Some people experience skin irritation when handling papaya.

Quick ways

Peel a small papaya, cut it into chunks and whirl in the blender to make a purée. Mix with two parts yogurt or softened ice cream. Put the mixture into parfait glasses, garnish with shredded coconut and freeze until solid. Serve.

Passion Fruit

Passion may be the last thing on your mind when you look at a perfectly ripe passion fruit. It tastes best when it looks its worst – all shrivelled up and wrinkled. But close your eyes and get ready to take a heady swallow of this divine fruit, which offers up a seductively sweet and sour mouthful, full of deeply exotic flavours!

Other names

Passion fruit has quite a few aliases. First, there's mountain sweet cup. Then there's *granadilla* or "little pomegranate," the name chosen by the Spanish settlers who were reminded of pomegranate when they discovered this fruit. In Brazil, it's called *maracuj*, in Colombia it's *maracuy*, and in Venezuela it's *parcha* or *parchita*.

Looks like/Tastes like

A passion fruit may be as small as an egg or as large as an apple, but usually is the size of a large plum. Round, with a tough shell that is ¼-inch thick, passion fruit comes in dusky purple, yellow, reddish, orange or taupe. The juicy, gelatinous pulp is filled with edible black or brown seeds (about the size of grape seeds). The flesh comes in a variety of colours: greeny-golden, orange, pinkish-green, and even white and colourless. The flavour is intense and complex, both sweet and sour and incredibly fragrant. The two main types are yellow or purple passion fruit.

Select it

A passion fruit is ripe when it is wizened, wrinkled and shrivelled. If you buy one with smooth skin, let it ripen at room temperature. Choose passion fruit that are heavy for their size and without any cracks, bruises or signs of mould.

Store it right

Ripen smooth-skinned passion fruit at room temperature. Ripe passion fruit should be consumed immediately or stored in a plastic bag for a couple of days. The flesh and juice can be frozen in freezer bags or freezer-safe containers for 6 months.

Prep it right

This is an easy fruit to deal with. Simply cut it in half and scoop out the flesh with a spoon. Or drink up the flesh right out of the shell. The seeds are edible, but not to everyone's taste. The flesh is never solid enough to cut or slice.

You can eat passion fruit raw or cooked. Make juice by blending the flesh and seeds in the mixer, then passing it through a fine sieve, muslin cloth or even a paper coffee filter. Add fruit juice or water until it reaches the desired consistency.

Culinary companions

Passion fruit goes well with other tropical fruits such as kiwi and banana. It also has an affinity with grapes, strawberries and

melon. Lime and lemon juice are other winners. Sweeten it up with honey, sugar, rum,
kirsch or maracuya (passion fruit liqueur).
Consider it with such dairy items as ice
cream, yogurt, custard or whipping cream.

Culinary destinations

The famous Australian dessert pavlova is
customarily topped with passion fruit pulp
and seeds. Passion fruit also makes a great
topping for yogurt, ice cream, shortcake or
cheesecake. Use the juice to create tropical
punches, nectars or cocktails, or try it in
marinades or salad dressings. Lightly cooked
passion fruit sauce adds zing to grilled poultry, pork or fish. Passion fruit makes an exotic jam or jelly.

To your health

There are 97 calories in a 3-½-ounce (100-g)
serving of passion fruit and only 20 calories
in a single passion fruit. Passion fruit is a
good source of dietary fibre, if you eat the
seeds. It's also high in vitamin C. Five passion fruits supply 50 per cent of your daily
vitamin C needs. Passion fruit is also a source
of beta carotene, which helps lower the risk
of heart disease, stroke, cataracts and lung
cancer. It's also a source of folate and potassium. Passion fruit works as a natural laxative,
but you need to eat the seeds, too!

Quick ways

When you're in the mood for a rich, tropical
treat, remove the pulp from several passion
fruits, sweeten it up with some sugar and
fold it into whipped cream. Serve in chilled
parfait glasses, garnished with fresh strawberry slices.

Peaches

Whenever I have a basket of Ontario-grown peaches on my counter, I'm in culinary bliss. Many a joyful moment is spent hanging over the sink slurping down peach after peach. And then there are the cooking opportunities! I'll spend hours lovingly canning what I believe to be a year's worth of peach salsa, only to have it disappear from my pantry by November.

Looks like/Tastes like

California alone grows 175 different varieties of peaches, so you can imagine how many varieties are found around the world. However, it takes a pretty dedicated peach lover to tell the subtle difference between any of them. Newer varieties have been developed to create a larger, firmer, more acidic peach than the older ones. But two distinct peach varieties are worth noticing: white peaches and donut peaches. **White** peaches have pale white flesh and a creamy-white skin splashed with fluorescent pink. They are sweeter than their yellow-fleshed cousins due to their low acid to sugar ratio. To my mind, **donut** peaches look more like a fritter than a donut. They're flat, with rounded sides that draw in toward the centre like a donut without a hole. A descendent of the flat Chinese peach, the donut peach has a yellow skin with a red blush. All peaches are classified as either **clingstone**, **freestone** or **semi-freestone**, but almost all of the clingstone peaches end up in cans.

Select it

Nothing is worse than a mouthful of cotton when you're expecting a mouthful of juicy, ripe peach. Choosing the right peach is tricky because peaches don't ripen further once picked. They get softer but they don't get sweeter. To make matters worse, many growers pick peaches before they are ready because unripe peaches travel better. So here's how to avoid any peach pitfalls: choose peaches by background colour, not blush. A red or pink blush is not always a good indicator of maturity – but a creamy or yellow background is essential. Most importantly, avoid peaches that show the slightest hint of green in the background. A ripe peach will yield to pressure along the seam and it should have a nice, aromatic peachy smell. Don't ever buy a rock-hard peach or, conversely, a wrinkled one. Tan circles or spots are early signs of decay.

Store it right

You can't ripen a peach at room temperature, no matter what people might say. The old paper bag routine will create a softer peach, but not a sweeter, riper one. So buy your peaches perfectly ripe and they'll hold a day or two at room temperature, away from direct sunlight. If you've bought a basket, don't leave the peaches in it. Take them out and store them in a single layer. Ripe peaches last up to a week, uncovered, in the fridge.

The easiest way to freeze peaches is the dry-pack method. Peel and slice 4 cups (1 L) of peach slices and arrange on a baking sheet. Mix ¼ teaspoon (1 mL) of ascorbic acid powder and ¼ cup white sugar in a small bowl. Sprinkle this mixture evenly over the sliced fruit. Freeze until solid (it takes a few hours). Transfer the fruit to a freezer bag as soon as it is solid to prevent freezer burn. Keep frozen up to 6 months.

Prep it right

To eat a fresh peach, just wash and bite (preferably over the sink). Before you cook, freeze, preserve or prepare a peach for a dessert, peel it. (Cooked peach skin is tough and unappealing.) The classic method is to blanch it in boiling water for 30 to 60 seconds. Remove with a slotted spoon and plunge into a bowl of ice water. Once the fruit is cool, the skin should slip off easily with a sharp knife. If not, repeat the process. You can also microwave a peach at high for 1 minute to loosen the skin.

Peeled and sliced peaches brown easily. Prevent this by brushing with fresh lemon or lime juice. Or sprinkle peach slices with a pinch of ascorbic acid (vitamin C powder). Or dip peaches briefly into acidulated water (3 tablespoons/45 mL of lemon juice to 1 quart/1 L of water).

Culinary destinations

Try a warm grilled peach salad on a bed of greens, sprinkled with blue cheese and dressed with balsamic vinaigrette. Or simply toss raw, peeled peaches into a green salad or a curried chicken salad. Peaches are perfect in preserves, whether they are jam, salsa, chutney or jelly. They even make a nice vinegar with tarragon. Peaches are classic in pie, and have been known to end up in crumbles, popovers, tarts and flans. A few spoonfuls of puréed peaches, combined with tequila, lime juice and a bit of sugar makes a remarkable cocktail. Don't forget peaches in your soup – combine them with squash for a savoury soup or with plums for a sweet dessert soup.

To your health

One medium peach (98 g) contains only 42 calories and is a source of potassium and dietary fibre.

Biting into a peach means not only taste, but a powerful boost of antioxidant vitamins A, C and E. Research has shown that people who eat foods high in antioxidants are less prone to heart disease, stroke, cataracts and some cancers. Peaches are also a source of fibre, both soluble and insoluble. Pectin, a soluble fibre found in peaches, lowers blood cholesterol, and insoluble fibre prevents constipation. Those who are allergic to peaches are often allergic to apricots, plums, cherries and almonds, too.

Quick ways

Layer a ready-to-use shortcake or flan cake with yogurt cheese (yogurt that has been drained overnight through a cheesecloth or coffee filter) mixed with honey (to taste) and a sprinkling of lemon zest. Arrange peach slices on top, sprinkle with cinnamon and serve.

Pears

Despite its ubiquity, the pear is a fruit people still get excited about. Its voluptuous shape and buttery texture have been seducing palates for centuries. There are an estimated 5,000 varieties.

Looks like/Tastes like

While most pears are typically bell-shaped, Asian pears are as round as an orange and other varieties are short, stubby and neckless. Skin colours range from green to yellow to russet to red, but one thing always remains constant: the flesh of a pear is white to cream-coloured. Pears have a core that contains inedible seeds. The skin is edible.

Among the thousands of varieties, the **Bartlett** pear (a.k.a. **Williams** in Europe) is the most common and favoured pear. This exceptionally sweet pear offers a slurpy, juicy, buttery soft bite when ripe. It's shaped like a bell and comes in two colours: green that ripens to yellow and red that ripens to crimson.

The **Anjou** pear is oval, stubby and short-necked. It's the most abundant and inexpensive winter pear. This French pear is very aromatic but not quite as sweet as the Bartlett.

Some would argue that the **Comice** is the best pear due to its fine texture, which is juicy and not even faintly granular. This is a plump, neckless pear with a thick, green skin that turns golden when ripe. The red variety turns dark red when ripe. **Seckels** is a small, bite-sized pear, developed in the United States. This excellent-tasting, short-necked pear is usually dark green with a dull red blush. The **Bosc** pear has a slender shape, elongated neck and a russet hue on a golden skin. It has a crunchier texture than other pears and it holds its shape well in baking or poaching. **Clapp's Favourite** is similarly shaped to a Bartlett but slightly more granular. Like the Bartlett, its green and sometimes russet skin turns yellow when ripe.

Asian Pears

The Asian pear is erroneously pegged as a cross between a pear and an apple. It's an easy mistake to make – since its texture is as crisp and firm as an apple and the flavour is distinctly pear-like. But the Asian pear is truly a pear, belonging to a separate genus than the "regular" pear. Indeed, it may be the grandfather of all those pears grown throughout North America, Europe and Australia.

Asian pears come under many names: *nashi* is the Japanese name, but it's also called **Oriental pear**, **Chinese pear**, **sand pear** and **apple pear**. The two best-known types – *nijisseiki* and *shinseiki* – are both Japanese. There are dozens of varieties of the Asian pear, grown throughout China, Japan, Taiwan, Korea and now, in the United States and Australia. Japanese varieties tend to be more flavourful and sweeter than Chinese.

Unlike regular pears, Asian pears ripen on the tree and are ready to eat when firm, crisp and, often, green. For best results, choose one that has a sweet aroma. Asian pears store well. They keep for a week at room temperature and for weeks in the fridge. However, they are very fragile and bruise easily. Try wrapping them in paper towel or tissue paper before storing in the crisper in a plastic bag. Asian pears do not freeze well and they are best eaten raw, rather than cooked. Although many urban supermarkets carry Asian pears, you'll find the best selection at Asian food markets.

Select it

Pears, like bananas, are a plan-ahead fruit best bought unripe and brought home for ripening. While it is tempting to buy ripe pears, you're likely to bruise them on the trip home. Besides, once fully ripe, pears do not last more than a day or two in the fridge. Look for smooth-skinned pears, free of surface markings.

Store it right

You can store unripe pears in the fridge. The cold will slow, but not stop, the ripening process. When you're ready to eat them, let them ripen at room temperature. It's a good idea to put half your purchase in the fridge and the other half at room temperature to stagger ripening. When storing at room temperature, remember to rotate the fruit daily. Ripening takes from 3 to 7 days (to speed it up put pears in a brown paper bag with a banana or apple). It's ripe when it gives slightly to pressure at the stem end. Don't wait until the whole fruit is soft or you'll have a mealy pear. Store ripe pears in the refrigerator crisper for 2 to 3 days. Pears do not freeze well.

Prep it right

Pears, at their most basic, are easy to prep: wash and bite in. Although the skin is edible, it can be peeled off easily with a knife. Try using an apple corer to remove the core or simply cut it out with a sharp knife. Pears brown quickly once cut. Sprinkle liberally with lemon juice as soon as it is cut.

Culinary destinations

Toss some pears into your next cranberry sauce at Thanksgiving...they offset the cranberries perfectly and reduce the amount of sugar needed. Try pears with ginger, whether in a chutney or a cobbler. Arrange sautéed pear slices on thick slices of whole wheat toast, dust with freshly grated Parmigiano-Reggiano and cook under the broiler until golden. Stuff pears with raisins, dates, sugar and spices then bake. Or make pear sauce instead of applesauce.

To your health

The most nutritional part of a pear is the skin, an excellent source of dietary fibre. There are 4 g of fibre in a single pear. Pears are a source of vitamin C, folate and potassium. There are only 98 calories in a medium pear. Asian pears have similar nutritional qualities to regular pears.

Pears contain pectin, a soluble fibre, that helps control cholesterol. They also contain cellulose, an insoluble fibre that promotes normal bowel function. Pears are a good source of boron, a trace mineral that helps the body retain calcium and magnesium, two bone-strengthening minerals. Recent studies suggest that boron can boost estrogen levels in post-menopausal women. Pears are one of the least allergenic foods around, making them a perfect first food for babies. High in levulose sugar, pears are a valuable aid to diabetics, who are able to digest this type of sugar more easily than glucose. Pears simmered with fennel seeds and honey is considered a good cough remedy.

Quick ways

To make pear sauce, peel and slice four pears into 1-inch (2.5-cm) chunks. Combine the pears, 1 cup (250 mL) water and the juice of half a lemon in a deep, microwave-safe, 2-½-quart (2.75-mL) casserole. Mix in ¼ to ½ cup (50 to 125 mL) of brown sugar and ½ teaspoon (2 mL) of cinnamon. Cook, uncovered, at high for 5 minutes. Stir. Cook another 5 minutes at high. If you want your sauce chunky, mash it with a fork or potato masher. If you want it smooth, whirl it in the blender. Cool to room temperature, then cover and refrigerate. Alternately, add a little bit of freshly grated ginger before cooking, or add a little almond extract once cooked.

Tip

Pears are a consumer's dream: they ripen best when off the tree.

Persimmon

In Japan, the persimmon is known as divine food. When you delve into a perfectly ripe, sensuous persimmon, you'll know why. But be forewarned: if your first bite is an "unripe bite" (of a Hachiya persimmon), you may swear off this fruit forever. An unripe Hachiya will pucker you up like no other.

Looks like/Tastes like

Persimmons taste like a combination of plum, honey, apricot, pumpkin and mango, exotically laced with perfume. Some persimmons are slightly spicy. It's one of the sweetest fruits in the world. There are hundreds of varieties of persimmon grown around the world but the two main commercial varieties are Hachiya and Fuyu. **Hachiya** persimmons are packed with mouth-puckering tannins (also found in much smaller quantities in tea, grapes and peaches) when they are not ripe. Once the persimmon is ripe, the tannins become inert and the astringency disappears. **Fuyu** persimmons (also called **Fuji** persimmons) are not astringent when unripe – just unsatisfying. The Fuyu is tomato-shaped and brilliant orange. The Hachiya is acorn-shaped, with a pointed tip and orange-red flesh and skin.

Select it

Look for persimmons with a fresh, green, stem end and leaves. Take a pass on any that are brittle and dry. The colour of the persimmon should be deep orange, not yellow, mustard or green. Don't even think of purchasing specimens that are cracked or split. Choose ones that are heavy in the hand.

Store it right

When it comes to ripeness, the Fuyu and Hachiya differ. Hachiya are ripe when very soft. An unripe Hachiya can take a number of weeks to ripen at room temperature. Fuyu, on the other hand, ripen at room temperature in just a couple of days and are still slightly firm when ripe, giving way to slight pressure like a peach. Once the fruit is ripe, eat it immediately or refrigerate in a plastic bag for up to 3 days.

To freeze ripe persimmon, purée the flesh in a blender or food processor with some lemon juice. Pack in small freezer containers and keep frozen for up to 6 weeks. Or freeze a Hachiya whole, after cutting off the tip and wrapping the whole fruit well in plastic.

Prep it right

The skin and flesh of the persimmon are edible, but sometimes the skin can be too tart to eat (check first). There may be no seeds, or they may be as many as a dozen in either variety. Fuyu can be peeled with a paring knife and cut into wedges or slices. Hachiya have a thicker, less appetizing skin than the Fuyu. Try cutting it in half and scooping out the jelly-like fruit with a spoon.

Culinary companions

Lemon or lime enliven the flavours of persimmon. The Japanese like it sprinkled with sake – rum, brandy, tequila and Grand Marnier are other options. Cinnamon, allspice, ginger and nutmeg add flavour. Cream it up with whipped cream, ice cream, yogurt, sour cream or cream cheese. Persimmons combine tastefully with nuts, be they almonds, walnuts, hazelnuts, pine nuts or pistachios.

Culinary destinations

Freeze a whole ripe Hachiya, and then serve it as sorbet with fresh grapes or drizzled with liqueur. Firm slices of Fuyu persimmon can be tossed into a fruit salad or added to a green salad with red onions and toasted walnuts. The squishy soft pulp of a Hachiya can be transformed into puddings, mousses or custards. You can substitute persimmon purée for pumpkin purée in quick breads and muffin recipes.

To your health

One (168 g) persimmon contains 117 calories and is high in dietary fibre, containing 6 g. Turn to persimmons for an excellent source of vitamin A, supplying 36 per cent of the Recommended Daily Intake (RDI). Persimmons are a source of vitamins C, E and B^6, potassium and folate.

Persimmons contain important antioxidant vitamins (A, C and E), which may reduce your risk of cancer and heart disease. Moreover, persimmons are a good source of fibre, which helps prevent constipation and maintain regularity.

Quick ways

Persimmons taste fine after they've spent 2 minutes under a broiler. First, cut a ripe Hachiya or Fuyu in half, remove the seeds, then drizzle with a little maple syrup and a sprinkle of allspice, nutmeg or cinnamon or a few drops of vanilla extract. Broil for 2 minutes and serve warm, with a dollop of yogurt or ice cream.

Tip

If you have a stubbornly unripe Hachiya, place it in an airtight container with a couple of drops of rum or brandy. This ripening trick should have it ready in less than a week.

Pineapple

A truly sweet, perfectly ripe pineapple is pure magic. When I first tasted the "real thing" after a childhood of canned pineapple, I went into culinary culture shock. I never knew a pineapple could taste so good. The trick is in the selection. Pineapples don't ripen after they've been picked, so choose this fruit carefully.

Other names
Pineapple is indigenous to Brazil, where it was dubbed *anana* by the Brazilian Indians. The French took the name and ran with it. The Spanish, however, looked at its pine cone shape and called it *piña*, which inspired the subsequent English name.

Looks like/Tastes like
Pineapples can grow up to 20 pounds (9 kg) but those grown commercially are generally 3 to 5 pounds (1.25 to 2 kg). The most common variety is the cone-shaped **Smooth Cayenne**. The **Red Spanish** is more square, with a tougher shell. A new variety, developed by Del Monte in Hawaii, is the **Golden Pineapple** – it's not only sweeter, but also contains three times the vitamin C. Two exotic varieties of pineapple are the Queen and the Cherimoya pineapple. The **Queen** is a miniature pineapple from South Africa, about half the size of a regular pineapple, with a sweet, edible core. The **Cherimoya** hails from Taiwan, and is an elongated pine-apple that you can pull apart, rather than slice. Each handful reaps a small, sweet and juicy section.

Select it
More myths surround choosing a ripe pineapple than perhaps any other fruit. Forget the old tip about pulling a leaf from the crown – whether the leaf breaks off easily or not has no bearing on ripeness. Thumping also doesn't tell you anything. What matters is the foliage: look for crisp, green leaves that show no signs of yellowing or turning brown. And use your nose. The ideal odour is sweet and fragrant. Never buy a pineapple that smells sour or fermented. A pineapple should be firm, without any soft areas. Furthermore, colour doesn't matter. A ripe pineapple can be totally green or yellow – it all depends on the variety.

Store it right
Store a pineapple for a day or two at room temperature, out of direct sunlight, to reduce acidity (although this won't increase sweetness). Plus, a pineapple tastes better and is juicier when served at room temperature. But if you don't plan to eat your pineapple within 48 hours, store it in a plastic bag in the refrigerator. Better still, prep the pineapple and store it in its juice in an airtight container, where it will keep for up to a week.

Prep it right

Don't let a pineapple's anatomy discourage you from buying one. If you're not an experienced pineapple carver, start with something simple: cut off the top and bottom then slice crosswise, making wheels about an inch (2.5 cm) thick. Pare off the peel from the individual slices, making sure to remove the eyes and the inner core. Here's another easy approach: slice the whole pineapple lengthwise into large quarters. Use a small serrated knife to cut the fruit away from the shell, as you would a melon away from its rind. Then trim off the core in one lengthwise slice. Once you've graduated from these two methods and want a more challenging task, try this: slice the top and bottom off the pineapple. Stand the pineapple up on the cutting board and pare off the skin with long, lengthwise cuts from top to bottom. Notice that the remaining eyes form a spiral pattern along the pineapple. Follow the spiral, cutting a groove into the flesh, which not only removes all the eyes but also forms a beautiful pattern. But if all that slicing and dicing is too formidable for you, shop at a store that sells fresh, pared pineapple.

Culinary destinations

Try it in fresh fruit salad, on a cheesecake or in a yogurt smoothie. Pineapple grills well and can be part of a savoury pork and bell pepper kebab. For a dessert kebab, team it with melon and peaches. Pineapple makes a good salsa, chutney and even a curry. Toss it into a pilaf, throw it in a stir-fry with chicken and cashews, or wrap it with bacon and broil for an appetizer.

To your health

A 1-cup (250-mL) serving of diced pineapple (155 g) contains just 75 calories. It is an excellent source of vitamin C, supplying 38 per cent of the Recommended Daily Intake (RDI). It is also a source of potassium, thiamin and dietary fibre.

Pineapples contain powerful bromelain enzymes, which have been shown in numerous studies to help healing, reduce inflammation (as a result of injuries) and speed up repair. Accordingly, pineapple is a good food to eat right after surgery or an injury. Pineapple has long been considered a digestive and now, with the discovery of its enzymes, we know why a little bit of pineapple at the end of a meal helps digestion. Moreover, it reduces blood clotting and may also remove plaque from arterial walls, making this fruit a heart-healthy food, too.

Quick ways

Marinate chunks of pineapple and cantaloupe in equal parts of orange juice and brandy for 15 minutes. Thread on to skewers and grill until golden. Serve with chopped fresh mint.

Plums

When there are plums in your fruit bowl, you know it is summertime. I love the surprising splash of colour plums offer up with that first bite . . . you never know what gorgeous shade of luscious flesh will be lurking beneath that blue, purple or almost-black wrapper. That remarkable contrast of colours is as beguiling as the taste. Yellow and green plums can also astonish – most people don't realize how sweet they can be.

Looks like/Tastes like

The world of plums can be very confusing. With some 200 varieties, it's hard to know your Damson from your Santa Rosa. Plums can be as small as a cherry and as large as a baseball. They may be oval or round, sweet to tart, with skin colours covering a wide range: green, yellow, red, purple, blue and black. There are two main types of plums – Japanese and European. **Japanese** plums are green, yellow, bright red or crimson, but never purple. They are juicy plums with a yellow or reddish flesh and they arrive earlier in the season than their European relatives. Common varieties include **Santa Rosa, Laroda, Early Golden** and **Vanier**. European plums are sometimes called **prune** plums; they are smaller, firmer and less juicy than Japanese. These are the plums that are dried into prunes. They're perfect for baking, stewing and preserving but they also taste great fresh. The small and tart-tasting **Damson**

belongs to this group, as do the **Italian**, **President** and **Empress**.

Select it

Plums, like peaches and nectarines, don't ripen after picking, so be sure to select them ripe. Touch them first. A ripe plum should have a little spring – when you press it gently, it will bounce back. The end opposite from the stem end (a.k.a. the blossom end) should be slightly soft. Smell it – a ripe plum should have a delectable perfume; however, the lighter varieties tend to be less fragrant than the dark ones. No matter what colour the plum is, look for uniform colour. Don't buy shrivelled plums or those that have brown spots or brownish discolouration. Unripe plums will soften at room temperature but they won't get any sweeter.

Store it right

Time is of the essence with a ripe plum. Eat it fast and don't expect to store it long, for it will overripen quickly. Put it in a paper bag and store in the fridge if you can't eat it right away. It will last a day or two.

Prep it right

Simply wash the plum and eat – the skin is edible but the pit is not. Or slice your plums. If you have a freestone plum, the pit will fall away easily. A semi-freestone plum can be sliced around the equator to the pit, then twisted to free the two halves. You may need to nudge out the pit with the tip of your knife. The only way to treat a clingstone plum is to cut the fruit away from the pit.

To remove the skin from a plum, blanch it in boiling water for 30 to 60 seconds. Remove with a slotted spoon and plunge into a bowl of ice water. Once the fruit is cool, the skin should slip off easily with a sharp knife. If not, repeat the process.

Tip
Plums are often cooked whole with the skin on. Prick the skin first before poaching, stewing, boiling or roasting a whole plum.

Culinary destinations
Try fresh, sliced plums with red grapes, strawberries and cherries in a white wine and framboise sauce for dessert. You can stuff a pork tenderloin with diced plums and traditional bread stuffing – and then glaze it with a plum chutney or plum jam. Try adding plums to your favourite Indian curry or toss them alongside a roast chicken 15 minutes before it is done. Sliced plums make an elegant topping for plain cheesecake and also work in tarts and flans.

To your health
There are 36 calories in a plum. Plums are a source of vitamins C and E, along with potassium and riboflavin. They also contain fibre.

Plums contain two important antioxidants (vitamins C and E), which may help reduce your risk of heart disease and cancer. Eat the skins and you benefit from the fibre in plums, especially cellulose, which is an insoluble fibre that can keep you regular and prevent constipation. Plums contain potassium

and no sodium, which is good news for heart health. Those allergic to plums are often also allergic to almonds, apricots, cherries and peaches.

Quick ways
Get ready to dip some spring rolls in homemade plum sauce. Purée six, peeled plums in a blender or food processor. Heat some oil in a wok or frying pan at medium high and stir-fry some garlic, fresh ginger and hot pepper flakes (if you like it hot) for just 30 seconds. Add the plum purée, a splash of vinegar and soy sauce to taste. Bring to a boil, then simmer for a few minutes. Add 1 teaspoon (5 mL) of corn starch mixed with 1 teaspoon (5 mL) of cold water if you want it slightly thicker. Serve.

GET FRESH!

Pomegranate

The pomegranate is a fun and messy fruit that children adore. Adults like it too, but prefer it already "shelled" without all the mess. It pays to learn how to unwrap a pomegranate, so that you can serve up some juicy arils as part of a sauce, salad, dessert or garnish. Remember to stock up during pomegranate season, for those jewel-like seeds store like a gem in the freezer.

Other names

The pomegranate is sometimes called a Chinese apple. In Spain, they call it *granada* and in France it is *grenade*, which helps to explain where the name grenadine (pomegranate syrup) originated.

Looks like/Tastes like

Pomegranates are round, orange-size and crowned by a turret-like calyx or blossom end. The pomegranate's thin, leathery skin ranges in colour from green to yellow to red to purple, but is most commonly red or pinkish-red. The interior of a pomegranate is bursting with hundreds of tiny, edible seeds packed into compartments called arils and separated by bitter, cream-coloured membranes or pith. The aril is a translucent brilliant-red pulp that has a fragrant, berry-like, sweet and sour flavour.

There are many types of pomegranates cultivated around the world. One of the most popular varieties in North America is called **Wonderful**, perhaps the best pomegranate to choose for juicing. The **Early Wonderful** is better for eating out of hand. **Green globe** has green skin and is excellent quality. **Granada** is a little less tart than Wonderful and ripens earlier. **Fleshman** is pink inside and out, with soft seeds and a very sweet flavour.

Select it

Pomegranates are available from fall to early winter. For best results, choose fruit that is heavy for its size. And give it a little squeeze – if powdery clouds puff out of the crown you've found a dud that is dusty and dry inside. Look for specimens that are large and richly coloured and have a few cracks.

Store it right

Whole, unpeeled pomegranates will store in the fridge for up to 3 months, but once cut, a pomegranate deteriorates quickly. Wrap cut pomegranates tightly with plastic wrap and store in the fridge. Better still, remove the seeds and store them in an airtight container in the fridge for a few days. Or freeze them in a single layer on a cookie sheet in the freezer until solid, pour into a freezer bag and keep frozen for up to 3 months. There is no need to defrost them before using.

Prep it right

Score the skin lightly, cutting lengthwise into quarters, without piercing the arils. Peel back the skin and pull them out. If you do this in a bowl of water, the arils will sink and the membranes will float, so you don't make such a big mess.

To make pomegranate juice, first prep a whole pomegranate by rolling it on a table with the palm of your hand to break the arils. You'll hear them pop. Simply pierce a small hole through the skin, stick in a straw and enjoy! Or pierce a hole, hold the pomegranate over a bowl and squeeze. One fruit yields about ⅓ cup (80 mL) of juice. To get the most juice from a pomegranate, use a manual citrus juicer or a food processor, and then strain the seeds out with a sieve.

You can eat a pomegranate out of hand. Or remove the ruby-red arils and sprinkle them over fruit salads or into savoury green salads. Pomegranate juice can be consumed raw or cooked. Think of it when you glaze poultry or ham, or try it in jellies, jams or chutneys.

Tip
Pomegranate juice stains; it is used to dye Persian rugs.

Culinary destinations
Tangy pomegranate juice is used like lemon juice in many Mediterranean and Middle Eastern preparations, such as Lebanese okra simmered in pomegranate juice or the traditional Mediterranean dip of hot and sweet peppers, walnuts and pomegranates called muhammara. Try substituting pomegranate juice with lemon juice in any of your recipes, especially curries, soups or vinaigrettes. Simmer pomegranate juice until reduced in half, add sugar and lemon juice to taste, and use as a glaze for carrots, parsnips or sweet potatoes.

To your health
Pomegranates are a good source of potassium. One medium pomegranate contains 398 mg, about the same as that found in a banana. Pomegranates are also a source of vitamins C and E. There are 104 calories found in one pomegranate.

Pomegranates contain powerful antioxidants (vitamins C and E), which help fight cancer. As a potassium-rich fruit, pomegranates may help to regulate your blood pressure, preventing heart disease. Recent research suggests that pomegranate extract has antiviral properties and can kill off viruses associated with the common cold, herpes and diarrhea.

Quick ways
Toss together one head of Boston lettuce with the seeds and juice of one pomegranate, one cubed ripe avocado and the sections of one orange. Dress in a light vinaigrette, season with salt and freshly milled black pepper and serve immediately.

Trivia
What do pomegranates and condoms have in common? Researchers at Nottingham University in the United Kingdom discovered in 1996 that extracts of pomegranate can kill viruses, including the HIV virus. Now they're looking into ways to market this research and a pomegranate-based chemical coating on condoms is just one of those ideas!

Pummelo

The giant of the citrus family, pummelos have long been favoured in Asia. The Chinese believe that a pummelo is a sign of fortune and prosperity and that good things happen to those who eat it. Besides, it tastes good.

Other names

Pummelo is often spelled pomelo. In the United States and West Indies, the name Shaddock is also used. Adam's apple is another common moniker.

Looks like/Tastes like

The largest citrus fruit, pummelos range in size from that of a large grapefruit to a basketball. Some pummelos weigh 22 pounds (10 kg), but most are about the size of a small cantaloupe. Pummelos are round or pear-shaped, with a slightly conical stem end. The green or greenish-yellow rind is thick and aromatic. The white, pale yellow or pink flesh has a coarser, drier texture than grapefruit, but it is sweeter than grapefruit without any bitterness.

Pink Pummelo has a Thai heritage but it's also grown in California. It looks like a pink grapefruit with a pebbled rind and bright yellow skin. **Chandler** is the most common pummelo. It has a delicious sweet pink flesh and seeds. Three pummelo-grapefruit crosses are of note: look out for **Oroblanco**, **Melogold** and **Pomelit** – they are all super sweet.

Select it

Choose heavy, filled-out and fragrant fruits. A pummelo is ripe when it is golden yellow and heady with aroma.

Store it right

You can store a pummelo at room temperature or put it in a perforated plastic bag in the crisper of your refrigerator for better last-ability.

Prep it right

A pummelo cannot be eaten with a spoon like a grapefruit. It is best peeled, with all the pith and thick white membrane removed. In fact, you can also peel the entire membrane off each single section, since pummelo flesh holds its shape, even once peeled. Rather than use your fingers, use a sharp knife to slice off the stem and blossom end, cutting right to the flesh. Make four to five cuts lengthwise into the rind without cutting to the flesh. Pull off the rind, then peel the membrane off each section.

Use pummelo as you would grapefruit, in fruit salads, green salads and desserts, or simply eat it out of hand. The thick soft rind can be candied or preserved in a marmalade.

Culinary companions

Pummelo is enhanced by such sweeteners as brown sugar, honey and maple syrup. It tastes delicious with ice cream, yogurt, mascarpone, cottage cheese and farmer's cheese.

It works well with lemon, lime or orange juice. Seasonings include fresh ginger, nutmeg, cinnamon, anise, mint and hot peppers. Almonds and almond extract are other winners.

Culinary destinations

Baste some peeled pummelo sections lightly with oil or melted butter, dust with brown sugar and place briefly under a hot broiler. Break the sections into vermicelli-like strands, splash with Pernod and serve between courses as a refreshing palate cleanser. Sprinkle with salt, lime juice and cayenne pepper as a spicy appetizer. Or put pummelo sections into a salad with endive, radicchio and avocado with a chive vinaigrette. Toss a few sections into a pasta salad with grilled chicken or use as a garnish when serving grilled fish.

To your health

One cup (250 mL) of pummelo sections (190 g) contains 72 calories and a whopping 115 mg of vitamin C, almost twice the Recommended Daily Intake (RDI). Pummelo is a source of dietary fibre, potassium and magnesium.

In Asia, pummelo is often served after a meal as a digestive. Pummelos are an excellent source of vitamin C, which not only reduces the severity of colds but also plays an important role in maintaining good health. For instance, vitamin C helps the body absorb the iron in foods better, which in turn prevents anemia and fatigue. Team iron-rich foods with pummelo to increase iron absorption. Vitamin C also forms collagen, the cement that builds healthy teeth, skin and bones. Lastly, vitamin C improves immunity, helping to fight off cancer and other diseases.

Trivia

The pummelo is the ancestor of the grapefruit, which wasn't born until the 1700s, as a natural cross between the sweet orange and pummelo.

Raspberries

Summer just wouldn't taste the same at our cottage if it weren't for those wild raspberries. Braving scratchy canes and the inevitable mosquitoes, we pounce on the fruit-heavy bushes, gobbling as fast as we pick. There's never much to show after a family raspberry hunt, except stained fingers, happy faces and half-filled containers.

Looks like/Tastes like

Red continues to reign as the favourite raspberry variety. You'll find it in a range of reddish hues, from pink to crimson. It thrives in moderate climates with warm summer days and cool evenings. **Black** raspberries grow in the warmer climes of the southern United States. Small and seedy, they have a mild, tart flavour. **Purple** raspberries are a hybrid of the red and black. **Golden** or **yellow** raspberries have a sweeter, milder flavour than red.

Select it

Look for firm, dry berries with good colour and a seductive perfume. Stay away from any that are shrivelled or overly soft. Likewise, don't buy any with the hull attached – they've been picked too early and will be tart. Check for mildew. Pass up cartons that are stained with juice, indicating a layer of crushed berries at the bottom.

Store it right

Handle raspberries gently. Check the carton contents and remove any crushed berries. Avoid mould, in the shape of little white dots. Store in the fridge, preferably in one layer, with a paper towel on the top and bottom, covered loosely with plastic wrap. They'll keep no more than a few days. If you purchase pick-your-own berries, store them in a cooler during the trip home.

Raspberries freeze well. Once they are clean and dry, arrange them in a single layer on a baking sheet in your freezer. When they are frozen solid (45 minutes to 1 hour), transfer them to a freezer bag and store for up to 6 months.

Prep it right

Wash raspberries carefully under running water, using the spray attachment of your kitchen spout, if possible. For really delicate berries, mist with a plant sprayer. Dry them carefully using paper towels or clean dish towels. Don't soak berries in water – they absorb it like a sponge and lose flavour.

Culinary companions

Raspberries team up well with other berries, summer fruits and tropical fruits such as mango or kiwi. They also work with mint and tarragon. Dairy possibilities are limitless.

Culinary destinations

Make a raspberry and mustard sauce for veal or chicken. Throw a few berries in a blender for a smoothie. Make a sweet dessert soup simmered with lemon, cinnamon and cloves, and then served chilled with a swirl of sour cream. This berry is a favourite with bakers: it's in pies, cobblers, tarts, muffins, crisps and bread puddings.

To your health

Get them while you can: raspberries are teeming with nutrients! Raspberries are an excellent source of vitamin C and fibre. There are 6.6 g of fibre in 1 cup (250 mL) of raw raspberries, which fulfills 20 per cent of an adult's daily fibre needs. They also contain folate, iron and potassium.

The insoluble fibre found in raspberries helps to prevent constipation, and the soluble fibre helps control cholesterol levels. Both red and black raspberries contain anthocyanins, a pigment responsible for their red, violet and blue colours. Black raspberries contain high concentrations of this important phytochemical, boasting more than seven times the amount found in red raspberries. Anthocyanins have been shown in studies to have numerous health benefits, such as preventing cancer and heart disease, controlling diabetes, improving circulation, reducing eye strain and even combatting the loss of memory and motor skills associated with aging. Raspberries also contain ellagic acid, another cancer-fighting substance also found in gooseberries, blackberries and strawberries, and it doesn't break down during cooking.

On the negative side, raspberries contain oxalic acid, which interferes with calcium and iron absorption and is best avoided by those who have kidney or bladder stones.

They also contain salicylate, which can cause an allergic reaction in aspirin-sensitive people.

Quick ways

It's easy to make your own raspberry vinegar. Heat ½ cup (125 mL) of white wine vinegar to boiling and pour over 1 cup (250 mL) of clean and dry raspberries. Cover and steep at room temperature (out of direct sunlight) for 3 days. Strain the mixture and discard pulp. Put raspberry/vinegar mixture in a small pot, add 2 teaspoons (10 mL) honey and heat until dissolved. Pour into a clean bottle and refrigerate.

Trivia

Raspberries are the only cane berries that come free of their hulls and caps when picked, making them the most fragile berry of all.

Rhubarb

What is the first sign of spring? For many, it's a red-breasted robin. But for gardeners and rhubarb-lovers, it's the thought of all those sweet and sour desserts on the horizon as rhubarb starts poking through the soil.

Other names
Rhubarb is sometimes called pie plant and wine plant.

Looks like/Tastes like
There are two main types: **field grown** (with dark red, green or striated stalks) and **hothouse** (with light pink stalks). Rhubarb resembles celery stalks, ranging in colour from ruby-red to pink to green. The inedible – poisonous, in fact – leaves are shaped like huge elephant ears. Rhubarb has a distinct, tangy taste, but it is easily dominated by other cooking flavours.

Select it
Look for firm, crisp stalks. When snapped, these stalks release juice if they're fresh. The leaves should be perky and fresh looking. Colour doesn't indicate ripeness, but red rhubarb is sweeter and juicier than green, which is higher in dietary fibre.

Store it right
Wrap rhubarb in damp paper towels (to keep the stalks moist) and place them in a plastic bag in the refrigerator for up to a week.

Rhubarb is easy to freeze. Chop into 1-inch (2.5-cm) pieces and place directly into freezer bags. Rhubarb will freeze for up to 1 year and there's no need to defrost before cooking.

Prep it right
Rhubarb is easy to work with. Simply cut off the leaves, trim the ends, wash and start chopping!

Rhubarb is very sour and requires sweetening. Cook it with sugar, honey, maple syrup or other sweeteners. You'll need about ½ cup (125 mL) of sugar per pound (500 g) of rhubarb. To reduce the sugar content, pair rhubarb with sweet fruits such as apple, strawberry or pineapple. It tastes sweeter once it's cooked, so add just the minimum of sugar before cooking, and add more later if necessary. Rhubarb browns naturally when cooked. Avoid aluminum or cast-iron pans, or it will darken due to the acids reacting to the metals. You can bake chopped rhubarb in a 300°F (150°C) oven in a covered glass baking dish until tender (about 30 minutes per pound/500 g). Or try stewing chopped rhubarb in a saucepan with just enough water or fruit juice to cover. Bring to a boil and then simmer, covered, for 5 to 7 minutes or until tender. After the rhubarb is cooked, add sugar or honey and cook for a few more minutes until it's dissolved.

Culinary companions

Rhubarb teams up well with many fruits: strawberries, raspberries, mangoes, apples, pears and pineapple. Citrus juice and zest work well with rhubarb. Freshly grated, dried or candied ginger brings out the best in rhubarb. Other companions include cinnamon and vanilla.

Culinary destinations

No wonder rhubarb is also known as pie plant. It makes the perfect springtime pie, tart, flan, crisp or crumble. It also works well in muffins and quick breads. Consider rhubarb sauce over veal cutlets, chicken breasts, duck or grilled fish. Rhubarb can stand solo or work in a fruit duet when making chutneys, compotes or jams.

To your health

One cup (250 mL) of raw rhubarb contains only 26 calories, compared to 1 cup (250 mL) of cooked and sweetened rhubarb at 280 calories. One cup (250 mL) raw contains 10 mg of vitamin C. It's also a source of potassium, magnesium and calcium. However, rhubarb contains high levels of oxalic acid, which binds up calcium and prevents absorption.

Researchers at the University of Alberta are awaiting patent approval for a dried rhubarb dietary supplement. What's the fuss? Rhubarb has long been considered a folk remedy for constipation, but now science has confirmed not only rhubarb's laxative powers, but also its ability to reduce cholesterol levels. Rhubarb is extremely high in the kind of fibre that rids the body of "bad" LDL cholesterol that clogs arteries. In the meantime, it increases levels of "good" HDL cholesterol. Researchers say it outshines oat bran and even pectin as a cholesterol-reducing food.

But don't eat the leaves! Rhubarb leaves contain toxic levels of oxalic acid.

If you're prone to kidney or bladder stones, avoid rhubarb due to its high oxalic acid content.

Trivia

An Italian aperitif called Rabarbaro is made from rhubarb.

We commonly call rhubarb a fruit, due to its high acid and pectate content. But it is technically a vegetable, belonging to the same family as buckwheat and sorrel.

Star Fruit

Move over kiwi, star fruit is the new garnish in town! Chances are you've seen a slice of this gorgeous, golden-yellow fruit adorning a gourmet meal. But star fruit is more than just a pretty face. It delivers a crisp, juicy mouthful with a tropical mix of flavours.

Other names

The proper, scientific name for this fruit is carambola, but most people call it star fruit. It's also called five-angled fruit, five corners or five fingers. In the West Indies, it is called *granadilla*.

Looks like/Tastes like

"What star?" ask most people when they first see this fruit whole. Glossy and oval, the star fruit is from 3 to 6 inches long and has five, longitudinal ridges. Once it is sliced crosswise, a star-shape is formed. Some varieties contain a few small, flat and inedible seeds. The skin colour is most commonly yellow, but it ranges from green to gold to orange. One variety is white. The edible skin contains a natural wax that makes it shiny. The translucent flesh is greenish yellow.

There are 20 different varieties of star fruit. One of the best known is the sour-sweet **Golden Star**. **Arkin** is very sweet, but slightly bland. Depending on the variety and ripeness, a star fruit can be incredibly sour, or sweet and sour, or sweet. The crisp, juicy, citrusy flesh hints of apple and grape flavours.

Select it

Choose a shiny, plump, firm star fruit with no brown spots or wrinkles. A perfectly ripe star fruit will have a thin brown line along the ridges. Green star fruit are underripe. The thicker the ribs, the sweeter the flavour. Ripe star fruit has a floral, fruity aroma and no traces of green on the skin. Look for it sold in specialty produce and Asian stores.

Store it right

Star fruit will ripen at room temperature. Speed up the process by putting it in a paper bag with an apple or banana. Store ripe star fruit in a perforated plastic bag in the crisper where it will last for up to a week. Star fruit slices freeze well. Arrange slices in a single layer on a baking sheet and freeze until solid. Transfer to a freezer bag and freeze for up to 6 months.

Prep it right

Everything is edible in a star fruit except the seeds. If the skin is thick, you may want to peel it lightly. Some people slice off the unappealing brown strip along the ridges of a ripe star fruit. You can eat a star fruit out of hand or sliced. It's easy to juice: just cut it in half, crosswise, and juice it like an orange with a citrus juicer. Or, purée in a blender or food processor and pass through a sieve to remove seeds and unwanted fibres. You can sauté, grill, stir-fry or bake star fruit. Slice it into fruit salads, toss it with greens or use it as a garnish for a pasta or rice salad.

Culinary destinations

Try it in a sauté with ginger, lemon zest and shrimp. Bake some white fish fillets in a wine sauce with a blanket of star fruit slices. Simply sautéed in butter with fresh herbs, star fruit slices make a classic garnish for grilled poultry or fish. Thread it on a skewer to make a fresh fruit kebab with strawberries, bananas and grapes or team it up with a savoury combination of marinated chicken cubes and sweet red peppers. Star fruit, particularly sour varieties, are stellar in preserves, be it chutney, salsas, relishes, jellies and jams. Kids love finding a star fruit slice in the middle of a pancake. Consider it on your next cream cheese and bagel. For a fancy appetizer, serve star fruit wrapped in prosciutto. For parties, float star fruit slices in your punch bowl.

Culinary companions

Star fruit has a particular affinity for Asian flavours such as curry spices (cardamom, cloves, turmeric, mace, nutmeg, ground coriander, cumin and cinnamon) and fresh ginger. Complementary fresh herbs include tarragon, basil, fresh coriander, chives and parsley. Bland, sweet cheeses are a good pick whether it is cream cheese, ricotta or cottage cheese. It pairs well with all citrus and is heavenly with avocados, too. Spirited companions for star fruit include rum, Frangelico, Cointreau and Triple Sec.

To your health

There are only 30 calories in a medium (91 g) star fruit. It is high in vitamin C and a source of potassium, folate and fibre.

A common Asian snack is half-ripe star fruit dipped in salt. Not only does it taste good, but this snack helps to replace body fluids lost through perspiration in hot, tropical climates. According to traditional Chinese medicine, star fruit is a diuretic. Star fruit contains high levels of oxalic acid, which interferes with calcium and iron absorption. Foods high in oxalates should be avoided by people with kidney or bladder stones.

Trivia

Very sour star fruit are used to clean copper and brassware in Asia.

Tip
Buy some fresh star fruit in season and freeze it in slices. That way you'll have a year round supply of this exotic garnish for special events. Kids also love munching on these "star popsicles!"

Strawberries

It used to be that strawberries were the harbinger of summer. The short season allowed but a limited love affair with this very special berry. But today, if you're an urban dweller, chances are you can get your strawberry fix year round.

Other names
Wild strawberries are sometimes called alpines.

Select it
Look for bright red, slightly shiny, ripe berries with fresh green caps. Once picked, a strawberry doesn't ripen any more. Choose carefully to avoid berries with green or white shoulders (the areas below the hull). Don't buy a box of berries if you see any mouldy berries on top. Mould travels fast and may have ruined the rest of the box. And stay away from berries packed in juice-stained containers. An imported berry with a lot of mileage is an unlikely candidate for great taste. Your odds are always better when you buy local.

Store it right
Strawberries do not keep well. Gobble them up as fast as you can. Most keep no more than 3 days. Pick berries over before storing in the fridge. Remove any damaged, crushed or mouldy ones. Store unwashed, with hulls intact, preferably in a single layer, on paper towel, uncovered. Strawberries freeze well. Put washed and dried strawberries (whole or sliced) in one layer on a large tray or cookie sheet and freeze until firm (about an hour). Pour them into a freezer bag, draw out as much air as possible and you've got summer in the freezer for about a year.

Prep it right
Keep the hull on when washing strawberries. They absorb water quickly and taking the hull off makes each one a super sponge and it will lose flavour. Wash them gently under softly running water and never soak them. Once they're washed, dry them immediately with paper towels. If you're serving them whole, keep the hull on – it makes it easier to dip or plop into your mouth. For a garnish, dehull and make lengthwise slices that stop just before the tip end. Fan out and serve.

Culinary destinations
You've heard of strawberry pancakes and crepes, so for something different, try a strawberry omelette. Fold some inside the omelette and leave a few to sprinkle on top, too. Toss some strawberries in your next spinach salad. Or try them with avocados, Boston lettuce and some orange slices. Creamy yogurt dips, sweet or savoury, are great for strawberry dipping. Melted chocolate doesn't hurt, either. Chop strawberries up and mix with your favourite cream cheese.

This is a nutritional spread that most kids love, despite the fact that it's "good for you."

To your health

In the berry batch, strawberries win the contest for vitamin C content. Just 1 cup (250 mL) sliced strawberries contains 94 mg of vitamin C, which is one and a half times your daily needs. Ounce for ounce, strawberries have the same vitamin C content as oranges. Strawberries are a source of folate, potassium and dietary fibre.

Strawberries contain phytochemicals called flavonoids, which are thought to boost the antioxidant effects of vitamin C – something that strawberries are very high in. With both vitamin C and flavonoids working in conjunction, your risk of heart disease and cancer may be reduced. Strawberries contain another cancer-fighting substance called ellagic acid. It doesn't break down when food is cooked, so that means pies, jams, jellies and preserves are better for us than we ever imagined.

Unfortunately, many conventionally grown strawberries test high in pesticide residues. Buy organically grown produce to avoid that risk. Moreover, strawberries are a highly allergenic food. Introduce them into a baby's diet watchfully and ask guests about food allergies before serving them strawberries.

Quick ways

1. Strawberry salsa time! Dice 2 cups (500 mL) of washed strawberries. Mix with some chopped onion, lime juice, a little salt and sugar (to taste) and some chopped fresh coriander. Heat it up with some cayenne powder, Tabasco sauce or fresh jalapeño peppers. Serve on grilled fish or chicken, as a dip with taco chips or as an appetizer, spooned on top of fresh avocado slices.

2. Try some sweet and sour strawberries, the northern Italian way. Wash and slice a pint of strawberries. Sprinkle with 2 tablespoons (30 mL) of sugar and chill in the fridge for about 2 hours. Toss gently, then stir in 2 tablespoons (30 mL) of good quality balsamic vinegar. Marinate in the fridge for another 30 minutes and then serve chilled, tossing gently one more time before serving. Garnish with freshly ground black pepper.

Trivia

What's the difference between strawberry jam and strawberry preserves? Both are cooked with sugar (and sometimes pectin) to create a soft, spreadable consistency, but the distinction is that in jam fruit is crushed or cut up – in a preserve the fruit's original shape is maintained.

Vegetables

Artichokes

Many people avoid the artichoke because of its strange anatomy. But if you cook them whole, they're easy to prepare. This fine vegetable is meant to be savoured, much like a good lobster. Serve some up on a weekend evening when you have the time to relish each leaf, dipping your way slowly to the luscious heart.

Other names
The common nickname for an artichoke is choke.

Looks like/Tastes like
There are as many as 50 varieties of artichokes around the world, but the most commonly found is the **Green Globe**, an Italian type. Artichokes come in different sizes: baby, medium and jumbo. Surprisingly, **baby** artichokes are not artichokes that are picked young. In fact, all three sizes grow on a single plant: the **jumbo** ones on the centre stalk, the **medium** ones on the sides and the babies, at the base. An artichoke looks like a big, green unopened flower bud, which makes sense since the artichoke is the edible flower bud of a thistle. It's picked just before it blooms. You'll discover that spring and summer artichokes look and taste slightly different than fall and winter artichokes.

Select it
Choose artichokes that are heavy for their size. In winter and spring, choose ones that have an even green colour and are compact and firm. If the leaves have begun to unfold, the artichoke is past its prime. Summer and fall artichokes are somewhat flared and more conical in shape. Bronze-tipped leaves are caused by exposure to light frost, a natural occurrence that doesn't harm their taste at all. Look for a green stem end with no holes or signs of drying. Avoid artichokes with dark bruised spots or black, wilted leaves.

Store it right
Artichokes last longest in a plastic bag in your refrigerator crisper. Sprinkle with a little water or spritz with a mister before closing the bag. They'll last no more than a week.

Prep it right
To serve an artichoke whole, trim away the outer leaves and slice a half inch (1 cm) off the top to create a flat top. Some people like to cut off the stem so an artichoke can sit up on a plate. If you do, be sure to reserve the stem, because it's edible and tasty.

To quarter or slice an artichoke, bend back the outer leaves until they snap off easily near the base. Continue to bend back leaves until you reach a central core of pale, tender green leaves. Scrape the stem base of the artichoke to smooth off the rough areas where the leaves were broken off. Halve the artichoke, and remove the fuzzy choke (babies don't have one) with a spoon or sharp knife. Cut lengthwise again into quarters or slice thinly.

The easiest way to serve an artichoke is to steam or boil it until it is tender, then serve with a dip. The classic dip is melted butter and lemon juice. Lower-fat options include salsa, buttermilk or herb dressings and roasted red pepper purée. Try trimming artichokes into quarters, sautéing with olive oil, garlic and herbs, and serving on pasta.

Tip

When trimming an artichoke, keep a fresh lemon at your side. As you trim, rub the cut areas with the lemon to stop browning. Alternatively, drop the trimmed artichokes into a bowl of acidulated water (3 tablespoons/45 mL of lemon juice or vinegar in 4 cups/1 L of water).

Culinary companions

Delicious companions to artichokes include lemon juice, butter, olive oil, garlic, tarragon, rosemary, sage, bay leaves, parsley, thyme, fennel seeds, capers, green onions, Parmigiano-Reggiano and goat cheese.

To your health

One medium artichoke (120 g) contains 60 calories and 6.4 g of dietary fibre, making it an excellent source. Artichokes are also an excellent source of folate and magnesium and a source of calcium, iron, phosphorous, potassium, vitamin C, thiamin, riboflavin, niacin and vitamin B[6].

Artichokes contain an organic acid called cynarin, which stimulates sweetness receptors in some people. That's why wine can taste strange when drunk with artichokes and why water can taste sweet. Cynarin is also associated with lowering blood cholesterol but studies are not conclusive. Artichokes are a traditional remedy for indigestion and the liver.

Arugula

When this green first became trendy, everyone was stumbling on its mouthful of a name. If you don' t like to say "ah-ROO-guh-lah" then call it rocket, like they do in Britain.

Other names
Other names include *roquette* (in French), Mediterranean rocket, Italian cress, rugula and tira.

Looks like/Tastes like
Arugula has dark green, flat, serrated leaves shaped like oak leaves. Young arugula leaves are 2 to 3 inches (5 to 8 cm) long but mature leaves can measure up to 8 inches (20 cm) long. Small, young leaves have a sweet, nutty and mild taste. Big leaves can be very spicy, slightly bitter and peppery. Arugula is commonly sold with its roots attached, and is usually displayed by the fresh herbs or specialty salad greens.

The two main varieties are wild and cultivated – ironically, the wild type is now cultivated. Arugula still grows wild in France and Italy.

Select it
Look for lively, crisp greens with no signs of yellowing. Avoid arugula that is limp or soggy. Choose small leaves for salads and large ones for cooking.

Store it right
Keep the roots attached until you are ready to use it. Arugula likes a dry environment, so wrap it in paper towel and place in a plastic bag in your crisper.

Prep it right
Trim the leaves from the stalks and roots. Discard the stalks or reserve for stock. Arugula leaves can be very sandy, so wash them in several changes of water. Dry in a salad spinner or blot dry with a clean kitchen or paper towel.

You can treat arugula like a salad green, an herb or a green leafy vegetable. Small arugula leaves are best for salads (baby arugula is added to most mesclun salad mixes). Toss it with radicchio leaves for a classic Italian combination, team it up with less audacious leaves like bibb or Boston lettuce or let it star on its own. When cooking arugula, give it a light touch – a quick sauté until it wilts is all it needs. Larger leaves lose their bitterness when cooked.

Tip
Home gardeners take note: this green is easy to grow, even in containers. You can seed it all summer long for an everlasting crop. Plus, you can eat those arugula flowers.

Culinary destinations

Shred some arugula and toss it into omelettes, quiches and risotto. Wilt some and mix with hot pasta and roasted garlic. Pile some fresh leaves in your next sandwich or make a trendy arugula and goat cheese pizza.

Culinary companions

Arugula works with many different flavours. Team it up with walnuts and hazelnuts, as well as their oils. In salads, it shines under a red wine, sherry or balsamic vinegar dressing. Salad options include blood oranges, avocado slices, tomatoes, pine nuts, fresh figs, hard-cooked eggs, fresh berries or grilled onions. Get cheesy with pecorino Romano, Parmigiano-Reggiano, goat cheese or Gruyère.

To your health

Arugula is a nutritional superstar among salad greens. It has more calcium than most other salad greens. A 2-cup (40-g) serving of raw arugula contains only 10 calories and is a source of calcium, vitamins C, A, E and folate.

Arugula is a card-carrying member of the illustrious Cruciferous Club (cabbage family). Research shows that this veggie group contains phytochemicals that trigger enzymes that ward off cancer. Meanwhile, the beta carotene found in arugula may offer protection against heart disease, cataracts and premature aging of the skin.

Quick ways

Throw two peeled cloves of garlic down the tube attachment of your food processor while it's running. Add a clean bunch of arugula leaves, a small handful of walnuts and a ½ cup (125 mL) of Parmigiano-Reggiano cheese. Pulse several times. Add 3 tablespoons (45 mL) of extra virgin olive oil and salt to taste. Process to a smooth paste. Serve this pesto with hot pasta or spread it on a pizza crust, topped with grilled shrimp, tomato slices and mozzarella cheese.

Tip
Tell your produce manager to stop misting the arugula! Moisture causes deterioration.

Asparagus

You know it's spring when asparagus pops up in your store. Feast on it while supplies last . . . and consider freezing some for a winter day.

Looks like/Tastes like
The most common type of asparagus is **green**. **White** asparagus, popular in Europe, is finding more growers in North America. Watch out for **purple** asparagus, the newest type to emerge.

Select it
Look for straight, crisp, nicely rounded spears with deep green or purplish tips that are closed and compact. Avoid partially open, wilted or sandy tips. Check out the stem ends, too: they should be moist and green, and not grey, dry or cracked. Size is a matter of preference and doesn't indicate maturity. But do try to pick out a bunch of spears of equal size to ensure even cooking.

Store it right
Keep asparagus refrigerated and moist. Asparagus lose roughly half of their vitamin C content within 2 days if stored at room temperature. Keep in a plastic bag in the refrigerator crisper with the stem ends wrapped in a damp paper towel. Or stand them upright in a jug of water, covered with a plastic bag in the fridge. Remove any rubber bands before storing – they constrict and hasten rotting. Storage time is limited to 2 or 3 days. Eat as soon as possible.

Prep it right
Asparagus is grown in sandy soil and can surprise with a gritty mouthful if you don't wash the spears carefully. Wash them under running water or dunk them in a sink full of water to remove sand and dirt.

Should you snap or cut off the ends? Snapping is your best option since it detaches the inedible, woody part of the asparagus and doesn't remove any of the edible part – a risk you take when using a knife. To snap, hold the asparagus at the centre of the stalk with one hand and at the base with the other hand. Bend the stalk gently until it snaps.

Another dilemma: to peel or not to peel? Thin asparagus spears don't warrant the task but thick stalks have a more fibrous, woody skin that is best peeled off. Use a potato or vegetable peeler and start at the base, peeling upward.

To boil asparagus, put an inch (2.5 cm) or so of water in a large skillet. Bring to a boil. Turn off the heat temporarily (so as not to burn your hands in the steam) and place the asparagus so it lies flat in the skillet; turn the heat back on and cook, uncovered, until tender (3 to 5 minutes, depending on thickness). Keep the lid off so your asparagus keeps its green colour.

Roasting intensifies the sumptuous flavours of asparagus. Simply toss 1 pound

(500 g) of washed and trimmed spears in 2 tablespoons (30 mL) of olive oil and 1 table-spoon (15 mL) of lemon juice or balsamic vinegar. Spread in a single layer on a baking sheet lined with parchment paper. Sprinkle with salt. Roast in a 400°F (200°C) oven until tender, about 6 to 15 minutes, depending on the thickness of the asparagus. Sprinkle with freshly grated Parmigiano-Reggiano and serve.

You can also steam asparagus standing upright in a special, asparagus cooker.

Culinary companions

Asparagus goes well with so many things: butter, olive oil, sesame oil, hazelnut or walnut oil, lemon juice and zest, hollandaise sauce, basil, tarragon, thyme, parsley, hazelnuts, walnuts, pine nuts, sesame seeds, goat cheese, Gruyère, Parmigiano-Reggiano, mustard, garlic, ginger, green onions, soy sauce, oyster sauce, shallots, and so on.

To your health

Seven spears (100 g) of asparagus contains only 24 calories and provides a whopping two thirds of your total daily needs in folate. Asparagus is a source of vitamins C and A, iron, phosphorous, potassium, thiamin and riboflavin. White asparagus contains fewer vitamins than green.

Asparagus is a natural diuretic that can help prevent water retention. Some people notice after eating asparagus that their urine has a pungent smell. Studies show that about 40 per cent of the population is affected by this harmless reaction, caused when the body metabolizes sulphur compounds found in asparagus. People with gout should avoid asparagus as it is high in purines, which can raise uric acid levels. Asparagus is high in folate, a B-complex vitamin that may prevent cardiovascular disease. Recent studies

have shown that folate can reduce high homocysteine levels, which increase the risk of heart attack. Folate also prevents neural tube defects in fetuses and may also protect against cancer of the colon and cervix.

Quick ways

Got some leftover asparagus spears from dinner? Take a fresh, flour tortilla, spread on a thin layer of goat cheese and then arrange a thin slice of prosciutto and a few stalks of cooked asparagus. Wrap and serve.

Avocado

Yes, it's true – avocados are a high-fat food. But that shouldn't stop you from making them part of a healthy diet. This vegetable (technically a fruit) boasts a creamy, luxuriant taste and a bounty of nutrients.

Other names

The avocado's pebbly, dark green skin prompted the nickname alligator pears. They're also referred to as butter or green pears.

Looks like/Tastes like

The **Haas** (also known as **California** avocado since it comprises most of the state's avocado production) has thick, pebbled skin that ripens from a dark green to a purplish black. Thanks to a high oil content (one of the highest among avocados), Haas has a rich, buttery texture. It averages about half a pound (250 g) in weight. The **Fuerte** has a thin, green skin, even when ripe. Expect a milder flavour than the Haas and a more pronounced pear shape. The **Bacon** is green and smooth skinned, too. The **Zutano** is yellow-green with a shiny, smooth skin. Florida varieties include the **Booth**, **Lula** and **Waldin**. Florida avocados tend to be larger than California ones, and contain less fat and fewer calories. However, they also lack the rich texture of their California counterparts.

Select it

An avocado can require up to a week to ripen. Take this into consideration when making your purchase. Look for avocados with a good green colour that are heavy for their size. Avoid overripe avocados. An overripe Haas will be dark black; other varieties will be green or crimson. Any overripe avocado has a dry and crackly skin, and when you press lightly on the surface your fingers leave a dent. The flesh of an overripe avocado is inedible and black, while a ripe avocado offers up soft, spoonable flesh. A just-ripe avocado, on the other hand, can be sliced.

Store it right

For best results, keep avocados out of the fridge. Cold temperatures alter their flavour and interrupt the ripening process. To speed up ripening, store them in a closed paper bag with a banana or apple. To store mashed avocado or guacamole, press the plastic wrap against the surface to keep air out (oxygen turns avocado flesh from green to brown). When storing leftover avocado, leave it in its skin, with the pit intact, and brush some lemon juice over the surface before wrapping with plastic. Mashed avocado and dip can be frozen for several months in a freezer-safe container.

Prep it right

Peeling an avocado is a messy, difficult job, especially if the avocado is under- or overripe. For best results, cut it lengthwise (or even crosswise, to produce "rings"), and twist the two halves gently to separate them. Pry out the pit with the tip of a knife or spoon. When an avocado is ripe, you can cut the flesh and pry out the slices without removing the skin. Or you can put the halved avocado on a cutting board – skin side up – and peel the skin off after making lengthwise, skin-deep incisions. Alternatively, just spoon out the flesh – the easiest and best thing to do if you're making a dip.

When working with avocados, keep some fresh lime or lemon juice nearby. A little spritz goes a long way to keep it green, not brown. Slice, mash or purée avocado. You can't cook it, though – it turns bitter.

Culinary destinations

Avocados are the perfect choice for guacamole or any other dip. They can be whirled in a blender to make a salad dressing, cold soup or even a milkshake. Many people are surprised to learn that avocados can go either way: savoury or sweet. Mash avocado with sugar and fresh lime juice, and fold in whipped cream, cream cheese or ricotta to make a delicious pie filling or pudding. A slice or two of avocado makes a club sandwich, hamburger or cheese-melt very special. Avocados and alfalfa sprouts are a classic California combination – try them in tortilla wraps, stuffed in a pita pocket or rolled up with sweet Japanese rice for sushi.

To your health

Most fruits and vegetables are fat-free, but not the avocado. There are a whopping 17 g of fat in a 3-½-ounce (100-g) serving of Haas avocado, compared to 8 g in the same size serving of a Florida avocado.

Avocados contain more potassium, ounce for ounce, than a banana. One serving

(3 ½ ounces/100 g) of avocados can contain from 488 to 634 mg of potassium, depending on the variety (California avocados contain more). Avocados are high in folate and fibre and a source of iron, thiamin, riboflavin, niacin and vitamins C, A, E and B[6]. There are 177 calories in one serving of California avocado and 112 calories in the same serving of Florida avocado.

Due to the high potassium and ample protein found in avocados, this food is a good choice for athletes. Although the avocado is high in fat, fortunately it is high in unsaturated fat, which has been shown in studies to reduce cholesterol. Plus, valuable vitamin E is stored in that fat.

Small amounts of avocado can contribute to heart health, thanks to the high levels of potassium and vitamin E. In the meantime, avocados are an excellent source of folate, which studies show may prevent heart disease.

Quick ways

Guacamole is an easy, quick preparation that can be used as a dip, sauce or garnish. Mash one avocado with 2 tablespoons (30 mL) each of finely chopped tomatoes and green onions. Crush or chop one clove of garlic and add it to the mixture, along with some fresh lime juice, a pinch or two of hot pepper and some fresh, chopped coriander.

Tip
It's a myth that you can stop a bowl of guacamole from turning brown by storing it with the pit immersed in the bowl.

Beans

Easy to grow, a snap to prepare, beans are a wonderful gift from Nature. All of the following beans are categorized as "edible pod beans." They're the babies of the bean family, picked before they turn into mature beans that are grown for drying such as kidney, Romano or black-eyed pea.

Looks like/Tastes like

Snap beans (a.k.a. **string** beans) are the most ubiquitous. There are three kinds: green, yellow and purple. These beans are actually a type of immature kidney bean. Yellow and purple (**Royal Burgundy**) snap beans are sometimes called **wax** beans. The yellow variety has a mild, slightly buttery taste and the purple variety turns green when cooked.

Haricot vert is the French cultivated snap bean. These skinny beans are more dainty and slender than their snap cousins, and they're best when very young, no more than 3 inches (8 cm) long.

Wide-podded **Romano** beans (a.k.a. **Italian green** beans) are flat and broad, sometimes twice the heft of snap beans.

Chinese long green beans (also called **yard-long** or **asparagus** beans) are indigenous to Asia and can measure up to 18 inches (46 cm) in length. They have a slightly crunchier, tougher texture than string beans and a milder flavour. They are a close relative of the black-eyed pea.

Select it

Look for beans that have a vivid, fresh colour and a velvety feel. Avoid those with rusty spots or scars. Snap beans should, as the name implies, snap when bent in half. If they don't, they aren't fresh and may be too tough to eat. If seeds are visible through the pod, pass those beans up. That means they are too mature and will taste tough and insipid.

Store it right

Put beans in a perforated plastic bag and store them in the crisper. Fresh beans will last for up to 4 days.

Prep it right

"Top and tail" is the old adage in prepping beans. The top is the stem end, and needs removing. Some people like to do it by hand, one by one. Alternatively, line up a bunch of beans on a cutting board and use a knife. Whether you need to remove the tail (or tip) is a matter of taste. Small, fresh beans look lovely cooked whole with their tips still attached. Or you can "French" your beans, cutting them lengthwise into thin strips.

Cook your beans whole, Frenched or cut on the diagonal. They can be steamed, boiled or microwaved. If thick and whole, beans are best blanched first before sautéing or stir-frying. Cook until just tender and bright, emerald green.

Culinary companions

Beans go well with butter, olive oil, mayonnaise, yogurt and cream sauces, pesto and olives. Nuts are a natural for beans. Choose almonds, peanuts, pecans, pine nuts or cashews. Chinese seasonings such as soy sauce, ginger, oyster sauce, black bean sauce and sesame oil all complement beans. Herbs that go well with beans include basil, parsley, dill, chives, thyme, rosemary and sage. Zest, be it orange or lemon, works well with beans. Tomatoes, sweet peppers, onions and potatoes can all team up with beans with success.

To your health

One cup (110 g) of raw green beans has only 34 calories, no fat and 2 g of protein. Beans are high in vitamin C and folate and a source of vitamin A, potassium, riboflavin and thiamin. Green beans have six times more beta carotene than yellow beans.

Beans are rich in fibre, both soluble and insoluble. The soluble fibre in beans can help reduce cholesterol. Insoluble fibre prevents constipation.

Quick ways

Sauté 2 cloves of garlic and 1 onion, chopped, until tender. Add ½ pound (250 g) of fresh beans, 3 chopped tomatoes, a drained can of white kidney beans, and some parsley, thyme and rosemary. Braise until the beans are tender. Sprinkle with freshly grated Parmigiano-Reggiano cheese.

Trivia

Eat your beans while they're fresh! A recent study reported that fresh green beans left for 3 days in the store and 3 days in a home refrigerator retained only 36 per cent of their vitamin C, while frozen green beans had twice as much.

Beans were named string beans due to the stringy and woody nature of their pods. But geneticists solved that problem breeding the string right out of the beans.

Beets

What's more comforting on a cold winter day than a hot beet slathered with butter? Then there are beets in the summertime. Marinate them, pickle them or toss them into a hundred and one salads. This sweet little orb is versatile, inexpensive and totally colourful. Plus, when you buy fresh beets with their greens attached, you get a bonus vegetable. Beet greens are not only edible, but highly nutritious, too.

Other names

Red beets, root beets and table beets – these are all names for beets. Sugar beets are not meant for eating. They contain 20 per cent sucrose (compared to 10 per cent in table beets) and are cultivated specifically for sugar production.

Looks like/Tastes like

The most common beet is **red** and round. But beets can be long and tapered and even oval-shaped. They range from the size of a golf ball to baseball size. Less common, but growing fast in popularity, are beets that come in different colours. Watch out for **white** and **golden** beets, which don't stain and are milder than red beets. More playful is the Italian variety, called **Chioggia**, with its pinwheel, red-and-white striped flesh and remarkably sweet flavour. All of these varieties look spectacular in a salad. Don't add red beets until the last minute, for they will stain the other ingredients.

Select it

The best time to scout for beets is in early summer when you'll find small beets the size of golf balls. These tender delicacies cook up much faster than their larger counterparts. In general, the smaller the beet, the more tender it will be. Avoid overly large beets (over 2 ½ inches/6 cm in diameter). They may be tough and woody.

Check out the tops. Beets are sometimes sold with their greens still attached and the freshness of the greens will reflect the freshness of the root. Look for perky greens, preferably thin ribbed.

> ### Tip
> *When you buy a bunch, look for beets of equal size so that they' ll cook evenly.*

Store it right

If you have bought beet roots with their greens attached, cut off the greens, leaving 1 to 2 inches (2.5 to 5 cm) of stem on the beet, which helps to lock in nutrients during cooking. (When greens are attached to root vegetables, they leach nutrients from them.) Store beets and greens separately. The greens are highly perishable so eat them right away or store 1 or 2 days in a plastic bag in the refrigerator. The roots, stored in a perforated plastic bag in the crisper, will last up to 3 weeks. Once cooked, beets last for up to a week in the refrigerator.

Prep it right

Wash beets carefully. The outer skin can tear easily and the beet will bleed. It's best to cook your beets whole. If you cut them before you cook them, the deep crimson colour will leach out and your beets will turn a dull brown. To prevent excess bleeding, leave 2 inches (5 cm) of the stem attached to the root and don't trim the tap root until after it's cooked. The entire leaf and stem is edible, but most people trim off the stems.

You can steam, boil, bake, roast or microwave beets. One of the easiest ways to cook them is wrapped in foil, like a potato, at 375°F (190°C) until tender. Or you can simply arrange washed beets on a baking sheet and roast. A large beet may take more than an hour, while a small one takes only 30 minutes. Once the beets are cool, cut at each end and the skins slip off easily. To help beets keep their colour when cooked in water, add 2 tablespoons (30 mL) of lemon juice or vinegar. If you need a beet-fix, but don't have time to cook them whole, try grating raw beets and sautéing in olive oil with a squirt of lemon juice for about 10 minutes.

Beet greens can be boiled, steamed, sautéed or stir-fried. They bleed a crimson-hued liquid once cooked.

Culinary companions

The sweet sensations of beets stand up to many complementary flavours. Fresh herbs for beets include tarragon, thyme, parsley, dill, chives, mint or coriander. Try beets the Spanish way with a little anise seed, or bathe them in something creamy, such as buttermilk, yogurt or sour cream. Give beets a bite with a dollop of mustard or horseradish. They work well with salty cheeses, citrus fruit and a range of vinegars. Beet greens can be cooked with garlic, ginger, onions, Chinese seasonings and lemon juice.

To your health

A serving of 2 cooked beets (100 g) contains 44 calories and provides 36 per cent of the Recommended Daily Intake (RDI) for folate. Beets are also a source of potassium, vitamin C, magnesium and iron. A ½-cup (125-mL) serving of cooked beet greens (72 g) contains 19 calories and is an excellent source of beta carotene and high in vitamin C and potassium. Beet greens are a source of fibre, calcium, iron, vitamin B6, folate, riboflavin and thiamin.

Turn to beets for a spectacular source of folate, a B-complex vitamin that can reduce a woman's risk of having a baby with a neural tube defect (such as spina bifida) if consumed before conceiving and during early pregnancy. Folate may also reduce the risk of colon and cervical cancer and may also contribute to heart health, too.

Beet roots and tops contain oxalic acid, which can interfere with the absorption of minerals such as calcium and iron. People who have kidney stones should avoid beets and beet greens due to the high oxalate content.

Trivia

Beets on your burger? Yes, that's the preference in Australia, where sliced beets and pineapples are popular toppings on the Down Under hamburger.

Belgian Endive

Why are these little, white bundles in the lettuce section of your grocer so darn expensive? Pity those poor Belgian endives, for they never get to see the light of day. They grow forced from a root, buried in a mound of soil. It's a time-consuming agricultural method that creates a crisp, special taste with a gourmet price tag.

Other names
Belgian endive belongs to the chicory family. It's also called witloof chicory, chicon, radicchio, French endive and goat's beard.

Looks like/Tastes like
These bundles of white, smooth leaves look like unshucked cobs of corn, only smaller. They are 4 to 6 inches (10 to 15 cm) long and tapered, with small yellow leaves. Some varieties have a pink blush.

Select it
Look for firm, full heads with yellow leaf tips. The whiter the better. If the ends are green-tinged, pass them up, because they'll be bitter. Belgian endive often comes wrapped in royal-blue paper that keeps it shielded from the light during transport. Most is still grown in Belgium.

Store it right
Wrap Belgian endive in paper towel and store it in a paper bag in the crisper where it will last for 2 to 3 days.

Prep it right
Remove any damaged leaves and rinse the Belgian endive quickly in water. Avoid soaking it in water which makes the endive bitter. Remove the small, bitter inch-long cone situated at the root end. Belgium endive will brown when cut, so sprinkle liberally with lemon juice or hold in acidulated water (3 tablespoons/45 mL of lemon juice or vinegar to 1 quart/1 L of water) until you are ready to use it.

Belgian endive is an excellent salad ingredient and can also be stuffed and served as an hors d'oeuvre. You can cook it too: braise, roast or purée it.

Culinary companions
Belgian endive can team up with a lot of different ingredients such as beets, apples, walnuts, avocado, star fruit, currants, mushrooms, sorrel, smoked chicken or cheese.

Culinary destinations
Put Belgian endive in a salad: it blends well with tart greens such as radicchio and arugula, and contrasts well with mild greens such as bibb or Boston lettuce. For a change, cut it crosswise into rings for a salad. Stuff the cup-shaped leaves with goat cheese, bean purée, crab meat salad or smoked salmon cream cheese. Put Belgian endive alongside your next roast or toss it with a variety of vegetables, herbs and oil for oven

roasting. Try it braised, then sprinkled with Gruyère and placed under the broiler for a few minutes.

To your health

A head of Belgian endive (53 g) contains only 9 calories. It is a source of iron and folate, both of which help prevent anemia.

Europeans traditionally believe that bitter salad greens such as Belgian endive can stimulate digestive fluids and liver function. It's also a folk remedy for gout and rheumatism.

Broccoli

Sometimes I have to slap my own hand from reaching for broccoli each and every time I see it at my green grocer. I never tire of broccoli's sweet, pungent flavours or its emerald green colour. Whether broccoli is part of an Oriental stir fry or drizzled with a little extra virgin olive oil and blanketed with a snowy layer of Parmigiano-Reggiano, it is easy, fast and delicious.

Looks like/Tastes like

Standard green broccoli is also called **Italian green** or **Calabrese**. **Purple sprouting** broccoli is the original broccoli predecessor, and was used throughout Europe until the Italian variety swooped the continent. It turns green when cooked. **Broccoli Romanesco** is pale, yellowish green with spirals that form a pointed head.

Standard green broccoli has thick, green stalks that branch out into clusters of tight, unopened buds. There are grey-green leaves on the stems and around the florets. Kids like to call broccoli "trees" – which says it all. Purple sprouting broccoli is more leaves and stalks than bud clusters.

Select it

Look for firm, crisp broccoli with deep colour. The head should be tightly budded. Avoid broccoli with loose, yellowed buds or buds that have flowered. The more slender the stem, the better. Thick stems can be fibrous and woody. Avoid butt ends that are dry, cracked or hollow. Fresh broccoli should have a sweet, mild smell, not a strong, cabbagey odour.

Store it right

Store broccoli in an open plastic bag or a sealed, perforated plastic bag. Broccoli stored too long converts its sugar into fibre. That's why winter broccoli is never as sweet as summer-fresh broccoli. The sooner you eat it the better.

Tip
Keep the lid off when cooking broccoli – this results in bright green colours.

Prep it right

Simply wash broccoli well, cut off the florets and trim the stems. Don't toss those stems in the garbage – peeling is all a stem needs to taste great. Serve peeled stems raw with a dip, or brown-bag them with carrot and celery sticks. Florets cook faster than stems. If you peel stems and cut them on the diagonal into coins, they'll cook in the same time as florets. When cooking broccoli florets with long stems attached, cut an "X" at the bottom of the peeled stem to help speed up the cooking time. Don't toss the leaves away either, as they're packed with beta carotene. Add them to the cooking broccoli or reserve for soups or stocks. Broccoli is easy to prepare: steam, blanch, sauté, stir-fry, bake or microwave it. Cook broccoli until just tender to ensure sweet flavour, an emerald green colour and a pleasant crunch. Overcooking increases cooking smells and destroys colour.

Culinary companions

Broccoli has a wide range of complementary flavours. It works well with dairy, be it milk, buttermilk, cheeses, yogurt or sour cream. Mediterranean ingredients such as olive oil, capers, anchovies, hot peppers and olives are delicious with broccoli. Try it with such Asian sensations as sesame oil, oyster sauce, soy sauce, black bean sauce, ginger, garlic and shiitake mushrooms.

To your health

Broccoli is often hailed as one of the healthiest foods you can eat. A 1-cup (156-g) serving of cooked broccoli contains only 44 calories but supplies almost twice the Recommended Daily Intake (RDI) for vitamin C, containing 116 mg. The same serving of broccoli is also an excellent source of folate (35 per cent of the RDI) and vitamin E (26 per cent of the RDI). It's high in beta carotene, plus it's a source of calcium, iron, potassium, riboflavin and vitamin B^6.

Broccoli is rich in such phytochemicals as flavonoids (antioxidants) and indoles, which help protect against cancer and lower your risk of heart disease, stroke and cataracts. Broccoli is high in fibre (4.5 g of fibre in 1 cup (250 mL) of cooked broccoli) and works as a natural laxative, preventing constipation. High in folate, broccoli is a must for women planning to get pregnant since studies show that a diet high in folate reduces the risk of neural tube defects in fetuses.

Trivia

Hate the taste of broccoli? Researchers have a great excuse for those who can't stand its taste. Consider yourself a "super taster!" That's what researchers dubbed ¼ of the population after studies revealed that 1 out of 4 people has a sensitivity to bitter tastes found in fruits, vegetables and other consumables.

Brussels Sprouts

You could say that Brussels sprouts were never on my mother's culinary A-list when I was growing up. Consequently, I never knew this vegetable existed until I moved out into my own apartment. Suddenly, I'd found this "exotic" vegetable that was cheap, ubiquitous and deliciously satisfying when steamed, anointed in butter and spritzed with fresh lemon juice.

Looks like/Tastes like
It's a wonder that trendy chefs haven't tried to pass these off as "baby cabbages," because that's what they look and taste like.

Select it
Look for dense, firm heads with bright green colour. Small specimens taste better than large. Pick similar-sized Brussels sprouts to ensure even cooking. Brussels sprouts sold loose in a bin are a better choice than those hidden under cellophane in a 10-ounce (280-g) carton. (You never know what lurks at the bottom of those cartons.) And speaking of lurking, bugs love Brussels sprouts. Watch out for their calling cards: tiny holes or soot-like smudges on the leaves. Let your nose lead the way. Fresh Brussels sprouts should smell sweet, not off-putting.

Tip
The best time of year for a Brussels sprout feast is the fall, after the first frost or two. Sprouts taste better once they've been frostbitten.

Store it right
Store Brussel sprouts in your crisper, unwashed. Brussels sprouts do well in a perforated plastic bag or wrapped in paper towel in a regular plastic bag. Eat within 2 or 3 days. The longer you wait, the stronger they will taste.

Prep it right
Remove discoloured or damaged outer leaves. If you have bought organically grown produce and the outer leaves look perky and green, keep them on – outer leaves contain the most nutrients. But to minimize the risk of consuming pesticides, it's best to remove the outer leaves of conventionally grown produce.

To soak or not to soak? Due to the bug factor, some Brussels sprouts need a 10 to 15 minute soak in cold water to expel the little creatures. However, soaking means the loss of water-soluble nutrients. Speed up the soaking process by shaking the Brussels sprouts vigorously under the water. Farm-fresh Brussels sprouts are more likely to contain bugs than store bought – especially packaged – sprouts, which have already been washed and require only a quick rinse.

For best presentation, you may want to trim the stems. You can also score the stems with an "X" before cooking to allow the heat to penetrate the centre of whole, large Brussels sprouts. Little ones don't require this treatment.

Although you can eat Brussels sprouts raw, most people prefer them cooked. Brussels sprouts are most commonly cooked whole, but this method is best suited to boiling, steaming or baking, versus a quick stir-fry or sauté. To stir-fry or sauté, parboil Brussels sprouts first, rinse under cold water, slice, and then stir-fry or sauté. Or shred raw Brussels sprouts with a knife, then stir-fry. Overcooked Brussels sprouts give this veggie a bad name. Cook them until they are emerald green and tender (a fork should pierce through easily). The second you smell sulphur, stop the cooking.

Try them in a salad. Parboil, plunge in ice water, pat dry, and then mix with other salad ingredients. Or marinate in a vinaigrette for a few hours or overnight, and serve.

Culinary companions

If something is delectable with cabbage or cauliflower, it will work with Brussels sprouts, too. Fresh herbs include dill, thyme, parsley and oregano. Go nutty! Chestnuts and Brussels sprouts are an old English tradition, but almonds, pistachios, pecans, pine nuts and walnuts work fine, too. Mustard, caraway and curry spices are all complementary, as are cheeses, lemon and bacon.

To your health

A 1-cup (156-g) serving of cooked Brussels sprouts contains 60 calories and is an excellent source of dietary fibre, vitamin C and folate. Just one serving of Brussels sprouts supplies 150 per cent of the Recommended Daily Intake (RDI) for vitamin C and 41 per cent of the RDI for folate. Brussels sprouts are also high in potassium and vitamin B[6] and are a source of vitamin A, iron and calcium.

Brussels sprouts, like the other members of the cabbage family, contain many important phytochemicals (such as indole glucosinolates) and antioxidants, which may lower your risk of cancer. Since Brussels sprouts are a sensational source of folate, this veggie should be included in the diets of women who are pregnant or plan to become pregnant, as folate reduces the risk of neural tube defects in fetuses.

Quick ways

1. Try baking your Brussels sprouts. Parboil for 3 minutes, plunge in cold water, drain and arrange in an oiled casserole dish. Dot the Brussels sprouts with tiny dabs of butter, season with a pinch of mustard powder, salt and pepper, then sprinkle with ½ cup (125 mL) of chicken stock. Cover with grated cheddar cheese or Gruyère. Cook in a 350°F (180°C) oven until tender, about 20 minutes.
2. Pull all the leaves off a pound (500 g) of Brussels sprouts. Wash well. Sauté in butter, shallots and ½ teaspoon (2 mL) of caraway seeds. Serve.

Tip

It's best to cook Brussels sprouts with the lid off. That way you'll prevent the build-up of sulphurous gases. If steaming, take the lid off for a few seconds every 2 to 3 minutes.

Cabbage

Cheap and easy to cook with, cabbage has gained new stature as the leader of the Cruciferous Club. Cruciferous vegetables (members of the cabbage family) continue to astound researchers with their health-promoting qualities. So the next time you dig into a cabbage roll or enjoy a forkful of coleslaw, you can revel in the flavour while taking comfort in its cancer-fighting characteristics.

Other names
Cabbage is sometimes known as cole.

Looks like/Tastes like
There are three main types of cabbage: green, red and savoy. **Green** – the most common – has a mild flavour that can be enjoyed raw or cooked. A green cabbage head can be as small as a grapefruit or as large as a melon. **Red** cabbage has a deep reddish-purple colour. It often takes longer to cook than green. **Savoy** cabbage, sometimes called **curly** cabbage, is green, with ruffled, deeply ridged and veined leaves. Savoy's milder flavour and softer texture make it a good choice for salads and wraps.

There are three main varieties of **Chinese** cabbage (a.k.a. **celery cabbage**). The first and best known is **napa** cabbage. It is tight-headed, barrel-shaped and pale yellow to pale green. Napa grows about a foot (30 cm) long and is about 6 inches (15 cm) in diameter. There's also a loose-headed napa variety that

looks more like a light green head of romaine lettuce than a cabbage. The third variety is **Peking** (or **Tientsin**) cabbage, which is longer and more narrow than a napa. All Chinese cabbages have a milder, more delicate taste than green, red or Savoy cabbage.

Select it
Look for firm, solid, heavy heads with bright, fresh colour. The brighter the leaves, the fresher the cabbage. Avoid cabbages with outer leaves that have discoloured veins or worm damage. Sometimes you'll find tiny black spots on the leaves of Chinese cabbages, which are not a sign of deterioration. The spots occur naturally and are completely harmless.

Store it right
Store the whole head of cabbage in a perforated, plastic bag in the refrigerator crisper. It will retain its nutrients and, in the case of green or red cabbages, will keep up to 2 weeks. Savoy and Chinese cabbage may not keep as well. Once a cabbage is cut, it deteriorates quickly. Wrap up the cut end carefully and use it all up as soon as possible.

Prep it right
Remove the outermost leaves and any other leaves that are damaged. Cut out the tough core at the base of the cabbage. For Chinese cabbages, cut off 1 to 2 inches (2.5 to 5 cm)

at the base. To shred cabbage, simply cut the head in half and slice thinly. Raw cabbage is easily grated. Savoy cabbage leaves are soft and pliable when raw – perfect for cabbage rolls. You can also use green cabbage for rolls, but blanch it first. Remove the core and blanch the whole head of cabbage in boiling water until the leaves become soft and pliable – this way you'll be able to keep the leaves intact, which is difficult to do when they are raw and stiff.

Overcooked, boiled cabbage has given this veggie a bad reputation, mostly because it tastes and smells awful. Give cabbage a light touch when cooking and it will repay you with sweet flavours.

You can boil, steam, braise, stir-fry, sauté or bake cabbage. Try cabbage wedges in the steamer, or lightly braised red cabbage with a splash of red wine or balsamic vinegar. The first heads of green cabbage in spring are perfect for coleslaws and salads. To tame the taste of strong cabbage, try soaking it shredded in salted ice water for up to an hour. Chinese cabbage has a more delicate texture than regular cabbage, and requires less cooking time.

Tips
Chinese cooks line the bottom of bamboo steamers with cabbage leaves to stop foods from sticking to the steamer.

Toss a cube or two of bread in a steamer full of cabbage. The bread will help to soak up any sulphurous smells.

Culinary companions
Vinegars (especially balsamic, dark Chinese and fruit) or wine provide a delicious counterpoint to cabbage. Chinese seasonings work wonders with both Chinese and regular cabbage. Try soy sauce, tamari, ginger, garlic, sesame oil, oyster sauce, hot peppers and shiitake mushrooms. Indian flavours include black mustard seeds, fennel seeds, cayenne, cumin and curry powder. Other good additions include Dijon mustard, black pepper, dill, caraway, celery seed, sage, savoury, thyme, nutmeg and sugar.

To your health
One cup (89 g) of chopped, raw green cabbage contains only 22 calories and is high in vitamin C. The same amount of red cabbage contains almost twice as much vitamin C, supplying 50 mg or 83 per cent of the Recommended Daily Intake (RDI). Green cabbage, on the other hand, contains twice as much folate as red cabbage, supplying 17 per cent of the RDI. Both red, green and Savoy cabbage are a source of potassium and fibre, but only Savoy is a source of beta carotene.

The cabbage, and its many cruciferous family members, are some of the healthiest vegetables you can eat. All contain powerful phytochemicals such as sulphoraphanes, indoles and flavonoids, which have cancer-fighting abilities. The antioxidant vitamins such as vitamin C, A, E and selenium that are found in cabbage family members may lower your risk of heart disease, stroke and cataracts. Cabbage and its cousins are all sources of heart-healthy potassium. Folate and iron in cabbage work together to help prevent anemia.

Carrots

Baby boomers were raised on that carrot-toting rabbit, Bugs Bunny. His favourite line was "What's up doc?" Now we all know the answer: Beta carotene.

Looks like/Tastes like

The two main carrot varieties are **regular** and **baby**. But there are many variations in between. Carrots can be long and thin, straight and narrow (**Nantes**), more red than orange (**Scarlet Nantes**), the shape and size of a golf ball (**Thumbelina**), or twice as high in beta carotene (**Park's Beta Champ Hybrid**). You can find them in yellow, white and even purple, but orange is the most common.

Select it

Look for firm, crisp and smooth carrots with good, rich colour and no blemishes. If there's greenery attached, the carrot is probably freshly harvested, but if the tops are yellow or dry, pass them up. Also, inspect the carrot's "shoulders" just below the carrot top. If they're deep green, the carrot is probably bitter. Avoid cracks, which often lead to a woody core.

Store it right

When purchasing carrots that still have their tops, remove the tops before storing – otherwise they draw moisture and vitamins from the root, causing wilting and toughening. Store carrots in a perforated plastic bag in the crisper. But don't tuck them beside apples. The ethylene gas emitted by this fruit will make your carrots bitter.

Tips

A hairy carrot is an old carrot.

Consider going organic when it comes to carrots. That way you can reap the benefits of the carrot's skin, worry-free. Besides, carrots and many other root vegetables, are particularly prone to high levels of residue from pesticide and other farm chemicals, especially nitrates.

Prep it right

Most people automatically peel their carrots. Think twice before you do. Many of a carrot's nutrients are stored just below the skin surface. Try scraping them lightly or brushing well under running water. Some carrot connoisseurs remove the core to eliminate bitterness. It's a tedious task, which can only be done once a carrot is cooked and cut lengthwise into quarters – then the core can be pulled out with the tip of a sharp knife.

Carrots can be cooked whole, cut into coins, julienned, grated, slivered, and so on. Boil, sauté, stir-fry, braise, roast or microwave your carrots. Of course, carrots are great raw, too.

Culinary companions

Carrots are compatible with almost every herb and spice. Fresh herbs include coriander, tarragon, dill, basil, chervil, chives, mint, sage and savoury. Spices include allspice, caraway, cardamom, cinnamon, cloves, cumin, ground coriander, cayenne and curry powder. You can sweeten up carrots with a glaze (consider marmalade, maple syrup, honey or brown sugar), and they can go savoury with capers, olives and vinegar, too. Chinese seasonings such as soy sauce, ginger and sesame oil taste great on carrots.

Culinary destinations

Raw carrots are perfect in crudités and lunch boxes. Grated carrots work neatly in a tortilla wrap-up and also add colour and sweetness to a garden salad. Try mixing grated carrots with low-fat cream cheese or cashew butter for a sandwich spread. Sneaky parents are known to toss grated carrots into spaghetti sauce to secretly boost the family's beta carotene levels. Carrots are a treat in cake, muffins and even homemade cookies. In India, they make carrot purée, thicken it with butter, flour, spices and sugar, and serve it for dessert. Try steaming some carrots with whole cloves, for a subtle but terrific taste sensation. Carrots can snuggle up to any roast and can stand up to the long simmering of a soup. Simply steamed or boiled, they are magical with a knob of butter or a simple vinaigrette.

To your health

If you had to pick only one vegetable in life, your body would thank you if you chose carrots. They are the most abundant source of beta carotene (which your body converts to vitamin A), which is why this important antioxidant vitamin is named after the carrot. In fact, just two small carrots (100 g)

provide almost three times the Recommended Daily Intake (RDI) of vitamin A. And although cooking destroys some of the nutrients in most vegetables, it actually enhances the bio-availability of beta carotene. That's because heat breaks down the tough, cellular walls that encase beta carotene. A 3-½-ounce (100-g) serving of raw carrots contains only 43 calories and is a source of dietary fibre, magnesium, potassium, vitamins C and B⁶, thiamin and folate.

Beta carotene is a powerful antioxidant that helps protect against cancer, especially lung cancer. Studies show that a diet high in beta carotene can also prevent age-related macular degeneration, one of the leading causes of blindness in the aged. Likewise, carrots help prevent cataracts. While much of the focus has been put on vitamin C as an immune booster, recent studies show that beta carotene boosts defences against both bacterial and viral infections. The high pectin content in carrots (found in the soluble fibre) helps reduce cholesterol and prevent heart disease. That same fibre also works to fight diarrhea. You'll get more benefits from whole carrots than from carrot juice. Moreover, older carrots contain more beta carotene than spring carrots.

Trivia

Washed and peeled baby carrots are a retailing success story. Even though baby carrots cost more, most consumers are thrilled to buy them. But did you know that most of these carrots aren't technically "babies"? In fact, they're the product of a high-tech machine that cuts baby-sized carrots out of full-sized ones and, in some cases, puts green food colouring at the stem end for authenticity.

Cauliflower

The sight of a cauliflower fresh from the garden is enough to take my breath away. Thanks to the tender care of farmers who gather the outer leaves like a tent over the forming bud, we are gifted with a snowy white vegetable that delivers both taste and aesthetics.

Looks like/Tastes like

Most commonly, cauliflower is white, inspiring such poetic varietal names as **Snowball** or **White Sails**. In the early 1980s, a hybrid was developed and dubbed "broccoflower." It has a lime green head (technically called a curd) that is more tender than cauliflower and sweeter than broccoli. Growers like it since it takes less work to harvest than white cauliflower. Buy, store and cook with broccoflower as you would cauliflower. **Purple** and **golden** cauliflower have been developed, too.

Select it

Look for a firm, clean, white head of cauliflower with no yellow or brown tinge on the florets, which indicates aging. The florets should be tightly formed – not spread out. Inspect the leaves – they should be crisp, bright and green.

Store it right

Store cauliflower in a perforated plastic bag in the fridge. It will keep for up to 5 days but every day it is stored it will lose a bit of sweetness. Cut cauliflower deteriorates more rapidly than whole.

Prep it right

First, cut off the edible outer leaves, which have a slightly stronger taste than the head. (Use these leaves in soup, stocks or cook alongside cauliflower.) Cut out the core and, if your cauliflower is less than perfect, slice off any yellow tinge on the head. If you don't want to cook it whole, break off the florets at the base with your hands or a knife. Be sure to break them into similarly sized pieces to ensure even cooking. You can also slice up a cauliflower, which is quick and easy but less attractive than florets.

You can steam, sauté, boil, microwave, bake or roast cauliflower. To keep the colour as white as possible, boil it in acidulated water (add 3 tablespoons/45 mL lemon juice or vinegar to 1 quart/1 L water) or poach it in milk. Likewise, soak raw cauliflower in acidulated water before serving it in a relish tray or crudité. The trick to cauliflower is to cook it until just tender, before it starts to smell sulphurous. Overcooked cauliflower gives this fine veggie a bad and mushy name for itself.

Culinary companions

Cauliflower combines well with fresh or dried herbs, such as dill, chives, parsley, tarragon, oregano, marjoram, savory, rosemary and fresh coriander. It also works well with mustard, fennel and celery seeds. Cauli-flower's fundamentally bland flavour has been spiced up over the centuries in Indian cuisine: it's a match made in heaven for curry powder, ginger, garlic, cumin, turmeric, ground coriander, fenugreek and nutmeg. European tastes bring cauliflower and cheese together: try Gruyère, Parmigiano-Reggiano, Romano, Jarlsberg, cheddar, ricotta or goat cheese.

Culinary destinations

Cauliflower can be roasted with paprika, stir-fried with green onions, ginger and ground pork, or baked in a tomato sauce topped with cheese. Thick and creamy soups are a perfect place for cauliflower florets, whether they are with potatoes and leeks, or chives and cheddar. Cauliflower florets are the perfect addition to an omelette, quiche or frittata. Try it with pasta, tossed with anchovies, garlic and bread crumbs. And if you're trying to convince children of cauli-flower's attributes, they often like it best raw (or blanched) dipped in peanut sauce.

To your health

Cauliflower, like most veggies, is low in fat, with just 25 calories in 1 cup (250 mL). A 3-½-ounce (100-g) serving is an excellent source of vitamin C and folate, and a source of magnesium, potassium and vitamin B^6. For maximum folate intake, eat your cauli-flower raw – some 80 per cent of this water-soluble B vitamin is lost in cooking. Although white cauliflower contains no beta carotene, you will find it in broccoflower and purple cauliflower. Cauliflower contains many important phytochemicals such as fla-vonoids, indoles and sulphoraphanes.

Cauliflower is a member of the illustrious Cruciferous Club (cabbage family) which contain many phytochemicals and flavonoids that have cancer-fighting poten-tial. Vitamin C is an antioxidant that may lower the risk of heart disease and stroke. Folate is an important nutrient for women. Not only does it help prevent anemia, but folate can reduce the risk of neural tube defects in a developing fetus by 50 per cent when women planning to get pregnant or already pregnant have a diet high in folate.

Quick ways

Break up a head of cauliflower into florets and parboil them in a large pot of salted water for 3 to 5 minutes or until al dente (chewy). Drain, rinse with cold water and drain again. Heat some canola oil at medi-um high in a sauté pan and throw in 1 tea-spoon (5 mL) each of cumin and mustard seeds. Stir until the seeds pop, reduce the heat and toss in the drained cauliflower. Sauté until cooked through. Serve.

Trivia

Ever wondered why cauliflower costs more than cabbage or broccoli? It's all in the head. Growers protect that chalk-white head from the sun's rays by tying the leaves in a protec-tive tent over it. Extra labour in the fields means more dollars from you at the check-out counter.

Tip

Cauliflower may discolour when cooked in aluminum or cast-iron pots.

Celeriac

Expand your root vegetable repertoire with celeriac. You can eat it raw or cooked. Not surprisingly, it tastes like celery, but it mimics parsley and is slightly nutty, too.

Other names

The most common alias for celeriac is celery root, but don't let the name fool you. Celeriac is not the root of common celery but the root of a special variety cultivated specifically for its enlarged root. Other names include celery knob and turnip root celery.

Looks like/Tastes like

Knobby and gnarly, celeriac is irregularly shaped with clumps of rootlets sticking out. The skin is tan-brown, hiding an ivory-white interior. Celeriac is sometimes sold without its greens attached, which look like baby celery ribs. Celeriacs range in size, but on average, are the size of a turnip.

Select it

Choose a small and firm celeriac that is heavy for its size. If it's light and large, the centre may be spongy, tough or dry. Opt for a minimum of rootlets and knobs, and try to find one that is as regularly shaped as possible to facilitate peeling. Soft spots are to be avoided – they indicate decay.

Store it right

Wrapped in a plastic bag, celeriac lasts in your refrigerator for several weeks.

Prep it right

Pare off the roots, knobs and any greens. You need a sharp knife for this job – a vegetable peeler won't work. Some people like to pare it like an apple, while others pare off the top and bottom, and then pare it in lengthwise strips. Once it is peeled, work quickly to grate, shred, slice or dice the celeriac since it tends to discolour. Store the "prepped" celeriac in acidulated water (3 tablespoons/45 mL of lemon juice or vinegar to 4 cups/1 L of water) to keep it white until you are ready to cook with it.

The French *céleri rémoulade* is what put celeriac on the culinary map, so to speak. In this classic recipe, celeriac is grated and tossed in a creamy vinaigrette with mustard. You can serve celeriac raw in any type of salad, but first spritz it with lemon juice to prevent it from turning brown.

Celeriac also makes a nice cooked veggie, but don't overcook it, for it will become mushy and lackluster in flavour. You can dice it into cubes or slice it into sticks, then steam or boil – serve with butter or olive oil and a sprinkling of fresh chives, tarragon or basil. Celeriac is perfect for soups or purées and, when you're in a pinch, it can stand in for regular celery in most recipes. Toss it with herbs, olive oil, salt and pepper and roast in a 375°F (190°C) oven until soft and golden brown.

Culinary companions
Celeriac works well with parsley, dill, basil, tarragon and chives. Mustard, hot pepper and horseradish are wonderful perk-me-ups, too.

To your health
Celeriac is not exactly on the Top Ten List for nutrients. One 3-½-ounce (100-g) serving of cooked celeriac contains only 27 calories and is a source of vitamins C and B[6], and phosphorous. It's nutritionally similar to celery, containing slightly more folate and iron than its lunch-bag cousin.

Quick ways
Here's a quick celeriac coleslaw: grate 1 cup (250 mL) each of celeriac, carrots and jicama. Sprinkle with 1 tablespoon (15 mL) lemon juice and mix with 3 tablespoons (45 mL) low-fat creamy salad dressing. To intensify the flavours, let it stand in the fridge for at least an hour before serving.

Tip
Grate celeriac or chop it up finely and toss into tuna, salmon or chicken salad sandwiches.

Celery

Celery really needs no introductions – most of us take this veggie for granted. The crisp, clean bite of celery makes it a winner among children, a boon to calorie-conscious snackers and the foundation upon which many a soup, stew or sauce is built.

Looks like/Tastes like

The variety of celery most often found in stores today is the bright green **Pascal**. **Golden Heart**, a white variety, was once fashionable but it's rarely seen these days. **Chinese** celery, available in Asian food stores, looks like a slender, smaller, greener version of regular celery with extra leaves. The stalks are thinner (½ inch/1 cm) and the base is only 1 or 2 inches (2.5 or 5 cm) in diameter. The taste is stronger than regular celery and it's seldom used raw.

Select it

Look for firm, unblemished ribs and tightly formed stalks. Avoid limp or rubbery celery. Check the leaves and opt for green, crisp foliage rather than yellow and wilted. The darker the green, the stronger its taste. Plus it has more nutrients. A caveat: dark green celery may be more bitter and stringy than lighter versions.

Store it right

Celery stores for 2 weeks or more in a plastic bag in your refrigerator. This veggie is frost sensitive – keep it away from the coldest parts of your fridge (side walls and back). Don't wash or trim it until just before using. If you mist it with water occasionally, you'll stop it from drying out.

Prep it right

Most people just use the stalks of celery, trimmed at both ends without the leaves. Use a vegetable brush or vegetable peeler to clean it carefully, removing any dirt and grime lodged within the outer fibres. You can de-string tough ribs by using a small kitchen knife and pulling the strings off gently as you remove leaf ends. For soups and stews, celery is usually chopped finely. For a change of pace, try cutting it into small strips (¼ inch/6 mm wide and 3 inches/8 cm long) for stews, soups or sauces.

Celery can be eaten raw or cooked. It's a must for tuna, salmon, egg or chicken salad mixtures. It works in many other salad preparations too, such as potato or pasta. Sticks stuffed with cheese – whether it's a processed cheese spread for the kids or Gorgonzola for the adults – are an easy snack or hors d'oeuvre. Some people consider the tender ribs in the centre, or heart, to be the best part of celery. Try braising in stock with leeks or carrots, or braise them on their own, until tender, sprinkle with cheese, and cook under a broiler until the cheese melts. Don't throw out the leaves! They're full of nutrients and have a flavour like parsley. Steam until tender and then sauté in olive oil with garlic or shallots. Reserve trimmed leaves and toss them in your next homemade stock.

Culinary companions
Cheese and celery are made for each other, so try the entire range from Roquefort to cream cheese. Hard cheeses can be shred and sprinkled over cooked celery. Herbs such as tarragon, dill, thyme, basil and rosemary all complement celery.

To your health
Like cucumbers and iceberg lettuce, celery is a low-calorie veggie full of water – 95 per cent, to be exact. There are fewer than 10 calories per stalk. A 1-cup (120-g) serving of raw, chopped celery is a source of vitamin C, potassium, folate and fibre. Celery leaves contain more calcium, iron, potassium and vitamins A and C than do the stalks.

There's hope that future studies will reveal a definite link between eating celery and lowered blood pressure. Celery is a traditional Vietnamese remedy for high blood pressure. Plus a chemical known to reduce blood pressure has been isolated in celery and used in experiments effectively. But in the meantime, as a source of potassium, celery is a certified heart-healthy food. Stressed out? Eat some celery, for it has long been regarded in folk medicine as a calming food. It's probably best to buy organically grown celery, since conventionally grown celery is prone to high nitrate levels, because of the use of nitrate fertilizers.

Trivia
Celery is a member of the carrot family!

Tip
Reach for fresh celery leaves when you're out of fresh parsley. It's a tasty substitute.

Chayote

This vegetable has more names than an international spy! Chayote is the most commonly used name in North America, unless you live in Louisiana, where mirliton is the name of choice. In the West Indies, it's called christophene, in honour of Christopher Columbus. Other monikers include chu-chu, cho-cho, vegetable pear and pepinella. But if you call it chayote, here's how to pronounce it: chy-O-tay.

Looks like/Tastes like
Chayote looks like a green apple that's been flattened and has a number of deep folds in the skin. It comes in apple-green, white and forest green. Depending on the variety, chayote are smooth-skinned or have a few prickly spines dotted over the surface. The flesh is white and crisp, containing a single, large white, oval seed. Chayote tastes like a mix of zucchini, green beans and cucumber.

Tip
The cooked seed is edible and tastes like a cross between a lima bean and an almond. Many chayote lovers claim the seed is the best part – try cooking it alongside the flesh.

Trivia
Chayote is actually a variety of American squash, belonging to the Cucurbitaceae (cucumber) family. It was once a principal food of the Aztecs and Mayans.

Select it
Chayote range in size from 8 ounces (250 g) to a pound (500 g). Look for small chayote that are firm, unblemished and free of bruises.

Store it right
Chayote keeps very well, lasting up to a month or more in a humid spot in your fridge. Place it in a plastic bag in the crisper and keep it away from really cold spots in the fridge – such as on the refrigerator floor or beside a wall – since chayote is frost sensitive.

You can freeze chayote, just like summer squash. See instructions on page 190.

Prep it right
A chayote's skin is edible, but some varieties are more tender and thin than others. You can remove the skin with a vegetable peeler or sharp knife before cooking, or peel it off with your fingers once it's cooked. Strangely, when it's peeled, raw chayote oozes a sticky white fluid that can irritate the skin, so wear gloves if you are sensitive and peel it under running water. For best results, cut a chayote in half lengthwise, remove the seed and then peel away the skin.

You can eat chayote raw or cooked. Slice it into salads, serve it in a crudité or marinate raw slices in lime juice, hot pepper flakes and salt. Chayote can be steamed, boiled, sautéed, stir-fried, baked or roasted just like summer squash. It is often stuffed and also makes a delicate soup.

Culinary companions
You can dress up chayote's bland flavours with assertive seasonings such as hot peppers or garlic, or you can enhance its delicate nature with dairy products and fresh herbs such as tarragon, rosemary, chives, chervil, basil or marjoram. Lime or lemon juice are good partners for chayote as are tomatoes and potatoes. Chayote goes well with crab and shrimp, cheeses (Parmigiano-Reggiano, Gruyère, cheddar and Monterey Jack) and bread crumbs.

Culinary destinations
Try chayote in a Louisiana-style casserole with onions, garlic, hot peppers, thyme, bay leaves, white wine and tomatoes, or put it in an omelette with tomatoes, onions and hot peppers. Stuff it with seafood, or purée and blend it into a refreshing cold soup with chives. Chayote is technically a fruit but most often eaten as a vegetable, so recipes can go either way. The Chinese like to stuff it with a savoury blend of ground pork, green onions and ginger, while the Mexicans stuff it with a sweet concoction of crushed pound cake, eggs, raisins, sugar and spices. When it is simply sautéed in butter with green onions, a splash of white wine and a sprinkling of fresh thyme and oregano, chayote shines!

Tip
In the Caribbean, chayote is used in marinades to tenderize meat.

To your health
A 1-cup (160-g) serving of cooked chayote contains only 38 calories and is a good source of fibre, supplying 4.4 g in a single serving. Chayote is a source of vitamins C and B^6, folate, potassium and magnesium.

Turn to chayote for an excellent supply of dietary fibre. Studies show that fibre in the diet helps to reduce cholesterol, prevent constipation and maintain regularity.

Chinese Greens

If you love green leafy vegetables, expand your horizons with Chinese greens. You'll see mountains of these fresh greens on display at any Chinatown, with numerous varieties to choose from. And while you're there, pick up some fresh ginger, oyster sauce and sesame oil – three tools of the trade that make those greens taste great.

Looks like/Tastes like

BOK CHOY Most people have met **bok choy**. It's the best-known Chinese green and is sold in most urban supermarkets. Bok choy has snow-white stems, dark green, flat leaves and a slightly bulbous base. There are three main types of bok choy: regular, baby and Shanghai. **Regular** bok choy is up to 20 inches (50 cm) long, whereas **baby** bok choy is only 3 to 6 inches (8 to 15 cm) long. **Shanghai** bok choy is usually about 12 inches (30 cm) long and looks like the others except that it's green all over. It has olive-green stems and green leaves with no white veins. All types of bok choy may have flowers. Avoid any with a profusion of opened flowers (indicating over-maturity), although unopened buds are fine. Look for crisp stalks and perky leaves. Avoid those with split stalks and limp, lifeless leaves.

CHOY SUM It's not easy to tell your bok choy from your choy sum until you notice those pretty yellow flowers. Choy sum or "flowering cabbage" has white stalks that are slightly more grooved than bok choy. The green leaves have white veins like bok choy but are more ruffled. Everything is edible and the best part is the flowering stem. Look for small and tender specimens with crisp stalks, perky greens and open yellow flowers.

CHINESE BROCCOLI While "regular" or common broccoli is commonly used in Chinese cuisine, the more authentic vegetable is *gai lan* or **Chinese broccoli**. Like its cousin, Chinese broccoli has deep green, smooth stalks, but the stalks are more narrow and richer in flavour. Unlike regular broccoli's big flowering heads, Chinese broccoli has a few, unopened flower buds (some may be open and white in colour). While regular broccoli has only a few, small leaves, Chinese broccoli has big, thick, deep green leaves. Buy specimens with as few opened buds as possible. Everything is edible.

CHINESE BROCCOLI RAAB It's too bad that this Chinese green is less common than the others, for **Chinese broccoli raab** is sweet, delicious and buttery tasting. *You cai* literally means "oil vegetable" and it's a variety of the rapeseed plant of canola oil fame. As with choy sum, the flowering centre stalk is the most succulent feature of the plant, but everything is edible. Look for long, narrow green stems with long green, oval leaves and yellow flowers or unopened buds.

Select it
When selecting Chinese greens, look for bright green colour, crisp stalks with no cracks or bruises and perky green leaves. Don't buy lifeless, limp greens.

Store it right
All Chinese greens are best eaten as soon as possible but can be stored for a few days. Wrap them in paper towel, then store in a perforated plastic bag in your refrigerator crisper.

Prep it right
All Chinese greens require thorough washing. Fill a sink or very large bowl with water and swish greens vigorously, rubbing the leaves and stalks with your fingers to free away any dirt. Change the water and rinse again several times until the water runs clear. Baby varieties can be cooked whole but be certain to wash well. Leaves always cook faster than stalks.

Chinese greens are perfect for stir-fries, of course, but that's not all. Consider steaming or blanching baby varieties whole and then drizzling a little sesame oil and oyster sauce over them. Big bok choy leaves can be blanched whole and used to wrap vegetables or noodles. Let Chinese greens star in their own stir-fry, or team them up with other vegetables, noodles or meat.

> ### Tip
> *When cutting Chinese greens for a stir-fry, remember to cut them into uniform sizes to ensure even cooking. Try cutting the stalks into 1-inch (2.5-cm) pieces and shredding the leaves into 1-inch (2.5-cm) thick ribbons.*

Culinary companions
Ginger, garlic, green onions, soy sauce, oyster sauce, chicken stock and canola oil all work well with Chinese greens. Fresh mushrooms and Chinese dried mushrooms are a great addition to stir-fried greens. More exotic additions include shrimp paste, yellow bean paste, dried shrimp and hot chili paste.

Culinary destinations
Add some shredded Chinese greens to your next stir-fried noodles or pasta dish. Put them in a soup just before serving. Add them to stir-fried rice or even a risotto. Many of these baby greens are perfect in a salad.

To your health
Chinese greens are a healthy choice. All contain high levels of beta carotene and vitamin C, two powerful antioxidants. A 1-cup (170-g) serving of cooked bok choy contains only 20 calories and is an excellent source of folate and vitamins C and A. Bok choy is also a source of calcium, iron, magnesium and potassium. All Chinese greens are high in folate and are a source of dietary fibre, potassium and calcium. The darker the leaf, the more beta carotene it contains.

All these Chinese greens are members of the cabbage family, making them card-carrying members of the illustrious Cruciferous Club – a group of vegetables that researchers have focused on due to their cancer-fighting abilities. Chinese greens, like their other cabbage cousins, contain powerful phytochemicals called indoles and sulphoraphanes that block cancer-causing substances before they can damage cells. These phytochemicals also suppress tumour growth and induce protective enzymes in the body. The only downside to Chinese greens is that they can cause gas and bloating in some people.

Quick ways

Once you have perfected the basic Chinese greens stir-fry you can walk into any Chinese grocery store, choose a Chinese green you have never seen before and stir-fry it successfully. Here's how: heat 2 tablespoons (30 mL) of canola oil in a wok. Once the oil's hot, add some garlic, ginger or green onions and stir-fry a few seconds. Add the stalks and stir-fry for a few minutes or until they become slightly tender. Add chopped leaves and stir. If the wok becomes too dry at any point, add a few spoonfuls of water or chicken stock. Stir-fry until the greens are tender but still bright green. Season with salt and serve.

Collards

Although "a mess o' greens" (a.k.a. collard greens) has been standard fare in Mississippi and Alabama for almost a century, collards seem like the new kid in town here in the North. Here's a veggie bursting with nutrients and cancer-fighting potential. You'll find that collards need more cooking than other leafy greens to smooth out the texture and flavour.

Looks like/Tastes like
Collards have big, round, flat green leaves that encircle thick, inedible stalks. Both stalk and leaf are the same shade of army-green. Collards taste like cabbage but have a smoky element that can be accentuated with ham, salt pork or sausage.

Select it
Choose dark green, firm leaves that are not wilted. The smaller the collard greens the sweeter. Look for thin (no thicker than a pencil) stalks.

Store it right
Collards can last in a plastic bag for up to a week, but get tougher with age.

Prep it right
Unless you have very young collard greens, it is advisable to cut and discard the centre rib and stalk.

Collards can be steamed, sautéed or boiled, but require 15 to 30 minutes of cooking. They are best braised, slowly, combined with other ingredients, or added to soups and stews. Whole leaves can be blanched and used to wrap foods for baking or steaming.

Culinary companions
The collard greens' best friend is pork. Salted or smoked, pork in the shape of bacon, ham or sausages is a match made in heaven. Ham hocks and pork rind are other options. Collards can withstand the heat of fresh or dried hot peppers and also have a surprising affinity with oranges, whether as juice or zest. Potatoes and polenta are two mild starches that offset the strong taste of collards.

Culinary destinations
Collards can be braised with other greens in chicken stock and finished with balsamic vinegar. To cook Southern-style, combine collards with ham hocks, hot peppers and ham and braise for up to an hour. Try them braised in Chinese red sauce – a combination of soy sauce, cooking sherry, ginger, garlic and star anise. Collards are featured in Portuguese potato soup.

To your health
One cup (190 g) of cooked collards contains only 49 calories and is an excellent source of fibre. There are 5.3 g of fibre in that same serving, along with 176 mcg of folate (80 per cent of the Recommended Daily Intake, or RDI) and 35 mg of vitamin C (57 per cent of

the RDI). Besides offering an enormous amount of folate and vitamin C in just one serving, collards are also an excellent source of vitamin A (59 per cent of the RDI). Collards are high in calcium and potassium, and low in sodium, and are a source of iron and riboflavin.

Few greens can match collards in nutritive power. Collard greens are a powerhouse of antioxidants, containing beta carotene, and vitamins C and E. As a member of the cabbage family, collards have been shown in studies to reduce the risk of cancer, heart disease and cataracts. Don't be surprised if you see collards in pill form sold at the health food stores one day!

Quick ways

Indian collards: put some whole potatoes and sliced collard leaves in a big pot of boiling water and cook until the potatoes are tender. Drain both and cut the potatoes into chunks once cool. Heat some oil in a frying pan and sauté some garlic and ginger. Add some whole black mustard seeds, hot pepper flakes and curry powder, along with the potatoes and collards. Sauté for 3 minutes and serve with a squeeze of lemon.

Corn

While I'm loath to play favourites, I have to admit that fresh corn on the cob is at the very top of my vegetable list. I can eat it every day of the summer, tossing my waistline to the wind as I bathe it in butter and sprinkle it with salt. But to me, only part of corn's attraction is the taste. Just as important are the events I associate with it. Corn spells out summers at the cottage, shopping at roadside farm stands and eating dinner in the golden light of a sun setting over a Muskoka lake.

Looks like/Tastes like

There are more than 200 varieties of corn, divided into three main classes: **normal**, **sugar-enhanced** and **supersweet**. Each class has three different colour groups: yellow, white and bi-colour. Exotic colours include purple, red, blue and calico. Cobs can range in size from 2 feet (60 cm) long down to 2-inch (5-cm) miniatures.

Select it

When choosing fresh sweet corn, resist the urge to strip back the husks and peek at the kernels. You can't really tell if corn is fresh by just looking at the kernels. And besides, the husk serves as a natural wrapper, keeping it moist and fresh. Look for grass-green husks that are moist and tightly wrapped around the ear. Check the silk: it should be golden and moist, with no signs of decay. Look for a moist, fresh stem that's neither chalky nor yellowed. Read the individual kernels through the husk like braille. Avoid cobs with tiny kernels or gaps between kernels.

For best results, buy freshly picked corn early in the day from roadside or farmer's markets and make sure it's stored in the shade. Pack it in a cooler for the trip home. If you know there will be a delay between purchase and use, select supersweet corn. It stores and stays sweet longer.

Tip
When shopping in stores, look for corn that is kept refrigerated.

Store it right

Keep corn wrapped in a plastic bag in the fridge for up to 2 days, more if it's supersweet. The sugar in corn starts to turn into starch the moment the cob is picked from the stalk, turning it tough and less sweet. Chilling slows that process. Half of the sugar content in normal and sugar-enhanced varieties can be lost in a day if stored at room temperature. Supersweet stays fresher and sweeter longer than the other two varieties.

Corn freezes well. Blanch it first, slice off the kernels, store them in freezer bags and freeze.

Prep it right

Don't shuck corn until just before you plan to use it. Pull back the husks and tear them off at the bottom. Remove the silk with your fingers or use a dry vegetable brush. You can slice kernels off the cob when it is raw or cooked: stand an ear of corn upright in a wide bowl and cut downward with a sharp knife. Be careful to cut off only the top two thirds of the corn kernels, leaving the fibrous base of the kernels (the part that gets stuck in your teeth) on the husk. If you are making soup or stew, extract the juices and corn still left on the cob by running the dull side of a large cutting knife down the length of the ear. Separate the cut kernels with your fingers. If you want a fine-textured corn for creaming or soup, simply grate corn off the ear.

Corn is never eaten raw. There are several methods you can use to cook it on the cob: boiling, roasting, steaming and microwaving.

To boil, fill a large pot with cold water, bring to a boil, add corn and cook until tender (3 to 8 minutes). Don't add salt to the cooking water, because it toughens the kernels. You can add a splash of milk or pinch of sugar to cooking water to improve sweetness.

To roast corn on the grill: pull back husks gently, remove the silk and replace the husks, tying their ends with kitchen string. Soak in cold water at least 10 minutes before grilling so the husks won't burn. Small cobs take 15 minutes and large up to 30 minutes.

You can wrap shucked corn in aluminum foil, spread with herb butter and place on the grill or oven (425°F/230°C) to steam. The cooking time is the same as for grilling.

To microwave, cook corn in husks (without silk), or remove husks and wrap in parchment paper or microwave-safe paper towels. Cook on high 3 to 6 minutes.

Corn kernels can be sautéed, stir-fried and tossed in soups and stews. Try them in pancakes, puddings, soufflés, breads and muffins, too.

Trivia
There's a new gadget out there called a corn brush. It promises to remove all the silk without damaging any of the kernels.

Tip
When making corn soup, cook the cobs right in the stock for a richer flavour.

Culinary companions
Corn pairs well with fresh herbs, particularly fresh coriander, tarragon and sage. But parsley, rosemary, chives, mint, oregano, thyme, basil, chervil and lemon balm all work fine, too. Corn and butter are a match made in heaven, especially herb butters. Spices include cumin, hot dried peppers, curry, nutmeg, ginger and saffron. Lime juice, beans, peppers (sweet and hot), tomatoes and squash all combine beautifully with corn.

Culinary destinations
Corn appears in many soups, whether it's Chinese cream of corn with crab or rib-sticking corn chowder. Try a corn salsa with tomatoes and black beans or with cherry tomatoes and avocado. Toss it into a chili con carne, put it in some muffins with maple syrup and buttermilk, or fold it into a rich soufflé with red peppers and cheese. Cajun hash browns pair sautéed potatoes with corn, plus hot and sweet peppers and onions. When fresh lima beans are in season, make a simple corn succotash, or try fresh corn in cornbread with jalapeños and Monterey Jack cheese. When corn is roasted, it adds a chewy, smoky taste to summer salads.

To your health
One medium ear of corn (77 g) contains 83 calories. Fresh corn is a source of folate,

potassium, thiamin, niacin and magnesium. It's also a source of dietary fibre with 2.1 g in a medium ear of corn.

Corn is a leading source of lutein, a powerful phytochemical that may lower the risk of macular degeneration, a common age-related cause of vision loss. Lutein belongs to the carotene family and, as an antioxidant, it disarms free radicals, which cause a variety of age-related disorders. Meanwhile, the fibre in corn helps prevent constipation and may reduce the risk of certain cancers. Meanwhile, potassium in corn helps maintain normal blood pressure and heart function and may reduce the risk of heart attack and stroke.

Trivia
An ear of corn averages 800 kernels in 16 rows.

Cucumbers

Some food memories never fade, like one of the cucumber slice I bought in India, through a train window, in the early 1980s. It was the peak of the hot season and sweat was surging out of every pore of my body. We were stopped at a station and a tray of cucumber slices passed beneath me, balanced on a child's head. For a couple of rupees, I was rewarded by the most refreshing cucumber I've tasted in my life – even if it was dusted lightly with cayenne pepper!

Other names
Cukes are the nickname of choice.

Looks like/Tastes like
The two main types of cucumbers are "slicing" and "pickling." The **slicing** varieties fall under two main categories: field-grown and hothouse. **Field-grown** cucumbers are 6 to 9 inches (15 cm to 22.5 cm) long, have glossy, dark green skin and a tapering end. Most are waxed to retain moisture. **Hothouse** cucumbers are also known as **English** cucumbers (other names include **seedless, burpless** and **European**). While this long cucumber (from 12 to 24 inches/30 to 60 cm) is classified as seedless, the truth is it does contain some seeds (albeit fewer than the field-grown variety). Moreover, these seeds are smaller and more tender than those of a field-grown cucumber. Fewer seeds and a thinner skin make the hothouse cucumber more digestible than its field-grown cousin. Most hothouse cucumbers are not waxed, but are shrink-wrapped in plastic for better storage.

Pickling cucumbers are smaller and squatter than slicing cukes. They usually have bumpy, light green skins. **Kirbies** have a thin skin, crisp flesh and tiny seeds, making it a pickler that many people like to munch on fresh. **Gherkin** cucumbers can be as tiny as a little finger.

There are also exotic cucumbers to try. **Japanese** cucumbers look like shorter versions of hothouse cucumbers. These dark green, slender cucumbers have warty bumps. **Armenian** cucumbers have a pale green skin, soft seeds and are not always straight, but curled. The **lemon** cucumber is shaped like its name, but instead of bright yellow, it's pale yellow. This cuke doesn't ship well and is enjoyed mostly by home gardeners.

Select it
When buying any cucumbers, look for one that is firm and has no soft or mouldy spots. The colouring should be green with no signs of yellow. Small hothouse cucumbers tend to be more tender than large ones. Slender field-grown cucumbers have fewer seeds than fat ones do. Don't buy a field-grown cucumber that is bulging in the middle, which indicates a watery, tasteless flesh with too many seeds.

Store it right

Put field-grown cucumbers in a plastic bag and keep hothouse cucumbers in their original plastic wrapping. Both should head for the crisper. An uncut cuke lasts up to a week, but once you cut it, deterioration sets in quickly. Keep your cucumbers away from really cold spots in the fridge (the bottom shelves or against the back walls). Cukes don't like to get too chilly. Frost will turn a cucumber to mush.

Prep it right

The skin of a cucumber is edible but often waxed, especially in the case of field-grown cucumbers. When you don't peel a cucumber, wash it thoroughly. You can make cucumber slices more attractive by scraping the skin with a fork, before slicing. The tines create a striped pattern on the skin. To seed a cucumber, cut it in half lengthwise and scoop out the seeds with the tip of a spoon. Some cucumbers are bitter and benefit from salting or marinating. When cucumbers are salted, moisture leaches out of the flesh. Try draining them in a sieve as they marinate in salt, and squeeze out any excess moisture. You can slice, dice, julienne or grate a cucumber. Make ribbons of cold cucumber "pasta" with a vegetable peeler.

Most people think of cucumbers raw in salads or sandwiches. But they can also be gently cooked. Due to the high water content in cucumbers (95 per cent of a cucumber is water), this veggie gets very soggy if it is cooked too quickly at high temperatures or overcooked. Gently braise or poach it. If you want to stir-fry or sauté cucumbers, do so at low heat. The mellow, clean taste of cucumbers complements fish and chicken.

Tip

Many fruits and vegetables are covered with a wax coating to help retain moisture, inhibit mould growth, protect from damage and generally improve shelf-life. These waxes come from natural sources and are deemed safe to eat. The problem is, however, that you can't digest wax, so it travels through your digestive system without breaking down or being absorbed. Personally, I try to avoid eating wax and always peel off a skin that I think is waxed. However, it's not easy for consumers to know what's waxed and what's not. When in doubt, ask your store's produce manager or buy organically grown produce.

Culinary companions

Cucumbers and dill are magic together. Consider mint, tarragon, fresh coriander, basil and chives, too. Spices include cayenne and other hot peppers, roasted cumin and caraway. Almonds and pine nuts work well with cucumbers, as do sesame seeds. Oriental seasonings such as soy sauce, dark vinegar and sesame oil give cucumbers punch. Lemon juice, yogurt, garlic and green onions are other naturals.

Culinary destinations

Cucumber shines in the garlicky, yogurt Greek dip called tzatziki. Similarly, the Indian condiment raita pairs cucumber with yogurt. Try some cucumber in a buttermilk dressing with basil or make it into a sauce with dill for poached salmon. Sauté cucumber slices in butter until opaque and garnish with toasted sesame seeds. Kids love the gentle flavours of cucumber slices, and it's always a hit as a crudité.

To your health

A cup (119 g) of raw, peeled cucumber slices contains only 14 calories. Cucumbers are a source of magnesium, potassium, vitamins C and B^6 and folate. Many of the nutrients and phytochemicals are found in the skin. Unpeeled cucumber has twice as much beta carotene as peeled, but it still amounts to very little.

Eat cukes and your heart will thank you! Cucumbers (mostly the skin) contain phytochemicals called sterols, which have been shown in studies to reduce cholesterol. They also contain monoterpenes, which are potent antioxidants that may protect against heart disease and cancer. Coumarins are another cancer-fighting phytochemical found in cucumbers.

Quick ways

There are many interpretations of the Greek salad, but this is how it is served in most Greek villages: cut 1 cucumber into quarters, lengthwise, then chop it up into 1-inch (2.5-cm) chunks. Toss with half a sweet onion, thinly sliced, and a couple of juicy, ripe tomatoes cut into wedges. Crumble some fresh feta on top, sprinkle with dried oregano (rub it in your palms first, to release the flavours) and dress with some extra virgin olive oil and a little bit of vinegar or lemon juice. Season with salt and freshly ground black pepper to taste.

Trivia

Women have known through the centuries that cucumbers were good for the skin, making cucumber facial masks and other concoctions. Now science has confirmed it. Cucumbers contain alpha-hydroxy acids, the trendy new ingredient found in many skin-care products.

Dandelion

Just as one person's junk is another's treasure, one person's weed is another's delicacy. The dandelion is one of the most nutritious greens you can eat. Ounce for ounce, it has more calcium than milk and as much iron as spinach.

Other names

The name dandelion is derived from the French *dent de lion,* which means lion's tooth, in reference to the plant's jagged green leaves. It is sometimes called cow parsnip, probably because the long roots resemble parsnips and can be cooked as such. The Irish called it heart fever grass because of its ability to ease heartburn and aid digestion.

Looks like/Tastes like

Cultivated dandelions are much longer than the common weed. Some varieties are up to 18 inches (46 cm) long, with very pointy, dark green leaves. A new cultivated variety has red stalks and red veins through the green leaves. Both the stalks and leaves of dandelions are edible.

Some people liken dandelion to chicory. It's a bitter green and an acquired taste. The pale centre leaves have the mildest flavour. The crown of unopened buds also has a mild flavour. You can eat it all: leaves, stalks, roots, flowers and unopened buds.

Select it

When buying cultivated dandelions, look for crisp, fresh heads with no sign of wilting or brown spots. When picking dandelions, the smaller and paler the dandelion leaf, the better. Early spring is the best time to pick before the plants have flowered. Young leaves are less bitter and more tender.

Tip

Before you forage for wild dandelions, make certain that the soil is free of fertilizers, herbicides and pesticides. Most public lawns and golf courses are not safe picking grounds. Ditto for areas popular with dog walkers. Roadside vegetation (beside highways or small roads) is too polluted for safe picking. For best results, grow your own – it's easy!

Store it right

Store in a perforated plastic bag in your crisper. To reduce bitterness, stand your dandelions in water overnight in the fridge.

Prep it right

Wash the leaves and stalks carefully – they can be gritty. Young whole leaves look and taste great in a salad. Bigger leaves need cooking to become less bitter. Dandelion leaves are usually shredded or chopped like spinach before cooking. You can steam, boil or sauté dandelion greens. Try blanching first to remove bitterness, then sauté in a little butter or oil. Large roots can be peeled, then steamed, boiled or sautéed.

Culinary companions

Lemon is an essential partner for dandelions, smoothing off the rough edges and making its flavour shine. Due to its strong taste, dandelion pairs well with bland flavours, such as pasta, potatoes, bread, polenta and eggs. Good seasonings include garlic, green onions, basil and sage. Walnuts, pine nuts and walnut oil all work with dandelions, as do a variety of cheeses: cheddar, Parmigiano-Reggiano, blue cheese, Gorgonzola and goat cheese.

Culinary destinations

Dandelions make the perfect bitter green for salads. Consider teaming them up with an array of bitter and sweet greens or use them as an accent with such mild greens as butterhead or leaf lettuce. Good salad partners include beet slices, bacon, croutons, hard-boiled eggs, roasted walnuts and creamy dressings such as lemon poppyseed. Try shredded, sautéed dandelion greens in your next pasta – they work well with olive oil, garlic, grilled chicken slivers, sweet peppers, sun-dried tomatoes, pine nuts and pancetta. Add shredded dandelion to mashed potatoes or an omelette. Roll up a tortilla stuffed with cream cheese and fresh baby dandelion leaves.

To your health

Dandelions are an incredible source of beta carotene. One cup (105 g) of cooked dandelion greens contains a whopping 122 per cent of the Recommended Daily Intake (RDI). Dandelion greens are also an excellent source of vitamin E and a source of dietary fibre, calcium, iron, magnesium, potassium, vitamins C and B^6, thiamin, riboflavin and folate. There are only 35 calories in a 1-cup (250-mL) serving of cooked dandelion greens.

Dandelion greens are high in the antioxidants beta carotene and vitamin C, which can protect against cancer and heart disease. There is growing evidence that dandelion greens enhance liver function and may help prevent or cure gallstones. Like other bitter greens, dandelions remove toxic wastes from the blood and may help clear up chronic skin disorders. They are considered an effective diuretic and laxative.

Quick ways

Wilted dandelion salads are popular in France and Italy. Sauté lots of minced garlic in extra virgin olive oil with some pancetta or bacon, and then pour over the dandelion leaves. Toss with a splash a balsamic vinegar and sprinkle with toasted pine nuts and freshly grated Parmigiano-Reggiano cheese.

Tip
Deep-fry some whole sage leaves and shallot rings. Use these as edible garnishes for your next dandelion salad.

Eggplant

A culinary star in Mediterranean, Asian and Middle Eastern kitchens, the eggplant is still a bit of a mystery to the North American palate. Once you get to know this veggie, in its numerous varieties, you'll come to appreciate its easy-going nature and meaty texture.

Other names
Aubergine is the French name and preferred moniker in Britain. They call it *melanzana* in Italian and *bengan* in India.

Looks like/Tastes like
There are hundreds of types of eggplants grown around the world. Colours cover a range, be it white, purple, purple-black, green, orange-red and even striped. An eggplant can be as small as a grape or as big as a football. It might be pear-shaped, round or long and skinny.

The most common, North American variety is dark **purple** and globular, ranging from 1 to 5 pounds (500 g to 2.5 kg) in size. You'll find it in supermarkets. The **white** variety can be found at specialty food shops or farmer's markets.

Japanese or **Chinese** eggplants are smaller and elongated, from 1 to 2 inches (2.5 to 5 cm) in diameter and 5 to 10 inches (12.5 to 15 cm) in length. They're a violet colour, sometimes striated with white with a thin skin. These eggplants are more mild, sweet and tender than the North American variety.

Baby or **finger** eggplants, sometimes called **Italian**, can be only a few inches long and either narrow or plump.

Sicilian or **Rosa Blanco** eggplants are an Italian variety that are round and large (1 to 2 lbs/500 g to 1 kg) with light purple and white striped skin and a mild, meaty flavour.

Thai eggplants can look like a bunch of hard green grapes or like bird's eggs, with white and green colourings. They have quite a few seeds and a more crunchy texture than other eggplants. They are usually cooked whole in Thai curries.

In general, the lighter the hue, the milder the eggplant. Eggplants that have been kept in storage taste more bitter than farm-fresh. Even small, thin-skinned eggplants can taste bitter and unappealing if they're not fresh.

Select it
Look for a tight, shiny, patent-leather skin on your eggplant that is free of wrinkles, bruises or spongy spots. Give it a tap. If it sounds hollow, pass it up. Choose those that are heavy for their size.

Store it right
Eggplants are quite perishable. They like to stay dry – store them in a perforated plastic bag, wrapped in a paper towel to absorb moisture. They may keep up to a week but always taste best the day of purchase.

Prep it right

To salt or not? Dark-coloured eggplants with tough outer skins and lots of seeds benefit most from salting, which cuts down on bitterness and reduces the amount of oil required for cooking. Cut your eggplant into strips, rounds or cubes and sprinkle ½ teaspoon (2 mL) of salt per pound (500 g) of eggplant. Let stand in a colander for at least 30 minutes to sweat. Pat dry with a paper towel or rinse quickly with water and carefully pat dry.

Eggplant skin is edible. Small eggplants and Asian eggplants have a thin skin that doesn't need peeling but thicker skinned eggplants are best peeled.

Some eggplant flesh will brown when cut. Sprinkle with lemon juice to prevent browning. The flesh is also sensitive to the type of knife you use. Carbon knives can cause a bitter aftertaste and leave rust marks on the flesh, so use stainless steel.

Eggplants absorb more fat than any other vegetable. (In one experiment, a deep-fried eggplant absorbed up to four times more fat than French-fried potatoes!) Stay away from recipes calling for deep-frying or sautéing. Try baking, roasting, grilling, broiling, steaming or braising eggplant instead.

To bake a whole eggplant, pierce it several times with a fork and bake in a 400°F (200°C) oven for 30 to 40 minutes. Or cut in half, baste lightly with olive oil and cook on a nonstick baking sheet, cut-side down for 20 to 30 minutes.

Eggplant strips are a quick alternative. Cut peeled or unpeeled eggplant into slices that are ½ inch to 1 inch (1 cm to 2.5 cm) thick. Baste lightly with olive oil and grill on the barbecue or bake in a 400°F (200°C) oven. The broiler or a stove-top grill are other possibilities. Cook until golden brown.

Culinary destinations

Roasted or baked eggplant makes a great dip such as babaghanoush, eggplant caviar or Indian dip with yogurt. Use eggplant strips instead of meat in your next lasagna. Because of its meaty texture, eggplant often substitutes for meat in vegetarian preparations. Spread some sun-dried tomato pesto on baked eggplant rounds, then sprinkle some crumbled goat cheese on top and cook under the broiler until the cheese melts.

To your health

Eggplant is a source of folate and potassium, but it is otherwise low in vitamins and minerals. A 1-cup (99-g) serving of cooked eggplant contains 28 calories and supplies 246 mg of potassium, or about half of the amount found in a medium banana.

Eggplants contain phytochemicals called terpenes, which have cancer-fighting properties.

Trivia

The first, cultivated eggplants were white – hence the name.

Tip

Many eggplant dishes are better the next day. Most can be first enjoyed hot, with the leftovers served cold or at room temperature the following day.

Escarole

The first time I met escarole, it was a case of mistaken identity. I took it for a messy head of sweet lettuce, making it the star of a very unsavoury salad. Just one bite, and I knew I'd stumbled on to something new! While not everyone can appreciate the astringent, pleasantly bitter taste of this green, escarole can taste brilliant when you treat it with a little veggie respect.

Other names
The Italian name is *scarola*. Another name is batavia.

Looks like/Tastes like
Escarole belongs to the confusing chicory clan. What is chicory to one person is endive to another and radicchio to someone else. All these terms are used interchangeably, depending upon where you live in the world. But trust me, escarole, along with radicchio, Belgian endive and frizee, all belong to the chicory family.

Escarole has been known to masquerade as butterhead lettuce, but when you look closely, you'll see it is really escarole in disguise. Escarole's leaves are more fleshy than lettuce's with jagged, pointy edges, versus the softer ruffle of lettuce. You'll see a colour progression that is distinctly chicory-like: the inner leaves are almost white, turning light green then eventually dark green on the exterior. Escarole has a nutty, bitter taste. Outer leaves tend to taste more bitter than inner leaves.

Select it
Like any green, escarole looks crisp and perky when fresh. Avoid wilted or browned specimens. Check the core, opting for one that is white rather than brown. Choose escarole with a large, pale, blanched heart for a crisp taste and mild flavour. Pick one with a majority of lighter coloured leaves and you'll be rewarded with a milder flavour.

Store it right
Store escarole unwashed, in a perforated plastic bag in the crisper. It will last only a few days.

Prep it right
Wash escarole in several rinses of water. It can be very sandy.

You can serve it raw in salads – the inner, white and light green leaves are best for salads. Try it in soups or stir-fries. It mellows with braising. It can also go into pilafs, polenta and risottos.

Culinary companions
Kidney, chickpeas and navy beans work with escarole, as do fresh green beans. Sausages or spicy meatballs are traditionally paired with escarole in Italian cuisine. Nuts, raisins, shallots, avocado, hard-boiled eggs and oranges are all good salad ingredients with escarole.

Culinary destinations

Sauté escarole in olive oil, garlic, lemon juice and perhaps some hot pepper flakes for a spicy green side dish. Or sauté with olive oil, garlic, toasted pine nuts and raisins and serve on crusty bread as bruschetta. Try it in soup with onions, garlic, parsley, tomatoes and chickpeas.

To your health

Escarole is low in calories, with only 17 calories in a 2-cup (100-g) serving of raw leaves. It's an excellent source of folate, supplying 142 mcg or 64 per cent of the Recommended Daily Intake (RDI). Escarole is high in vitamin A and a source of iron, magnesium, potassium, vitamin C, thiamin and riboflavin.

Quick ways

Take a head of escarole and trim off any dark green leaves. Cut into long, thin strips. Cut a small head of romaine and a bunch of arugula in the same manner. Toss with olive oil and red wine vinegar. Garnish with garlicky croutons, shaved Parmigiano-Reggiano and a sprinkling of crumbled Gorgonzola.

Fava Beans

There's a few things you should know about fresh fava bean frenzy. The season comes and goes with a blink of an eye. Be on the lookout after your first sighting of a red-breasted robin in spring. In my neighbourhood, you've got to be tenacious, too. When fresh fava frenzy erupts on the Danforth in Toronto, I'm elbow-to-elbow with the city's finest fava pickers, and if I'm not quick, my Greek and Italian counterparts will clean out all the best beans before I do.

Other names

Fava beans have many aliases. In Britain, they're called broad beans or even English or Windsor beans. Other names include horse and Italian beans.

Looks like/Tastes like

A fresh fava bean pod is green, about 5 inches (12.5 cm) long and 1 inch (2.5 cm) wide. The pod is thicker and denser than a pea pod. The shelled bean resembles a baby lima bean. Fresh fava beans have a clean, sweet and slightly bitter taste. The younger the bean, the better. Young fava beans (in pods no larger than 3 inches/8 cm) are generally the sweetest and most tender.

Select it

Look for plump, fresh pods bulging with beans. You want to find fava pods that are as green as possible. Blackened, blemished or withered pods are to be avoided. You may see floppy pods as long as a foot (30 cm), but the small, crisp ones are the best. Look for them in Italian, Chinese and specialty food stores.

Store it right

This veggie is perishable. Eat right away and don't expect it to enjoy a fridge life of more than a few days. Store unshelled, in a plastic bag in the crisper. You can blanch, peel and freeze fava beans that keep for up to 6 months.

Prep it right

It's true: fava beans are labour-intensive. Not only do you have to shell them, but the beans need to be individually peeled, also. Actually, it's a matter of taste. Those who relish bitter flavours rarely peel fava beans – but novices should peel first, then sample. Blanch fava beans (1 to 3 minutes), drain, rinse in ice water and then peel. Slit each skin with your thumbnail (or a knife) and the bean will pop out.

If you find some really young fava beans (no longer than 3 inches/8 cm) or you grow your own, you can cook these – pod and all – like sugar snap peas. But most fava beans require shelling and peeling. Once peeled, most fava beans only need to be reheated, but that depends on the size and age. You can boil, steam or sauté fava beans. They work well in pasta sauces, bean salads, soups and purées. Italians eat them raw as an appetizer with coarse salt, dry ham, some crumbly cheese and vino, of course.

Culinary companions

Fava beans, like most beans, pair well with many herbs: try summer and winter savoury, sage, thyme, rosemary, dill, parsley and oregano. Pancetta, prosciutto and bacon all add taste to a fava bean dish. Other complementary ingredients include cheese (especially Parmigiano-Reggiano, pecorino and Romano) and yogurt. Lemon juice and zest add life to fava beans.

Culinary destinations

Try pancetta, green onions and fava beans on bow-tie pasta. Or throw some fresh fava beans in a risotto with fennel and green onions. Team it up with asparagus in a springtime frittata, or bake fava beans in a cream, nutmeg, thyme and Gruyère casserole. These beans can be simply sautéed with olive oil and garlic or made into a puréed bean dip (with garlic, lemon juice, olive oil, cumin and cayenne) as an appetizer.

To your health

There are only 110 calories in 1 cup (126 g) of fresh, raw fava beans. They're low in fat, high in fibre and a great source of vegetable protein. Fava beans are an excellent source of folate and a source of potassium, vitamin C and iron.

Fava beans, like other beans, are very high in fibre, especially soluble fibre, which reduces the risk of heart disease by lowering cholesterol. Just one serving of beans a day will lower your cholesterol and blood pressure and keep you regular.

Warning: Some people of Mediterranean descent have an enzyme deficiency that triggers a type of anemia if they eat fava beans.

Quick ways

Try fava beans Shanghai-style. Heat some canola or safflower oil in a wok, then add ½ cup (125 mL) chopped green onions. Stir-fry 1 minute, then add 2 cups (500 mL) shelled and peeled fava beans and ½ cup (125 mL) minced ham. Stir-fry 2 to 3 minutes, adding water or chicken stock if the wok becomes dry. Add ½ teaspoon (2 mL) sugar, 1 tablespoon (15 mL) cooking sherry and salt to taste. Serve on steamed white rice.

Trivia

There's archeological evidence that the fava bean is one of the first cultivated foods.

Fennel

Fennel is another one of those strange-look-ing, bulbous vegetables that many people are afraid to try. Muster up some gumption and discover the unique, fresh taste of fennel.

Other names
Fennel is often called fennel bulb, anise, sweet fennel, Florence fennel and in Italian circles *finnochio*.

Looks like/Tastes like
Fennel looks like a distorted head of celery, which makes sense, because they're cousins. The base of fennel is pale green to ivory white and three to four times as large as a celery base. (It's technically not a bulb but a stem end, for it grows above ground.) It has thin, celery-like stalks (except they are round in diameter, not concave like celery) with feathery, dill-like green tops.

Select it
Look for a firm, clean, rounded bulb (flatter ones are undeveloped). The stalks should be straight and closely spaced rather than spread out. Find a fennel with fresh, green fronds and avoid flowering ones, because they're too old. The greener the fennel base, the stronger the flavour. Avoid fennel that has brown spots, split stalks or a fibrous outer layer.

Store it right
Store fennel in a perforated plastic bag in your crisper. Leave the stalks and fronds on until you're ready to work with it. This veggie dries out quickly and will last no more than 3 to 4 days in your fridge.

Prep it right
You can eat fennel raw or cooked. But first it needs a little trimming: trim off the stalks and fronds. The stalks are too stringy to eat but can be used in soup stock. New fronds have a delicate flavour perfect as a dill-like herb or garnish. Coarse, dry fronds should be discarded. Wash well and remove any dry or fibrous outer layer. Slice lengthwise or crosswise, making chunks, cubes, thin slices or julienne strips. Or trim it and cook it whole or simply cut in half. Small, sweet fennel is best for salads. Fennel browns after being cut so put sliced fennel in acidulated water (3 tablespoons/45 mL of lemon juice or vinegar to 4 cups/1 L of water) or sprinkle liberally with lemon or lime juice.

Serve fennel raw, like celery, or use it in recipes calling for celery. Toss it into salads, or serve fennel sticks with a dip. Fennel has a pronounced, clean, licorice flavour that is muted when cooked. It can be steamed, boiled, braised, sautéed, roasted or grilled.

Culinary destinations
Fennel marries well with fish and seafood. Add chunks of fennel to fish stew, chowders

or bouillabaisse. Finely chopped fennel adds zip to a tuna, salmon or even sardine salad. Steam mussels with finely chopped fennel, onions and white wine. Serve fennel raw in a cold, Italian antipasto with a collection of fresh Parmigiano-Reggiano wedges, olives, prosciutto, roasted peppers and olives. Try oven-roasting fennel with red potatoes and green beans, or grill it in on the barbecue after steaming it lightly and brushing with olive oil.

Culinary companions

Fennel and fish go hand in hand. Fennel can be paired up with root vegetables, cheese, cream and a selection of alcohol, be it wine, Pernod or vermouth. Think Italian and French cuisines when preparing fennel.

To your health

Fennel is a low-calorie veggie that is filling and satisfying. One cup (87 g) of sliced, raw fennel contains only 27 calories. It's a source of potassium, magnesium, vitamin C and folate. The leaves contain beta carotene and vitamin C.

The high levels of potassium found in fennel may help prevent and regulate blood pressure.

Trivia

Fennel seeds are a common herb used in Indian, Middle Eastern and Mediterranean cooking. The seeds are harvested from the flowering fennel plant, different from the vegetable, which was first cultivated in Italy. Fennel seeds have stronger medicinal value than the vegetable.

Fiddleheads

They've been called Canada's national vegetable, yet I wonder if the average Canuck can
identify a fiddlehead. If you're a gardener, or
a wilderness forager, chances are you are well
acquainted with this wild and wonderful delicacy. But if you're a city dweller in search of a
new veggie, brimming with taste and nutrients, then mark May on your calendar . . . and
get ready for flavours of fiddlehead.

Looks like/Tastes like
Fiddleheads look like no other vegetable!
They are deep green, spiralled stems resembling tiny, coiled grass snakes, encased in
brown, papery scales. The taste is halfway
between asparagus and spinach. Some
people liken the taste to artichokes or even
wild mushrooms. Regardless, it's definitely
earthy, a little bit nutty and somewhat
grassy.

All types of ferns go through the fiddlehead stage just prior to unfurling into a large
feathery plant. However, many fern varieties
are carcinogenic, making them not safe to
eat. If you plan to pick your own, make sure
you stick to the **ostrich** fern (*Matteuccia
struthiopteris*), which is the only non-car-
cinogenic fern.

Select it
Choose small, deep green or bright green,
tightly coiled fiddleheads, no larger than
1 ½ inches (4 cm) in diameter. When fiddleheads are too big, they taste like a mouthful
of green wood and fibre. Whether you find a
dry brown casing on fiddleheads depend on
whether these light, papery scales have fallen
off during the trip from field to market.

Store it right
For best results, eat your fiddleheads the
same day you buy them. If you must store
them, wrap them in paper towels and place
in a perforated plastic bag in the refrigerator
crisper.

Fiddleheads freeze well. Blanch in boiling
water for 1 minute. Plunge in ice water. Dry
thoroughly and store in freezer bags or airtight containers.

Prep it right
Gently rub fiddleheads between your hands
to remove the brown scales or shake them
in a paper bag. The scales are bitter and unpalatable so you want to make sure they're
gone. Trim off the stem ends or tails.

Cook fiddleheads briefly, either by steaming or boiling until they are bright green.

You can also sauté fiddleheads – albeit
gently – so that they don't lose their whimsical shape.

Culinary destinations
Many people believe that the very finest
way to eat fiddleheads is simply: with a dab
of butter and a squirt of lemon juice. Try
steaming fiddleheads, then tossing in a

vinaigrette and serving at room temperature or cold. Or eat them the Japanese way, lightly steamed and splashed with a little soy sauce, sesame oil and sesame seeds. You can sauté fiddleheads with a little garlic until just tender then put in a casserole dish, sprinkle with freshly grated Parmigiano-Reggiano and broil until golden. Fiddleheads and mushrooms are a natural combination. Steam fiddleheads then serve with a porcini cream sauce or make a fiddlehead and mushroom frittata.

To your health

Fiddleheads are low in calories, contain no fat and are bursting with nutrients. A 3-½-ounce (100-g) serving of raw fiddleheads contains 34 calories and 26 mg of vitamin C (almost half of your daily needs). Besides being an excellent source of vitamin C, fiddleheads are an excellent source of vitamin A, high in niacin, and a source of magnesium, iron, potassium, zinc and phosphorous.

Turn to fiddleheads for their powerful antioxidant values. An excellent source of both vitamin C and beta carotene, fiddleheads may offer protection against heart disease, cancer, stroke and cataracts. Warning: Do not eat fiddleheads of any other variety but ostrich fern since they are carcinogenic.

Quick ways

Lightly steam a pound (500 g)of fiddleheads until they are tender and bright green. In a small bowl, combine 2 tablespoons (30 mL) of canola oil, 1 tsp (5 mL) of sesame oil, 1 tablespoon (15 mL) of rice vinegar, ½ teaspoon (2 mL) of sugar and 1 tablespoon (15 mL) of soy sauce. Toss with the fiddleheads while still warm and refrigerate for at least 4 hours. Serve cold or at room temperature, garnished with toasted sesame seeds.

Trivia

The Maliseet Indians of New Brunswick have a long tradition of harvesting and eating fiddleheads. They consider it a medicine as well as a food and they mark their canoes, wigwams and clothing with a fiddlehead-shaped symbol.

Jerusalem Artichoke

If there were ever a misnamed vegetable, it would have to be the Jerusalem artichoke. First of all, this veggie is simply not related to the artichoke. Secondly, the "Jerusalem" association is a mystery because this knobby little tuber is indigenous to North America and was first cultivated by North American natives. The Jerusalem artichoke is a member of the sunflower family and has been dubbed sunchoke in California – a name that still brings forth that artichoke connection!

Looks like/Tastes like

Jerusalem artichokes are edible tubers that look like fat knobs of fresh ginger. They are rough and knobby with a very thin, light brown to matte skin. Some are tinged with red or purple. The flesh is creamy white, crisp and juicy. They have a sweet nutty taste that is faintly reminiscent of artichokes.

Select it

Choose Jerusalem artichokes that are free of bruises, cracks, mould, wrinkles and blemishes. It should be firm, not limp and soggy. Avoid any that are tinged with green or have begun to sprout.

Store it right

Although they taste and look a bit like potatoes, Jerusalem artichokes don't last as well. Put them in a sealed plastic bag in the fridge where they'll last for no more than 2 weeks.

Keep raw Jerusalem artichokes away from really cold spots in your fridge, such as beside a wall or on the bottom shelf for they are frost sensitive. Don't freeze raw or cooked Jerusalem artichokes – they discolour and turn to mush.

Prep it right

You can eat Jerusalem artichokes raw or cooked. The skin is edible and not necessary to peel; however, they need a good scrub with a vegetable brush. Sliced Jerusalem artichokes will discolour. Put them in acidulated water (3 tablespoons/ 45 mL lemon juice or vinegar to 4 cups/1L of water) as you slice them. For salads, toss sliced or grated Jerusalem artichokes with plenty of lemon juice or vinegar to stop discolouration.

You can boil, roast, steam, deep-fry or bake Jerusalem artichokes but be sure you don't overcook them or they'll lose their taste and texture. Cook until just tender for best results.

Culinary destinations

Cut Jerusalem artichokes into vegetable sticks and serve with a dip. Toss slices in a vinaigrette with watercress, apples and walnuts. Deep-fry them like potatoes, make a creamy soup with leeks or put them into a rich gratin with cream, tarragon and Gruyère cheese.

To your health

Jerusalem artichokes are a leading vegetable source of iron. A 3-½-ounce (100-g) serving of raw sliced Jerusalem artichokes contains 24 per cent of your day's needs, which puts it on par with iron levels in meat, without the fat. The same serving contains 76 calories, and is high in thiamin and a source of potassium and niacin.

If you've never eaten a Jerusalem artichoke before, start slowly. This vegetable contains a carbohydrate known as inulin, which many people cannot digest efficiently. Inulin can cause flatulence and discomfort until your body starts to tolerate it better. Conversely, inulin is considered a diabetic-friendly carbohydrate since it resists digestion and may limit a rise in blood sugar levels after eating.

Tips

The calorie content of a Jerusalem artichoke varies according to how long it's been stored. The older the Jerusalem artichoke, the higher the sugar content – and its calories.

Increase your body's absorption of iron from Jerusalem artichokes by eating or drinking a food high in vitamin C during the same meal.

Quick ways

To pickle Jerusalem artichokes, all you need is the remaining liquid from a finished bottle of dill pickles. Fill the bottle with ¼-inch (6-mm) thick sticks of raw Jerusalem artichokes, refrigerate for 24 hours and you've got a new batch of pickles that will last in the fridge up to 2 weeks.

Jicama

Looks are deceiving. And so are the names that people call this squat little tuber. The jicama has been dubbed a "dusty old stone" and an "inert looking blob" by various food writers. But if you can get past the names and the humble looks, you'll discover a cheap, delightful vegetable that is sweet, crunchy and a cinch to prepare.

Other names

Here's how you say it: HEE-kama. It's also called yam bean, Mexican turnip, potato bean, *ahipa* or *saa got*.

Looks like/Tastes like

It looks like a tan-skinned turnip that has been slightly flattened at both ends. When you peel off the inedible skin, you'll find crisp, juicy, ivory-coloured flesh with an apple-like texture. At its prime, jicama tastes like a cross between an apple and a water chestnut.

Select it

Stay small when choosing jicama to make a sweet and juicy purchase. Jicama ranges from ½ pound (250 g) to 5 pounds (2 kg) in size, but the bigger it gets, the starchier. Big old jicamas taste like raw potatoes. Make sure it is heavy for its size, and you'll get a juicy specimen with a high water content. The skin should be smooth and taut, with no cuts or dark spots. Try scratching the skin: it should be paper thin. If you can't find jicama in your supermarket, look for it in Asian and Latin American stores.

Store it right

Place jicama in a plastic bag in your fridge. Whole jicama will keep for up to 3 weeks. Once cut, it deteriorates rapidly. Wrap tightly in plastic and use as soon as possible. Don't freeze jicama, as it will turn mushy and translucent.

Prep it right

Peel off the skin with a sharp knife or vegetable peeler, removing the layer of fibre found directly beneath the skin. Once cut, jicama dries out quickly. It's a good idea to soak cut jicama in water until right before you use it.

Jicama can be eaten raw or cooked. Toss it into salads or cut it into sticks and serve with a dip. Try it grated, julienned, diced or sliced. Sliced jicama gives crunch to a stir-fry. Cook it lightly so it doesn't lose that crunch. It can also be lightly steamed. Baste jicama with a little olive oil and roast in the oven like potatoes or cut it into ¼-inch (6-mm) thick slices, baste with oil and grill 1 minute per side. Add it to light, Asian-style soups during the last few minutes of cooking.

Culinary companions

Jicama works with mayonnaise, sour cream and yogurt. Mexican flavours such as lime juice, fresh coriander and jalapeño work well too. Go Asian with sesame oil, soy sauce, hoi sin sauce, ginger and garlic.

To your health

A 1-cup (120-g) serving of raw jicama contains 45 calories, no fat or cholesterol, and is a good source of dietary fibre. Jicama is high in vitamin C and a source of potassium and folate.

Eat jicama for heart and baby health. Jicama contains heart-friendly potassium and folate. Recent research shows that folate helps reduce high levels of homocysteine, associated with heart attacks and stroke. Women planning to get pregnant or already pregnant can reduce the risk of neural tube defects in a developing fetus by 50 per cent with a diet high in folate.

Quick ways

Here's a quick and easy Mexican-style jicama salad. Take 2 cups (500 mL) of thinly sliced jicama. Toss with the sections of 1 orange and ½ sweet onion such as a Wala Wala or Vidalia, thinly sliced. In a small bowl, mix the juice of 1 lime, ¼ teaspoon (1 mL) of cayenne, and 2 tablespoons (25 mL) of sunflower or canola oil. Toss and season with salt and freshly ground black pepper.

Tips

If a recipe calls for water chestnuts, you can use jicama as a terrific substitute.

Avoid carbon knives and cast-iron pots when preparing jicama, as they can discolour jicama.

Kale

Many people are surprised to learn that those gorgeous ornamental garden plants that look like open-leaf cabbages are actually kale. While I don't recommend robbing your neighbour's garden for a taste of this cruciferous treat, I do urge you to try the vegetable variety found at your green grocer. Besides, it makes a striking substitute for lettuce in salad platters.

Looks like/Tastes like

Easily identifiable, kale has frilly, dark green and sturdy leaves that are tied together to make one of the biggest "bunches" of greens you can buy. The colour may vary. It's usually dark green with a blue, purple or a crimson tinge. Kale's pungent, cabbagy flavour can be tempered into a gentle sweetness when cooked properly.

Select it

When buying kale, remember that big does not always mean better. Look for small leaves, about the size of an outstretched hand or a little bigger. If you stick to small leaves of kale, you'll be rewarded with a more tender, mild taste. Find kale with fresh, green colour and avoid any bunches with yellow or brown leaves.

Store it right

Kale loves the cold and in fact, some varieties are picked after a frost, which enhances the flavour. So store this veggie in the coldest part of your fridge. Nestle it in a plastic bag up against the fridge wall or on the bottom shelf. Although it lasts beautifully, with slow textural deterioration, the sweetness disappears with every day of delay and a stronger flavour develops over time. Eat it as soon as possible.

Prep it right

Wash kale well. Sand and grit stay lodged in those frilly leaves if you don't clean thoroughly. The stems are edible, but quite fibrous. It's best to use a knife to remove any stalks thicker than a pencil. Or use your hands and strip the leaves off the stalk with a gentle pull. You can cook the stalks, but they take longer than the leaves.

You can sauté, braise, boil, steam, bake or microwave kale. Consider parboiling it for a couple of minutes, draining well and then sautéing. Unlike other greens that reduce up to eight times their original size, raw kale only shrinks in half or by a quarter.

The older the kale, the more cooking it will require. It's done cooking when it is tender and sweet. Use older kale in soups, stews or gratins. It can also stand up to long-cooking grains like brown rice, bulgur or barley, making it perfect for pilafs.

Small young leaves can be tossed into salads. It makes a nice spicy addition to a mesclun mix. But chances are, you won't find it young enough in the store and will have to depend on your vegetable garden for it.

Culinary destinations

Add kale to a slow-cooking bean soup or stew. Stir-fry kale with plenty of fresh ginger, a sprinkling of sugar and a drizzle of sesame oil. Chopped kale can be braised with plenty of garlic and stock. Try it creamed with fresh herbs or put it in a lentil, barley and sage pilaf with almonds.

To your health

Kale is a nutritional superstar, packed sky-high with vitamins A and C. One cup (130 g) of cooked kale contains almost a day's supply of vitamin A and 53 mg of vitamin C, which is 88 per cent of the Recommended Daily Intake (RDI). Kale is a source of iron, which is absorbed more readily due to kale's high levels of vitamin C. Kale is also a source of vitamins E and B^6, calcium, magnesium, potassium, thiamin, riboflavin and folate.

Turn to kale for an antioxidant boost. The vitamin C, beta carotene and vitamin E in this vegetable may help strengthen your defence against cholesterol build-up. Kale is also teeming with important phytochemicals that may reduce the risk of cancer, heart disease and stroke.

Quick ways

Trim and discard the stems from a bunch of kale. Slice the leaves into thin ribbons with a knife. Grate 1 tablespoon (15 mL) of fresh, peeled ginger, using the smallest grate on your kitchen grater. Heat 1 tablespoon (15 mL) of vegetable oil in a skillet or wok at medium high, add the freshly grated ginger and a pinch of salt, then toss in the kale with the rinsing water still clinging to its leaves. Stir until tender (about 5 to 8 minutes). Sprinkle with ½ teaspoon (2 mL) of sugar and drizzle on 1 teaspoon (5 mL) of sesame oil. Serve.

Trivia

Kale is one of the more remarkable members of the Cruciferous Club because it is so nutrient-dense. The cabbage family have been named after the crucifix as they all bear cross-shaped, four-petalled flowers.

Tip

Even though a vegetable may contain a lot of calcium, our bodies can't necessarily absorb it. However, according to a recent study, kale ranks high in bioavailable calcium. For instance, you have to eat 15.5 servings of spinach or 5.2 servings of broccoli to absorb the same amount of calcium that can be absorbed from a glass of milk. But you only need 3.5 servings of kale to get the same amount of "absorbable" calcium as a glass of milk.

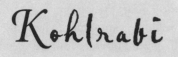

Kohlrabi

No stranger to the cuisines of Hungary, Germany and China, kohlrabi is still a mystery to most North American palates. When the leaves are removed, it looks like a light green meteor. Most folks are as inclined to try it as take a trip to Mars. But this veggie has a down-to-earth taste that delivers flavour, versatility and oodles of nutrition.

Other names

It's pronounced kohl-RAH-bee. The most common alias is cabbage turnip, which is the direct translation of the German name: *kohl* meaning cabbage, and *rabi,* meaning turnip.

Looks like/Tastes like

Kohlrabi is often called a root vegetable, but it's not. It's actually a rounded tuber that develops in the stem just above the ground. This turnip-shaped tuber, about the size of a tennis ball, has three varieties: **green**, **white** or **violet**. Its dark green, firm leaves grow out from the tuber at all angles. Despite the nickname, it doesn't taste like cabbage or turnip. It's the mildest-tasting member of the cabbage family, with a flavour not unlike broccoli stems, or a cross between a radish and a cucumber. The leaves taste like kale or collards.

Select it

When it comes to kohlrabi, the smaller the better. Choose bulbs no larger than 2 to 3 inches (5 to 8 cm) in diameter. Large ones are more tough and fibrous. Small ones are more delicate, don't require peeling and have a more mellow taste. If leaves are attached, you'll know how fresh the kohlrabi is. Look for crisp, firm, deeply coloured leaves. Make sure the bulb is free of cracks or visible fibres. Avoid any kohlrabi with soft spots.

Store it right

If the leaves are attached, remove them so they don't rob the bulb of nutrients. Stored separately in plastic bags, the leaves last a day or two, the bulb up to a week. To freeze, blanch cubed kohlrabi in salted water for 1 minute and then plunge into ice water. Dry thoroughly and store in freezer bags for up to a year.

Prep it right

If you have a small, very fresh kohlrabi, all you need to do is trim off all the stem ends and wash it well. Larger specimens need to be trimmed and peeled, taking care to remove all the large fibres lurking just below the skin. Alternatively, you can cook large kohlrabi with the skin on and remove it after cooking.

Kohlrabi can be eaten raw or cooked. It can be sliced or shredded for salads or cut into sticks for dipping. Or blanch briefly, plunge into ice water, drain and serve cold in salads for a more mellow flavour. Steam, boil or microwave until tender. Thin slices or shreds can be sautéed or stir-fried. Kohlrabi can be baked, roasted or braised, too. Large kohlrabi are perfect for stuffing. Peel, parboil, hollow out, stuff and then bake or braise. Add kohlrabi to soups or stews during the last 20 minutes of cooking.

Tip
Sadly, the striking purple hues of the violet kohlrabi turn to khaki green when cooked.

Culinary destinations
Make a slaw, substituting shredded kohlrabi for cabbage in your favourite recipe. Or serve shredded or matchstick-size kohlrabi with similarly shaped pieces of carrots and cucumbers, bathed in an Asian salad dressing of sesame oil, soy sauce, Chinese vinegar, garlic and salt. Grated raw kohlrabi can be tossed in an East Indian style salad with kidney beans and chickpeas with a spicy dressing laced with hot peppers, mustard seeds and fresh coriander. Raw kohlrabi is great as a crudité: try it with olives or an anchovy-based dip. The easiest way to serve kohlrabi is simply steamed and bathed in butter, sprinkled with fresh herbs. A more substantial dish is rib-sticking Hungarian chicken soup. Thinly sliced kohlrabi stir-fried with mushrooms is a classic Chinese combination.

To your health
There are only 47 calories in 1 cup (165 g) of cooked kohlrabi and an excellent supply of antioxidant vitamins C and E. That serving contains an impressive 89 mg of vitamin C, which is 148 per cent of the Recommended Daily Intake (RDI) and 2.7 mg of vitamin E or 27 per cent of the RDI. Kohlrabi is high in potassium and a source of dietary fibre, folate and vitamin B^6.

Here's another card-carrying member of the cabbage family, which may help reduce your risk of cancer, heart disease and cataracts. The walloping amounts of vitamin C in kohlrabi help ward off infection and speed healing. Kohlrabi is also full of antioxidants and phytochemicals which work in tandem to fight cancer. Meanwhile, the potassium in kohlrabi may help to regulate blood pressure and reduce the risk of heart disease.

Quick ways
Sauté a chopped onion and two garlic cloves in olive oil until tender. Add 2 cups (500 mL) each of kohlrabi and potatoes in matchstick slices, plus 4 spicy Italian sausages, whole and pricked. Sauté until the sausages are browned, then add ½ cup (125 mL) of tomato juice, ½ cup (125 mL) of chicken stock, chopped parsley and fennel seeds. Braise 20 minutes and serve.

Lettuce

When it comes to vegetables, lettuce ranks right up there with potatoes and tomatoes in the Mr. Popularity contest. When Canadian consumers go to the store, chances are they buy lettuce. In fact, they are most likely to purchase a head of iceberg – the nutritional loser among lettuces.

Looks like/Tastes like

There are four main types of lettuce: crisphead, butterhead, looseleaf and cos. Hundreds of varieties fall under these types. **Crisphead** lettuces are the ones with the crunch. **Iceberg** is the most famous variety and its name has become synonymous with the type. The crisp, compact leaves form a tight, cabbage-like head. The colour ranges from white in the interior to pale or medium green on the exterior. New varieties include red-leafed and red- and green-leafed crispheads. These lettuces have a mild, bland flavour, and can be cut and shredded like cabbage and even cut into wedges. Crispheads can withstand a thick and heavy dressing.

Butterhead lettuces include such varieties as **Boston**, **bibb**, **Limestone** and **Buttercrunch** and **Red Tip**. This lettuce boasts the softest leaf among all lettuces. The tender, almost floppy leaves form a loose, pretty head – Boston resembles a flowering rose while bibb has a smaller, cup-shaped head. The leaves come in green, red or bronze varieties. Its soft, buttery texture and sweet mild flavour make butterhead a good companion for stronger-tasting greens.

Looseleaf lettuces are sometimes called "cutting" or "bunching" lettuces since they don't form a head but rather a loose bunch of leaves. This lettuce is perfect for home gardeners and can be picked all summer long. (Once a leaf is cut at the stem, a new one grows back up again.) This type of lettuce boasts the greatest number of varieties (many of which are grown as baby lettuces for mesclun mixes): there's the popular **Oak Leaf**, the frizzy, gaudy red **Lollo Rosso** and the elongated **Deer Tongue**, to name a few. The flavour can range from mild to sweet to woody. Colours run from pale to dark green, deep crimson or bronze. Leaf shapes can vary, too: oval or oak-leaf-shaped, smooth, puckered, deeply curled, ruffled or frilly.

Cos or **romaine** lettuce has long, upright leaves that form a cylindrical head. The leaves (which are usually green, but can be found in red) have thick, crisp and juicy ribs. The strong texture of romaine stands up to cooking better than any other lettuce. The flavour can be sharper than other lettuces and pleasantly nutty.

Select it

It's pretty easy to know if lettuce looks fresh or not. Look for crisp, perky leaves and a clear colour. Avoid lettuce that has brown or yellow edges or soggy, dark brown areas.

Store it right

Before you store your lettuce, take off any bands holding the lettuce leaves together (they will eventually bruise and harm the leaves). Likewise, remove any bruised or wilted leaves or stems, which promote decay throughout the lettuce. If you want to wash greens before storing them, do so, but dry them carefully. Store lettuce in a perforated plastic bag in the crisper. Whether washed or not, greens last longer if they're wrapped in paper towels (or clean cloth or linen towels), and placed in a perforated plastic bag in the crisper. Leave your leaves intact – not torn, cut or shred, which causes loss of nutrients and speeds up deterioration.

Prep it right

Nothing spoils a salad faster than a gritty green. Be sure to wash all lettuce carefully. Gently separate the leaves and put them in a sink full of cool water with plenty of room for a thorough "swishing." Some greens require two to three rinses before the water runs clear. The next step – drying – is as important as the first step. Wet greens not only dilute a salad dressing but also stop it from adhering to the leaves. A salad spinner works best if you fluff up the greens after one spin, then spin again. You can also dry lettuce with clean towels. Don't tear, rip or cut your lettuce until just before serving or it will lose nutrients and freshness.

Lettuces are most commonly eaten raw, but you can cook with lettuce (especially romaine). Consider lettuce in a cold summer soup or a warm, creamed soup. Lettuce can be sautéed or stir-fried, braised, steamed or broiled.

Tip

If you're stuck with a mess of wet lettuce and no salad spinner in sight, try this fun alternative (out-of-doors). Put the greens in a clean pillowcase and spin the bag above your head. It works and creates quite a scene!

Culinary companions

Lettuces are interchangeable. You can easily substitute one type for another in salads. However, lettuces have come to be associated with certain dressings. Iceberg is usually paired with heavy dressings such as blue cheese, ranch or Thousand Islands. Looseleaf works with any type of vinaigrette, and also marries well with dozens of salad additions, such as sesame seeds, roasted red peppers, goat cheese, fresh herbs and so on. Butterhead lettuce calls for a citrus or wine vinaigrette, or a light, lemony mayonnaise or buttermilk dressing. If you can break away from the Caesar dressing, you'll find that romaine is perfect with balsamic vinegar, freshly grated Parmigiano-Reggiano, extra virgin olive oil, croutons and so on.

Culinary destinations

Lettuce is most commonly used raw in salads, but don't shy away from cooking with it. Try shredding up looseleaf or romaine and tossing it into your next homemade soup just before serving. Blanch romaine for 10 seconds, spread it with tuna salad or chickpea spread and roll it up for lunch. Or stuff a blanched romaine leaf with brown rice and mushrooms, top with grated cheese and bake until cooked through. Chinese stir-fried ground meat can be folded up in a cold, crisp, iceberg lettuce leaf.

Quick ways

1. For a quick and comforting vegetable side dish, try cutting a head of romaine into quarters lengthwise. Drizzle each quarter with a few spoonfuls of bottled Caesar dressing and a sprinkling of freshly grated Parmigiano-Reggiano. Broil until golden brown and serve.

2. Shred a head of romaine or looseleaf lettuce. Heat some oil in a wok and toss in some grated fresh ginger, chopped garlic, a little salt, a teaspoon (5 mL) of cooking sherry and the shredded lettuce. Stir-fry until wilted. Transfer to a serving plate and drizzle with oyster sauce.

To your health

Lettuce is low in calories. There are only 12 to 18 calories in a 3-½-ounce (100-g) serving of lettuce, depending on the variety. Romaine is the most nutritious lettuce and is an excellent source of folate and vitamin A, and is high in vitamin C, too. In fact, every variety of lettuce scores high in folate, even iceberg, which is also a source of vitamin C. Looseleaf lettuce is high in vitamins A and C and is a source of calcium, iron and potassium. Butterhead lettuce is an excellent source of folate and is a source of vitamins A and C, magnesium and potassium. Lettuce leaves with the darkest green colour contain the most beta carotene. Choose those more often.

The folate and iron found in lettuce make it a good food to help prevent or treat anemia. Folate is also linked with good heart health and can prevent birth defects. The antioxidants found in lettuce (beta carotene, vitamins C and E) are all associated with lower rates of cancer, heart disease, stroke and cataracts. In folk medicine the white "milk" that seeps out of cut lettuce is considered to have sedative qualities.

Trivia

As early as the 1920s, crisphead lettuces were transported great distances across the USA. The rail cars were piled high with ice to keep the lettuce fresh – hence the name iceberg.

The average Canadian eats 20 pounds (9 kg) of lettuce a year!

Mushrooms

Europeans tend to take their mushrooms seriously, and the people of Provence are no exception. When strolling through the outdoor market of Isle-sur-la-Sorgue a year ago, I was struck by a table of fungi. Piles of copper-hued boletes and chanterelles covered the surface of a huge table. These fruits of the forest had an earthy, woodsy aroma that transported me into culinary fantasies of rich and creamy golden sauces. Ahhhh . . . mushrooms.

Looks like/Tastes like

Mushrooms are manifold. Some 38,000 varieties exist. Here are the top nine to watch for:

The first mushroom to be commercially cultivated, the **white button** is still the leader of the domestic mushroom pack. Choose plump, clean ones that are a fresh white, cream or tan colour.

Criminis (a.k.a. **Italian brown, browntop, cremini** and **Roman**) look a lot like button mushrooms, but they have a darker-coloured cap that ranges from light tan to rich brown in colour. They are earthier, meatier and more intensely flavoured than their cousin the button.

The **portobello** (a.k.a. **portaballo, portabello** and **portobella**) is the biggest mushroom you can buy. The cap ranges from 2 to 8 inches (5 to 20 cm) in diameter, but averages in at 3 inches (8 cm). This large 'shroom is actually a large variety of the crimini. It has a rich, meaty taste, and can be served stuffed, grilled, braised or raw.

Shiitakes (a.k.a. **golden oak** mushrooms and **Chinese** mushrooms) originated in Asia but now many North American farmers have mastered the art of shiitake cultivation. They are tan to dark brown and look similar to buttons and criminis, except that the cap is wider and umbrella-shaped. Their flavour is rich and woodsy, developing a meaty texture when cooked.

Known as the "shellfish of the forest," **oyster** mushrooms are widely available and less expensive than other specialty mushrooms. They have a fluted cap that resembles a fan. Colours range from off-white to gray-brown. Oysters have a silky texture and mild flavour.

Native to Japan, **enoki** (a.k.a. **snow puffs** and **golden needles**) mushrooms are now commonly found in green grocers and specialty stores. They look like little Martian antennae: tiny white caps on long, thin trailing stems. Enoki have a sweet, crunchy, fresh flavour with a mild hint of citrus. They'll last only a few days in the fridge and toughen if cooked too long.

Shaped like trumpets with large frilly caps, **chanterelles** (*girolles* in France) range from gold to yellow-orange in colour. They vary in flavour from fruity (apricot-like) to earthy. Smell it: the more intense the aroma, the deeper the taste when cooked.

Morels are among the highest-priced mushrooms because they are usually picked in the wild. A pound of fresh morels can cost up to $60. This firm mushroom, with its conical, spongy cap, can be tiny or fist-sized. Colours range from ivory to yellow to black. Morels have a woodsy aroma and meaty texture with hints of hazelnut, smoke and nutmeg.

Boletes (*cèpes* in France and *porcini* in Italy) are more commonly sold dried than fresh. The colour ranges from white to beige to reddish brown. Boletes have thick, club-like stems and a satiny texture, accented by rich, sweet, earthy flavours.

Select it

Choose mushrooms that have uniform colour (either white, tan or brown depending on the variety) and are firm with tightly closed caps, especially for button and crimini. Mushrooms should be clean and dry, never slimy. Reject any bruised, discoloured or pitted mushrooms.

Tip

An old mushroom isn't necessarily a bad mushroom. As mushrooms mature, they darken in colour, the caps open and the flavour intensifies.

Store it right

Keep mushrooms in a vented paper bag and refrigerated for best results. If you must use a plastic bag, choose a perforated one. Shiitake and oyster mushrooms should be stored in a container with a damp cloth on top to prevent them from drying out. Most perishable are enoki, which last only a few days. White button, oyster, crimini and boletes stay fresh for up to a week. Shiitake and portobello up to 2 weeks. Do a nose check: if they smell sour – not earthy – their time is over. Mushrooms don't freeze well.

Tip

When you buy mushrooms in a grower-packaged tray, there's no need to transfer to a paper bag. These special packages allow the mushrooms to breathe and they last well.

Prep it right

Don't drown your mushrooms when you're washing them. Mushrooms soak up water like sponges, which thins out flavour and destroys nutrients. Instead, wipe them clean with a damp paper towel or mushroom brush. The butt end of the stem can be trimmed, but the cap and stem require no peeling. Morels should be sliced lengthwise before cleaning.

You can eat mushrooms raw or cooked, except morels, which are always served cooked. Try them in salads or marinate them. Sauté in butter or oil, spear on to kebabs, add to soups, stews and casseroles, or let them star in a pasta sauce. Mushrooms can be stir-fried, baked and breaded.

Culinary companions

Butter, olive oil, sesame oil and nut oils all accent the taste of mushrooms. Creamy additions are sublime: try cream, crème fraîche and sour cream. Cheeses suited to mushrooms include goat cheese, Gorgonzola, Boursin, blue and Stilton. Soy sauce emphasizes the earthy flavour, as do grains such as barley or rice. Garlic, roasted garlic, shallots, onions, green onions and chives can all team up with mushrooms, as do wine, sherry, vermouth and Madiera. Fresh herbs include rosemary, coriander, tarragon, chervil, thyme and parsley. Helpful additions are pine nuts, bread crumbs, pancetta and hot peppers.

Culinary destinations

Oyster mushrooms work well in Chinese stir-fries, cream sauces, gratins and breaded appetizers. Raw enoki are perfect in salads and sandwiches. Or cook them in stir-fries or spring rolls, or sautéed in whole bunches. Chanterelles complement chicken, game hens, veal and eggs. Toss them in a creamy pasta sauce or simply sauté in butter with shallots. The morel's honey-combed surface makes it ideal for sauces. It pairs well with poultry and makes a nice sauté with garlic and butter. Portobello are the finest grilling mushroom and offer lots of room to stuff. Shiitake are wonderful stir-fried and grilled, especially in Chinese preparations. White button is incredibly versatile – there's not much you can't do with it.

To your health

Mushrooms are extremely low in calories. A 1-cup (70-g) serving of raw mushroom slices contains only 18 calories and is fat-free. Mushrooms are a very good source of pantothenic acid (a member of the vitamin B-complex family) and a source of iron, potassium, zinc, niacin, folate and the antioxidant mineral selenium.

If you want to eat mushrooms for your health, turn to shiitake first. Japanese studies have revealed that these Asian mushrooms contain lenitan, a phytochemical that may help to boost immune activities against cancer and influenza viruses. Other tests show that shiitake may help lower cholesterol. All mushrooms are a source of the antioxidant mineral selenium, which may not only prevent cancer, but it may protect against heart disease, arthritis and accelerated aging. Warning: Many common species of wild mushrooms are poisonous. Never gather and eat wild mushrooms unless a mushroom expert has deemed them safe.

Trivia

Mushrooms are fungus, not vegetables.

Avocado

*Bok Choy
(foreground)
with Chinese
Cabbage*

Celeriac (foreground) with Fennel

Jerusalem Artichokes (also known as sunchokes) with a green Tomatillo

Kale (below)
Red Kale with
European Green
Cabbage (at left)

Kohlrabi
(red and white)

Honey Mushrooms (right) Shiitake Mushrooms (below)

Okra

Peppers (clockwise from bottom left): Banana Chili, Chilaca, Poblano, Jalapeño and Serrano

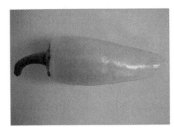

Radish Sprouts

Rapini

*Ruby Chard
(a variety of
Swiss Chard)*

Salsify (above) with Horseradish Root

Scallions

*Squash
(bottom left to
right): Delicata,
Hubbard and
Golden Nugget*

Tomatillos

Mustard Greens

Lots of folks are chomping on mustard greens and don't even know it! That's because mesclun greens – that popular and convenient mix of salad greens – contains two baby mustard greens: tatsoi and mizuna. Mature mustard greens are less well known. They have a peppery bite, can be cooked like spinach and are nutritional blockbusters.

Looks like/Tastes like

Tatsoi is an Oriental mustard with dark green (almost black) spoon-shaped leaves and white stems. It's sometimes called **flat Chinese cabbage** and is most often sold as baby leaves in mesclun mix.

Mizuna is another mesclun mix regular. It has light green, very deeply cut and notched foliage, giving it a feathery look. It is milder than most mustards and reminiscent of arugula but sweeter.

American mustard greens (or **Southern Curled**) can be found in specialty produce stores, farmer's markets and sometimes the supermarket. It's sold as a mature green and looks like a delicate version of kale – its kissing cousin. (All mustard greens are members of the cabbage family.) Southern Curled has jade green leaves that are crinkled or ruffled and more tender than kale. It delivers a hot, mustardy punch.

There are two types of **Chinese mustard** available in most Asian produce stores. One is known as **bamboo mustard cabbage**. It has green stalks and large oval leaves with serrated edges. It looks quite similar to Chinese broccoli raab (see page 112) but without the flowers. The taste is quite sweet and mild with a faint, mustardy bite. **Wrapped Heart mustard cabbage** is used primarily in Chinese soups or is pickled. It looks like a light green cabbage head wrapped up in a dark green baseball glove. This mustard green has a sharp and pungent taste.

Select it

Look for crisp leaves with vivid colour. When buying mature mustard greens rather than baby greens, choose the bunch with the smallest, youngest leaves, no longer than 8 inches (20 cm). Reject any with yellow, flabby, pitted leaves and thick fibrous stems.

Store it right

Use these greens as soon as possible. The delicate baby mustard greens deteriorate faster than their mature counterparts. All toughen with age. Wrap up the greens in paper towels and store in a tightly sealed plastic bag in the refrigerator crisper.

Prep it right

Wash mustard greens carefully. Even mesclun greens benefit from at least one good rinse. Trim off stems and centre ribs that are wider than a pencil.

Mature mustard greens can be steamed, boiled, sautéed or braised for 10 to 20 minutes.

The longer they cook, the softer the flavour becomes. You can cook them until just tender, but they will taste spicy. Baby mustard greens are best raw, in a salad or wedged into a sandwich or wrap.

Culinary companions

Mustard greens go well with Indian flavours such as fresh and ground coriander, cumin, turmeric, cayenne and black mustard seeds. Mediterranean flavours such as olive oil, garlic, oregano, hot pepper flakes and Parmigiano-Reggiano also complement mustard greens. Standard Southern treatment of mustard greens includes onions, garlic, ham, salt pork or bacon. Chinese seasonings go well, too: try soy sauce and oyster sauce. Beans, lentils, barley and sausages are other players.

Culinary destinations

Try young American mustard greens shredded coarsely in a salad with new potatoes and a mustard vinaigrette. Wilt some young mustard greens with a hot dressing of bacon fat, garlic, onions, balsamic vinegar and mustard seeds. Make a puréed mustard green soup seasoned with curry powder or add colour to a cream of potato soup with shredded mustard greens.

To your health

Mustard greens are nutritional powerhouses! One cup (140 g) of cooked mustard greens contains only 21 calories and is a source of fibre. Mustard greens are an excellent source of vitamin C, with 35 mg in that same serving, supplying 59 per cent of the Recommended Daily Intake (RDI). They are also an excellent source of folate and vitamin E, plus a source of calcium, iron, magnesium, potassium and vitamin B[6].

As a member of the Cruciferous Club, mustard greens offer a large range of health benefits. Besides reducing your risk of cancer, heart disease, stroke and cataracts, mustard greens may prevent or treat anemia. The potassium and high levels of vitamin E in mustard greens make them a heart-healthy vegetable green. High in folate, they are a wise food choice for women planning to become pregnant because a diet high in folate reduces the risk of neural tube defects, such as spina bifida, in fetuses.

Trivia

In the Southern United States, the cooking liquid leftover from mustard greens and collards is called "likker" and is used for dunking cornbread, or is reserved for use in soups and stews.

Tip

According to a recent study, mustard greens rank high in bioavailable calcium. Just 2 ½ servings (180 g) of mustard greens supply the same amount of bioavailable calcium as that contained in a glass of milk.

Okra

Okra will never win "The Most Popular" vegetable award, but in my books, it's a winner. The number-one complaint against it is its slime factor. Yet when okra transforms a Louisiana gumbo, the operative words are "velvety thick" – not slimy. Dressed up in an Indian saree of cumin, coriander and mustard seeds, okra is a unique and enticing vegetable side dish.

Other names
First cultivated in Ethiopia, okra was brought to America by the African slaves who called it "gombo." The name stuck when Southerners started making gumbo, a seafood stew thickened with okra. Other names for okra are lady fingers, ochro and bamia.

Looks like/Tastes like
The most popular variety is **green**, but a **burgundy baby** okra is growing in popularity. **Red** okra turns green when cooked. Some varieties have a smooth skin and others have a fuzzy one.

Torpedoes and lady's fingers come to mind when describing okra. These bright green edible pods have exterior ridges that run along the length of the vegetable. Okra contains numerous, edible soft seeds.

Select it
Look for small, bright green okra that is so crisp it should snap easily at the end when bent. You may find okra pods up to 6 inches (15 cm) long, but ignore the mythology of aphrodisiacs and stay with the smaller specimens (3 inches/8 cm or shorter). Any pods longer than that will be tough and fibrous (okra is used to make rope in many countries!). Look for a moist stem end, indicating freshness.

Store it right
Okra is allergic to time, moisture and frost. Your best bet is to eat it the day of purchase. If you can't, store okra in a paper bag or wrap in a paper towel and put it in a vented or perforated plastic bag. Keep it away from the refrigerator's cold spots such as beside a wall or on the bottom shelf.

Prep it right
If you have purchased a particularly fuzzy okra, you can de-fuzz it by wiping it softly with a paper towel or vegetable brush. Okra needs no peeling but it does benefit from light trimming at the stem and tips. But be careful! Once you pierce the inner capsule, the sticky juices will be released, invoking the dreaded sliminess. If you're preparing a soup or stew and want to take advantage of okra's thickening abilities, slice it in rounds and trim off the cap end completely.

One of the easiest ways to cook okra is steaming. Cook it until it is tender crisp. You can also sauté, microwave, boil, bake or roast okra.

*Some cookbooks advise soaking okra in
acidulated water (3 tablespoons/45 mL
of lemon juice or vinegar in 4 cups/1 L of
water) for at least an hour to reduce sliminess, but I find no benefits from this
process.*

Culinary destinations

Steam okra lightly until it turns emerald
green, let it cool and serve it as a crudité. Or
try it just out of the steamer with a buttery-
lemon or roasted pepper dip. Marinate
whole (slitted) okra pods in a vinaigrette,
then grill and serve in a warm salad with
leafy greens, tomatoes and fresh basil. Toss
okra in olive oil and Indian spices and roast
in the oven until tender. Put it in a curry, add
it to a gumbo, try it in tempura or put it in
your next tomato sauce and serve with
spaghetti.

To your health

One serving of cooked okra (about 10 pods
or 110 g) contains 32 calories and is a source
of fibre. Okra is high in folate and magnesium, and is a source of potassium, thiamin,
calcium and vitamins C, E and B[6].

Soluble fibres, most notably in the form of
pectin, are what make okra such a good
thickener in soups and stews. But that's not
all. Pectin is great for your health as it can
help lower cholesterol.

Onion Family

I'm biased. As far I'm concerned, anyone who claims to hate onions simply doesn't know a thing about good food. I just can't imagine a day of cooking without the seductive smell of sautéed garlic and onions wafting through my kitchen. And if it weren't for chives, the summer sensations of freshly sliced tomatoes and boiled new potatoes would be lost from my memory. Shallots, green onions, leeks and those lovely Vidalia onions are all indispensable elements of any good kitchen. Here's how to make them work for you, in yours.

Other names

Among the members of the onion family, it is the green onion that carries the most monikers. Commonly referred to as a scallion in the United States, the green onion is also called a bunching onion and spring onion. To confuse matters even more, they call them shallots in Louisiana.

Looks like/Tastes like

ONIONS The **common cooking** onion, or **yellow storage** onion can be as small as an apricot or as large as an orange. It is round or oval, with a heavy brown wrapper. It's a hot onion but the heat dissipates during cooking.

White (storage) onions are large and can easily weigh more than a pound (500 g). Cloaked in a white, papery skin, these onions have a slightly sharper, cleaner flavour than yellow onions and are used extensively in Mexican cooking. White onions don't last as long as yellows.

A **Spanish** onion is actually a very large yellow onion. Because of its high water content, Spanish onions are sweeter, crisper and milder than yellow onions. Remember **Bermuda** onions? They're actually Spanish onions.

Red onions have a reddish purple skin and flesh. Like Spanish onions, they are sweeter and crisper than yellows. The red onion has a thicker, coarser texture than a Spanish. These onions are perfect for the grill and terrific in salads. Watch out when adding them to sautés, because their red colour can bleed into the other ingredients.

Boiling onions are very small white or yellow onions, about 2 inches (5 cm) in diameter. Leave them whole when boiling or simmering in a stew.

Pearl onions are even smaller than boiling onions, about 1 inch (2.5 cm) to 1 ¼ inch (3 cm) in diameter. They have a thin white wrapper and a white flesh that is sweet and crisp. Pearl onions are perfect for marinating or pickling. Watch out for the **Pink Pearl** variety.

Creaming onions are fresh onions, sold by the bunch, each with a large white bulb still attached to a green stalk. Most often, these are yellow onions picked young, but sometimes they are overly mature green onions. Their crisp, clean flavour is hotter than green onions. Try them raw in salads or cooked.

Sweet Onions While their producers would have you think differently, the truth is most sweet onions taste the same – but oh, what a taste! We're talking juicy, crisp onions that can actually be eaten out of hand like an apple. None of these onions has much heat and all are about 80 to 85 per cent water. A sweet onion generally weighs in from ½ to ¾ pound (225 to 340 g). Best known is the **Vidalia** from Georgia, followed by the **Texas 1015 Supersweet**. There are **Mauis** from Hawaii, **Walla Wallas** from Washington, **Arizonas** and **California Imperials**. Even Ontario has come out with a sweet onion, called the **Norfolk**.

Garlic Some 300 varieties of garlic are grown around the world, but California garlic is perhaps the most common (about 90 per cent of the U.S. crop is grown there). The **California early** and **California late** are both white, averaging about 10 cloves per bulb. Many red, pink and purple tinged varieties are grown around the world. Despite the name, **elephant** garlic isn't a true garlic, but a member of the leek family. Its taste is much milder than true garlic. An elephant garlic can weigh up to a pound (500 g) and sometimes yields just one single clove, the size of a golfball. More commonly, you'll find 4 to 6 cloves in an elephant garlic.

Shallots More expensive than other onions, shallots are a small, tender, mildly flavoured onion that tastes like a cross between an onion and a garlic. A shallot grows in segmented cloves, like the garlic, but it usually has only 2 to 3 segments per shallot. Shallots come in copper, gold or grey papery skins and depending on the variety, may have white, yellow or pink-tinged flesh. The grey variety, grown in France, is not usually found in North American stores. It has a thicker skin than other shallots and holds its shape well when cooked. Shallots can be eaten raw or cooked. Used widely in French cuisine, shallots are also popular in Vietnamese and Thai cooking.

Leeks Leeks look like very large green onions with thick, tough green tops and a white, non-bulbing base. Like green onions, they are sold with roots attached. Unlike green onions, you don't want to eat them raw – they are tough, coarse and very hot. Once cooked, leeks develop a more complex flavour than onions, both mellow and astringent at the same time.

Green Onions The seeds of these long, slender onions are sown tightly together and harvested before they develop bulbs. They're essentially seedling onions and are usually about 12 to 18 inches (30 to 45 cm) long. Some varieties have a slightly swollen white bulb at the bottom while others have no bulb. **Tokyo** and **Feast** varieties both have an exceptionally long white end, about 2 to 3 times the length of the common variety. **Red Beard** variety has rhubarb-coloured stalks, with dark green leaves and a non-bulbing white tip. Green onions are mildly hot and can be eaten raw or cooked. Green onions are used heavily in Asian cooking, in trinity with garlic and ginger.

Chives Usually referred to as an herb, chives are the smallest member of the onion family. Like green onions, chives bear hollow green shoots but they are more tender and rarely thicker than ⅛ inch (3 mm). (A chive's tiny little bulb is never harvested for eating.) Besides **common chives**, there are **garlic chives**, also called **Chinese chives**. Garlic chives have broader and flatter stalks that are grey-green in colour. They taste more garlicky than oniony. Garlic chives can stand up to cooking better than common chives and are used in many Asian stir-fries.

Select it

When buying any dry onion (versus fresh ones, such as chives, leeks, green onions and creaming onions), look for a dry, papery skin that is taut, is unbroken and has no signs of mould. Squeeze your onions – make sure they feel very firm and have no soft spots. An onion should feel heavy in the hand, not light and airy. Avoid onions, garlic and shallots with green sprouts. Use your nose. If it smells, it's toast.

When purchasing fresh onions (chives, leeks, green onions and creaming onions), look for crisp, bright greens and smooth firm white bulbs. If leeks, green onions or creaming onions are slimy or soggy, they are past their prime. Dried and withered ones are also unacceptable. Smaller leeks often taste better than large leeks, especially in the dead of winter.

Store it right

Store dry onions, garlic and shallots in a dark, cool, well-ventilated spot. Many onions and shallots are sold in mesh or netted bags. Keep them in these bags – try hanging – to permit air circulation. Or store them in a basket or colander. Don't seal them up in a plastic bag – they'll rot in a flash. If stored properly, onions, garlic and shallots will last for a month or more.

Sweet onions are much more perishable than their cousins. Due to their higher water and sugar content, they bruise easily and shouldn't be stored touching each other. Try the pantyhose trick: arrange sweet onions in a clean pair of sheer pantyhose and tie a knot between each onion. Hang in a cool, dry place. Stored this way, they'll last a month to 6 weeks. For even longer storage, wrap each onion in aluminum foil and store in the refrigerator crisper where they'll keep for up to 6 months!

Chives, green onions, leeks and creaming onions must be refrigerated. Remove any rubber bands or ties – they promote decay. Wrapped in paper towel and placed in a perforated plastic bag, all these fresh onions can last up to a week or more.

You can freeze onions, leeks, shallots and garlic. Simply chop them and pack in a freezer bag. Chives and green onions freeze well, too. Chop them up, lay them out in a single layer on a baking sheet and flash-freeze until solid. Transfer to a freezer bag. There's no need to defrost them before using.

Tips

While many people like to store chopped garlic in oil, these preparations are potentially dangerous. When fresh garlic is stored in oil, the conditions are right for the growth of clostridium botulinum, which causes botulism – a deadly form of food poisoning. To be safe, always use garlic-in-oil preparations right after they are made and throw out the leftovers. This doesn' t apply to salad dressings containing vinegar or citrus juice, because the acid stops the growth of C. botulinum bacteria.

Don' t store onions and potatoes in the same spot. Both veggies emit a gas that causes the other veggie to rot faster!

Prep it right

To prep an onion, cut off the root and neck end and peel the skin off downward toward the root. An onion can be sliced whole in rounds, or sliced in half moons from an onion half.

To dice an **onion** quickly, take half a peeled onion, placing the cut side down on the cutting board. Make lengthwise, parallel cuts (the closer they are spaced, the smaller the dice will be). Then make crosswise slices, perpendicular to the lengthwise cuts. As you cut, the dice will appear. You can also grate an onion. Onions are best chopped by hand – a food processor turns them into mush. However, you can slice or grate onions in a food processor successfully.

The easiest way to peel a **garlic** clove is to smash it first with the flat side of a large knife on a cutting board. Or put it in the microwave and cook on high for no more than 5 seconds – this loosens the skin. The finer you chop a garlic, the stronger the flavour. Thus, crushed garlic has a more pungent flavour than sliced garlic.

A **shallot** can be peeled, sliced and diced like an onion.

Leeks require scrupulous washing – they're usually covered in sand, inside and out. If you are serving them whole, trim off the fibrous roots and the green, bitter leaves. Starting an inch (2.5 cm) from the bottom of the bulb, make a lengthwise cut to the top. Soak leeks in water for a few minutes then fan out the leaves and wash under running water. If your recipe calls for chopped leeks, washing is a breeze: simply chop and rinse well in a sink full of water.

Green onions should be washed and then trimmed. Cut away any wilted parts from the green ends and slice off the tip of the white root. Sometimes the outermost layer of skin is slimy or damaged, requiring removal. Both the white and green ends of the green onion are edible, although many recipes call for the white part only (it has a more oniony flavour). Green onions can be sliced lengthwise or crosswise. When a recipe calls for finely chopped green onions, make some lengthwise slits from the base, stopping where the white part ends. Then chop the green onion crosswise, to produce a fine dice.

Chives should be rinsed carefully and dried in paper towel. You can chop them finely with a knife or snip them with scissors.

Onions and sweet onions can be baked, stuffed, creamed, boiled, sautéed and deep-fried as rings. All onions become sweeter when cooked.

Good salad onions are Spanish, white and red onions, green onions and chives. White onions are particularly well suited for salsas, because their flavour doesn't get stronger with standing like other onions.

To caramelize onions, sauté them in oil or butter for 5 to 7 minutes. Avoid the temptation to stir constantly and allow them to brown. Once they are golden, add equal parts sugar and vinegar, then sauté another 10 minutes or until the onions are browned, tender and fragrant.

Tips

To remove garlic odour from your hands, rinse with lemon juice or scrub with salt, and then rinse with cool water.

Like onions but don't like crying? Leave your onion in the freezer for just 10 minutes prior to chopping and it will become a "no-tears" onion. Or peel it under running water.

You won't shed a tear when preparing sweet onions. These toothsome onions are low in pyruvate, the natural chemical – in other onions – that causes tearing.

Culinary destinations

Make a pasta sauce of caramelized onions, garlic, balsamic vinegar and mushrooms. Or warm up a wintry day with a bowl full of onion soup and Gruyère cheese. Try a French version of pizza with sweet onions, herbs, tomatoes, anchovies and black olives. Garlic may be ubiquitous in your cooking, but have you ever stuffed a chicken with 30 cloves or made a garlic soup? Shallots are great in a vinaigrette, but also delicious roasted or braised whole. Leeks are another forgotten vegetable. Try them baked (see recipe on page 227), or blanch and drizzle with a vinaigrette. You can also roast leeks in the oven, tossed with olive oil, oregano and salt. Green onions are used more than any other onion in Chinese cuisine. Try them in scallion pancakes, sliced on steamed fish with ginger or stir-fried with beef and dried tangerine peel. Chives and chive flowers are perfect in salads or as a garnish. They add a touch of heaven to fish, eggs, soups, potatoes and salad dressings – but use them as a finishing touch only as heat destroys their delicate flavour.

To your health

A medium sweet onion contains more calories than a yellow onion because it has a higher sugar content. There are 57 calories in a medium sweet onion and 41 in a medium yellow. Onions are a source of vitamin C, folate and potassium. They also contain fibre.

Garlic contains several key nutrients such as vitamin C, calcium, potassium and thiamin. But you'd have to eat 33 cloves of garlic to get half the Recommended Daily Intake (RDI) of vitamin C! There are 4 calories in a single clove of garlic.

Shallots are a source of vitamin C and A, along with folate. However, you'd have to eat more than a ½ cup (125 mL) of chopped raw shallots to get 15 per cent of your RDI of folate. There are 7 calories in a tablespoon (15 mL) of chopped shallots.

Leeks supply more folate and iron, ounce for ounce, than onions. One leek contains 38 calories and is a source of iron, vitamin C and folate.

One green onion contains 5 calories and is a source of folate and vitamin C.

Chives contain beta carotene, vitamin C, potassium and calcium, but all in small amounts. There are 3 calories in one tablespoon (15 mL) of chopped chives.

Not only do onions and garlic spice up your cooking, but they are also excellent for your health, especially when eaten raw. Sulphur compounds – that smelly stuff in onions and garlic that can make us cry – are the essential ingredients that fight cancer and help to stop blood from clotting. When you cook an onion or garlic, the sulphur dissipates. However, researchers still see health benefits in eating both raw and cooked onions and garlic. Onions have long been a traditional remedy for infectious diseases such as coughs, colds, bronchitis and gastric infections. Both onions and garlic are known to lower blood cholesterol. In fact, one study showed that one clove of raw garlic a day can reduce blood cholesterol from 9 to 12 per cent and can reduce blood pressure, too. As an all-round preventative food that can help boost your immune system, onions and garlic spice up your life!

Quick ways

To roast garlic, preheat the oven to 350°F (180°C). Take four heads of garlic and trim the top third off to expose the cloves. Put the garlic heads, root end down, in a small baking dish and fill with water or chicken stock until it covers the bottom third of the garlic.

Drizzle garlic with 1 teaspoon (5 mL) of olive oil and place a sprig of thyme on top of each one. Cover and bake for 1 hour or until tender. Once it is cool enough to handle, squeeze garlic out of each clove and add to sauces and dressings, or serve this creamy delight on a cracker or crostini as an appetizer.

Parsnips

Parsnips have never received the same great press as their cousin, the carrot. But here's a versatile root that tastes great nestled up against a roast, skewered on a kebab or simmered in a soup.

Tip
If you are lucky enough to find just-picked parsnips with fresh, green tops still attached, be sure to cut off the tops before storing. If the tops are left on, they rob the roots of nutrients.

Looks like/Tastes like

Parsnips look like bleached carrots, sometimes covered in hair-like roots. They have a mild, celery-like fragrance and a sweet, nutty, slightly pungent flavour.

Select it

A fresh parsnip – or one that has been properly stored – will offer up a buttery-soft, sweet mouthful. An old, tired parsnip, no matter the size, will be fibrous and insipid. Look for chalk-white parsnips with as few hair-like roots as possible. Avoid yellowed or beige parsnips. You want a firm root, never one that is flabby or limp. Stay away from cracked and split parsnips, too.

Store it right

Parsnips like it cold. In fact, parsnips that are harvested after the first frost or even snowfall are sweeter. Cold temperatures cause a parsnip's starches to convert into sugars. Find a cold spot in the fridge for these roots, such as the bottom shelves or near a wall. They'll keep for several weeks wrapped in a perforated plastic bag.

Prep it right

You can eat raw parsnips, but most people don't. They're a little too fibrous and pungent. Peel or scrub them well before cooking. You can also cook them first, and then remove the skins, but the skins don't exactly "slip" off. If you have a fibrous parsnip, remove the inner core for better flavour.

Parsnips can be steamed, boiled, braised, sautéed, baked, roasted or grilled. To speed things up, parboil parsnips first. When time is no issue, they can be slow-roasted or baked. Keep an eye on this root, though, because unlike carrots, parsnips turn from tender to mush in no time at all. Team them up with milder vegetables for best results. They can jazz up mashed potatoes but may clash with pungent vegetables such as kohlrabi or rutabaga.

Culinary companions

Toasted nuts and seeds such as walnuts, hazelnuts, pine nuts, sesame seeds and sunflower seeds all highlight the nutty taste of parsnips. Apples and pears complement parsnips too, whether in a winter salad or in a soup. Indian flavours such as fresh ginger, curry, fresh and ground coriander, nutmeg and cardamom all work with parsnips, as do many fresh herbs, such as parsley, thyme, chervil, tarragon, dill and rosemary. Citrus, be it zest or juice, is another winner.

To your health

One large parsnip (160 g) contains 129 calories and an incredible 6.4 g of fibre, making it a terrific source of this important nutrient. Parsnips are an excellent source of folate, with 93 mcg in a large parsnip or 42 per cent of the Recommended Daily Intake (RDI). High in magnesium, potassium and vitamins C and E, parsnips are also a source of calcium, iron, thiamin, riboflavin, niacin and vitamin B^6.

Parsnips are a high-fibre food, offering more than that found in many ready-to-eat cereals. Fibre in the diet can help prevent constipation and diseases of the bowel, and may prevent colon and rectal cancer. As an excellent source of folate, parsnips should be on the menu for pregnant women and women planning to become pregnant, because a diet high in folate can reduce the risk in half of having a baby with a neural tube defect such as spina bifida. Researchers have found many important phytochemicals in parsnips, such as terpenes, flavonoids and phenolic acid, all of which may protect against cancer.

Tips

There are only 60 calories in a ½-cup (125-mL) serving of cooked parsnips, making this root a lower-calorie choice than potatoes.

The colour of a parsnip tips you off that it doesn't contain any beta carotene, like its cousin, the carrot.

Peas

Fresh green peas are the essence of spring. Shuck them when you can, for the season is short. Fortunately for pea lovers, fresh snow peas and sugar snap peas are available year-round.

Looks like/Tastes like

There are three main types of peas: green peas, snow peas and sugar snap peas. **Green peas** are hidden beneath a large green pod, which is inflated by its seeds. The peas themselves are grey-green. Generally, the pod is discarded but tender young varieties have an edible pod. **Snow peas** have flat, tender pods (3 to 4 inches/8 to 10 cm long) protecting tiny, immature peas inside. The peas and pod are all edible and the colour is bright green. **Sugar snap peas** are a happy marriage of pea-strengths. Totally edible, they're a combination of the green and snow pea. Like green peas, they're slightly tubular, but just a tad smaller – averaging 2 ½ inches (6 cm) long. The pod walls are thicker than snow peas but more delicate than green peas. The peas inside the pod are more developed and defined than snow peas.

Select it

Look for young, fresh green peas with slightly immature pods, not yet bursting with peas. Good green colouring is important, but a few scratches or bruises are okay. Pods should be firm and supple – never limp or flaccid.

When choosing snow peas, look for bright green pods with a glossy, smooth finish. They should be so crisp they snap when they are folded. If you can see peas through the pod, pass them up. Remember, the flatter the better.

For good sugar snap peas, look for bright green, glossy and crisp specimens. Avoid any yellowed or bruised pods.

Store it right

Green peas are perishable. The sugar-to-starch conversion process starts the moment this veggie is picked. Eat them right away to enjoy their flighty sweetness. Snow peas and sugar snap peas last longer. If picked when crisp and fresh, sugar snap peas may last up to a week wrapped in a plastic bag in the refrigerator.

Prep it right

One pound (500 g) of unshelled green peas will yield about 1 cup (250 mL) shelled peas. To shuck, snap off the stem end and pull down the attached string like a zipper. Press on the seam and the pods open up like an oyster shell. Run your thumb under the peas to free them. It helps if you work over a bowl to catch the peas.

You can de-string snow and sugar snap peas as described above. Some peas need de-stringing on each side. (The Sugar Daddy snow pea variety is stringless.) But if your peas are fresh and young, they won't cry out for de-stringing.

Culinary destinations

You don't need to gussy up a fresh garden pea. It stands well alone, with a knob of butter. Snow peas and sugar snap peas are wonderful in stir-fries and, like garden peas, taste great in salads – even raw in a crudité. Peas are popular additions to many pasta and rice dishes, whether hot or cold.

To your health

One cup (160 g) of cooked green peas contains 134 calories and is an excellent source of dietary fibre, supplying 8.8 g. Garden peas are an excellent source of folate (45 per cent of the Recommended Daily Intake, or RDI) and thiamin, and are high in iron, magnesium and vitamin C. They are also a source of riboflavin, niacin and vitamins A and E. Sugar snap peas and snow peas offer most of the same nutrients as garden peas, but in slightly different levels. Moreover, edible-podded peas have half the calories per cup (250 mL) compared to green peas. Snow peas and sugar snap peas supply about half the fibre but much more vitamin C than green peas. There are 77 mg of vitamin C in 1 cup (160 g) of sugar snap peas, supplying more than your daily needs. Regardless of the comparisons, all kinds of peas offer great nutrition.

Peas are rich in fibre, both soluble and insoluble. Foods high in soluble fibre lower cholesterol and insoluble fibre prevents constipation. Peas and legumes are a good pick for diabetics as peas are digested slowly, which helps to steady the flow of blood sugar. Peas, especially green peas, are an excellent source of vitamin B^6, which helps to relieve pre-menstrual symptoms in some women.

Quick ways

Melt 2 tablespoons (30 mL) of butter in a frying pan and add 2 tablespoons (30 mL) of finely chopped shallots. Sauté until golden, and then add 1 pound (500 g) of sugar snap peas and cook until tender (about 3 to 5 minutes). Sprinkle with 1 teaspoon (5 mL) of grated orange zest and 1 tablespoon (15 mL) of chopped fresh basil. Serve.

Tip

Don't discard your green pea pods. Save them in the fridge or freeze them for the next time you make a stock. They're full of flavour.

Peppers – Hot

I'll never forget the time I was chopping fresh serrano peppers and my knife catapulted a fiery-hot seed smack into my eye. I have never cried so hard. Fortunately, my eye, my contact lens and my taste for hot peppers were collectively salvaged. Now I chop peppers wearing gloves – and have considered safety glasses, too.

Other names

Hot peppers are also called chile peppers, chili pepper or chilies.

Looks like/Tastes like

When it comes to peppers, the varieties are myriad. Here is a list of the most commonly found fresh hot peppers.

Jalapeño (pronounced ha-la-PAY-nyo) is perhaps the best-known hot pepper in Canada. It's a cone-shaped, chubby green pepper with a blunt tip. Jalapeños are about 2 inches (5 cm) long and have thick, meaty flesh. Try roasting and stuffing them, chopping them raw over nachos, or slipping them into cornbread. Medium hot.

Serrano peppers look like jalapeños, but are more elongated and slender. This bullet-shaped pepper is 1 ½ inches to 3 inches (4 to 6 cm) long. Like jalapeños, they are usually green, but sometimes show up red. Serranos are almost twice as hot as jalapeños: use half a serrano when a recipe calls for one jalapeño. Hot.

Thai chilies (a.k.a. **bird chilies**) pack a lot of heat into a tiny space. They're small and never more than an inch (2.5 cm) long. Just one Thai chili can equal the heat of a jalapeño 3 times its size. These tiny, tapered green and red peppers are usually sold in Asian stores, 20 to a package. Use them in Thai, Chinese and Indian cooking. Very hot.

Habanero peppers (fondly referred to as "habs" by pyromaniacs) are the King of Heat. Closely related (and identical in looks and flavour) is the **Scotch Bonnet** pepper from the Caribbean. While a jalapeño scores from 3,000 to 8,000 Scoville heat units, habaneros never go lower than 80,000 units and can reach as high as 577,000 units! Look for squat, lantern-shaped peppers, no wider than 2 inches (5 cm), in a rainbow of colours: red, yellow, green and orange. While most people can't get past the heat to discern any flavour, hot pepper aficionados claim that this pepper is the most flavourful. Try it in Jamaican jerk marinades, skull-and-crossbone chili pastes and other hot concoctions. The hottest.

Anaheim is the most commonly used hot pepper in the United States. Also known as the **California green chili** or **long green**, the Anaheim is about 6 inches (15 cm) long and 2 inches (5 cm) wide. Its slender, elongated shape make it perfect for roasting and stuffing. Mild.

The **poblano** is another stuff-able, mild type of pepper that appears in green or red. (It's technically called an **ancho** when it's dried, but the two terms are often confused.) The widest of all the fresh hot peppers, the poblano is heart-shaped and has a thick flesh, perfect for roasting. Mild.

Hungarian wax peppers come in sweet and hot varieties. Be sure to ask your grocer if it's hot or sweet before you buy. The hot ones are creamy yellow, pale green or red, about 5 to 6 inches (12.5 to 15 cm) long and an inch (2.5 cm) wide. This mild pepper is a good "starter pepper" for timid palates. Try them sliced into salads, stuffed raw with goat cheese or added to bean and grain dishes.

Select it

When choosing hot peppers, look for an unblemished, smooth, taut and bright skin. Avoid wrinkled peppers. Check the stem end, where mould or soft spots can develop. A fresh hot pepper feels firm and crisp. Green hot peppers tend to have a slightly more acidic and bitter flavour than their more ripe and red counterparts.

Store it right

When it comes to hot peppers, small ones tend to last longer than the large ones, and green ones last longer than red. So a big, red hot pepper is the most perishable. Most will last for a couple of weeks in a perforated plastic bag in your fridge crisper. If you're storing many peppers in a bag, check them regularly and discard any with mould or decay.

You can freeze peppers raw, blanched or roasted. Raw peppers can be chopped or frozen whole. It's best to flash-freeze them first on a baking sheet then transfer to a freezer bag. When you want to use a frozen whole pepper, don't bother defrosting it: simply slice or chop it while it is frozen, and start cooking. A raw pepper loses its crisp

texture when frozen and is not suitable for salads or raw preparations, but works wonders in cooked foods.

Roasted peppers can be frozen as is, black skin and all, or peeled, de-seeded and sliced, then frozen. If you don't want whole peppers or pepper pieces to clump together when frozen, flash-freeze them first on a baking sheet before transfering them to a freezer bag.

You can dry fresh hot peppers in a food dehydrator, or simply string them together on a thick thread and hang in a dry place (in the sun, if possible). Once they're dry, store these peppers in an airtight container, away from light or heat.

Prep it right

Handle hot peppers very carefully. It's wise to wear a thin pair of latex gloves when slicing and chopping them. Almost 90 per cent of a hot pepper's heat is located in the white ribs and membranes – not in the seeds. But the seeds do contain more heat than the flesh. Many cooks remove the ribs and seeds to get more flavour and less blinding heat from a hot pepper.

When cutting hot peppers, be careful not to touch your face or rub your eyes! Once you're finished, wash your hands (if you weren't wearing gloves) and the cutting board and utensils, too.

Hot peppers, raw or cooked, are most often used as a seasoning, added in small amounts to a dish. However, they can be roasted whole or stuffed and served as the main attraction. Dozens (if not hundreds) of sauces are made with hot peppers, be they chutneys, salsas, pepper sauces, sambals or relishes.

*Don' t expect 2 hot peppers, even of the
same variety and size, to be equally hot.
Every pepper can be different. To check a
pepper's heat, cut a small piece and put
your tongue to the flesh – if you plan to
use the white ribs and seeds, give them
the tongue-test too.*

Culinary companions

Hot peppers can combine with sweet foods
such as fruit salsas or pepper jellies as well as
savoury foods. Cheese works particularly
well with hot peppers, as do beans, tomatoes, sweet peppers and corn. All herbs and
spices can be combined with hot peppers. In
fact, there are few foods that hot peppers
cannot combine with.

Tip

*When the going gets too hot, don' t turn to
water. A sip of milk or a spoonful of yogurt
will squelch the heat better than anything.*

Culinary destinations

The options are endless . . . just about any
food is enhanced with a hot pepper kick!
Turn to Mexican, Southwestern and Tex-
Mex cooking for hot peppers in tacos, guacamole, chili con carne, enchiladas, burritos
and quesadillas. Caribbean flavours include
Jamaican jerk chicken and pepper pot stew.
Thai food is generally loaded with hot peppers, whether in a curry, salad or stir-fry.
Szechuan and Hunan cuisines of China are
particularly fiery and Indian foods blaze a
trail of heat from the south to the north.
You'll find hot peppers have slipped their
way into cuisines all the way around the
world.

To your health

When it comes to vitamin C, hot peppers are
nutritional superstars, and red hot peppers
are an equally astounding source of vitamin
A. The problem is that most people eat only
tiny quantities of peppers. But just one raw,
green hot pepper (45 g) contains 109 mg of
vitamin C, which is almost two times the
Recommended Daily Intake (RDI). A raw,
red hot pepper (45 g) contains the same
amount of vitamin C, plus 483 RE (retinol
equivalent, the unit of measurement for
vitamin A) of vitamin A, which provides 50
per cent of the RDI and is 14 times more
vitamin A than that found in a raw, green
hot pepper.

Hot peppers, especially red hot peppers,
are chock full of antioxidants (vitamin C
and beta carotene), which may protect the
body against degenerative diseases such as
cancer and heart disease. They're also loaded
with cancer-fighting plant pigments called
flavonoids. Other important phytochemicals
found in hot peppers include phenolic acid
and plant sterols, which have been shown in
studies to inhibit the formation of cancerous
tumours. Research also reveals that hot peppers have cholesterol-lowering and anti-
clotting properties. Moreover, hot peppers
stimulate the circulation and are a source of
potassium, making them an all-round heart-
healthy food.

It's long been thought that hot peppers
were bad for the digestion, but now science
tells us that hot peppers are a digestive stim-
ulant, increasing gastric acid and perhaps
even burning extra calories while doing so.
Although hot peppers may irritate hemor-
rhoids in susceptible people, there's no
evidence that they cause ulcers or other
digestive disturbances. Plus, hot peppers are
good for the respiratory system: they can
relieve nasal congestion, clear clogged air-

ways and perhaps even prevent asthma and allergies. Hot peppers are good for you ... but take it from me, if you aren't careful during preparation, they can irritate your skin and eyes.

Tip

If you'd like to spice up a stew or soup with hot peppers, but aren't sure how much, try this. Take a whole serrano or jalapeño pepper, slit it and add it to the pot. When the dish tastes hot enough, remove the pepper.

Quick ways

Here's a spicy way to start your day: sauté 2 green onions and a chopped jalapeño pepper in some butter in a frying pan. Add 4 lightly beaten eggs (seasoned with salt and pepper) and a handful of grated cheddar or Monterey Jack cheese, and a sprinkling of chopped fresh coriander. Scramble the eggs until they set. Wrap inside warm flour tortillas and serve.

Trivia

Capsaicin is the compound responsible for all that heat in hot peppers. This devilish compound actually burns the nerve endings in the mouth and tongue, sending pain signals to the brain. The brain responds by dispatching natural pain killers called endorphins, which provide a pleasurable, morphine-like rush. So a mouthful of peppers isn't exactly all pain, no gain. Moreover, it may be the endorphins that "chili-heads" are addicted to rather than the heat-producing capsaicin!

Peppers – Sweet

Sweet peppers are dear to my heart (and my stomach). I can't seem to eat enough of them. They have everything a fine vegetable needs in life: good looks, convenience and taste. Once roasted, these sweet things are transformed into melting mouthfuls of veggie decadence. Don't let roasting intimidate you – If you can burn a vegetable, you can roast a pepper!

Looks like/Tastes like

Bell peppers are one of the fastest-growing crops in Ontario, and that doesn't mean they're speedy growers from seed to harvest. It means that consumers can't get enough of this vegetable and growers can't add enough acreage. Once upon a time there was only the **green bell** pepper (a.k.a. the **pizza** pepper). Now, lone green has been joined by a rainbow of colours: yellow, orange, red and, more exotically, white, purple, black and salmon. These bell-shaped peppers are 3 to 4 inches (8 to 10 cm) tall. All unripe peppers start off green and that's why green peppers taste bitter. The sweeter the taste, the more ripe a pepper is. However, a ripe pepper never lasts as long as an unripe, green one.

Italian Sheppard peppers (a.k.a. **bull's horn**) are tapered to a point, look like a bull's horn (with a little imagination) and are about 6 to 7 inches (15 to 17.5 cm) long and 2 inches (5 cm) wide. These are the best roasting peppers, for their flesh is thick and sturdy, perfect for the job.

Cubanelle peppers are usually sold when they're light green, but they ripen to orange then red. These mildly flavoured peppers are tapered and similar in size to Italian Sheppards but have no shoulders at the stem.

Sweet banana peppers (a.k.a. **Sweet Hungarian wax**) are about 7 inches (17.5 cm) long tapering to a point, with square shoulders at the stem. These transparent, yellow peppers can be very sweet and are perfect on pizzas and salads.

The **pimento pepper** looks like a little, red pumpkin about 3 inches (8 cm) tall and 6 inches (15 cm) wide. Its thick walls and squat shape make it perfect for stuffing.

Select it

Look for peppers with smooth, taut, unblemished skin with deep colour. Avoid any wrinkled peppers or those with soft spots, bruises or cuts. Check the stem end, where soft spots or mould may be lurking. Peppers should feel heavy for their size.

Store it right

Store peppers in a perforated plastic bag in your crisper. Green peppers will last longer than red.

Prep it right

Simply wash the pepper, slice in half, remove the seeds and start chopping. Since the skin is slightly bitter, some people (not me) like to peel a pepper, which can be done with a sharp vegetable peeler.

There are several ways to roast a pepper. The easiest and fastest way is to roast peppers whole, on the grill. Turn them every few minutes until all sides are blackened and blistered. Or roast peppers in the oven. Preheat the oven to high and broil peppers on a baking sheet as close to the element as possible. Turn whole peppers until the skin is blackened and blistered on all sides. Either way, you can save time by cutting the peppers in half so that only one surface faces the element.

If you need to roast only one pepper, this method is handy, if you have a gas stove: turn the gas burner on high and place the pepper directly on the flame. Use tongs to turn the pepper until it is black all over. Leave roasted peppers to cool in a closed paper bag or a big bowl with a plate on top to cover. After 10 minutes the accumulated steam will make them easier to peel.

Roasted peppers keep in the fridge for a few days in a covered container. They can also be frozen. Put them directly into freezer bags and freeze. Or, if you want to be able to use only a portion of the peppers stored in a freezer bag, flash-freeze on a baking sheet in the freezer until they are solid, and then transfer them to a freezer bag.

Tip
Take advantage of peppers when they're in season. Invest in a bushel when you have time to linger by the barbecue and roast the entire bunch. Let your blackened peppers cool, then transfer them directly – 3 to a bag – into small freezer bags. Defrost, peel and serve all winter long!

Culinary destinations
Sweet peppers and pasta go hand in hand – add them to a plain tomato sauce, or sauté with chicken and sun-dried tomatoes. A whole, raw pepper makes a delicious edible salad bowl for rice, bean or tuna salads. Sweet peppers star in kebabs, Hungarian goulash and Italian antipastos.

Try sliced peppers stir-fried with black bean sauce and chicken, or steam green pepper chunks with a savoury Chinese shrimp stuffing. The cuisines of the Mediterranean have numerous renditions of baked, stuffed peppers filled with ground meat and rice. Nothing beats a grilled vegetable sandwich with roasted red peppers, goat cheese, arugula and crusty French bread.

To your health
Sweet peppers (along with kiwis and rose hips) are on the top of the list when it comes to vitamin C content. Ounce for ounce, you get 3 times as much vitamin C from a sweet red pepper as you do from an orange! One medium, sweet red pepper contains more than 3 times the Recommended Daily Intake (RDI) of vitamin C. Green peppers contain less vitamin C than red, but are still a terrific source of vitamin C. One medium green pepper contains 106 mg of vitamin C, which is one and a half times the RDI. Sweet red peppers are an excellent source of vitamin A. One medium sweet red pepper contains 67 per cent of the RDI, almost 10 times more vitamin A than a medium sweet green pepper. Sweet peppers, both green and red, are a source of dietary fibre, folate and potassium, too.

Due to their high vitamin C and A content, sweet peppers are rich in antioxidants. Studies show that diets high in antioxidants can protect against heart disease, stroke, cataracts and some cancers. Sweet peppers

contain many cancer-fighting phytochemicals, too, such as flavonoids, phenolic acids
and plant sterols.

Quick ways

For an easy appetizer, thinly slice 3 sweet
peppers of different colours. (Include a fresh
hot pepper too, if you like it hot.) Sauté
in olive oil until very soft – about 15 to 20
minutes – then add a tablespoon (15 mL)
of sugar, salt to taste and ¼ cup (50 mL)
of white wine. Sauté until the liquid is
absorbed. Cool to room temperature and
serve on crackers or crostini.

Plantain

This kissing cousin of the banana is worth get-ting to know. But be sure to cook it! Plantains, unlike their sweet yellow relatives, cannot be eaten raw.

Other names
Plantains are sometimes called Adam's fig, *plantanos*, jumbo, or cooking or vegetable bananas.

Looks like/Tastes like
Plantains look like large bananas, but are thicker skinned and flatter with three de-fined ridges. They are firmer than regular bananas and remain firm, even when ripe. Depending on their ripeness, plantains are green, yellow or black. Some varieties ripen from pink to red.

An unripe, green plantain tastes like a potato or squash. It is more starchy than sweet. A ripe black plantain has a sweeter, more banana-like flavour, but it is still pre-dominantly starchy in texture.

Select it
Choose a firm plantain with stem end and skin intact, without any cracks. It's okay if it appears bruised. Buy it green, yellow or almost black, depending on how you plan to use it and when. A black plantain must be used as soon as possible. If you can't find plantains in your supermarket, look in Asian, Latin American or Caribbean fresh produce stores.

Store it right
Store plantains at room temperature until ripe. A green plantain can take up to a week to ripen. To speed up the process, put it in a brown paper bag with a banana or apple. Once ripe (and really black), a plantain can be stored in the refrigerator for about 3 days, with no damage to its texture. But don't store unripe plantains in the fridge, because the cold ruins their texture and interferes with the ripening process. Ripe plantains can be frozen in their skins in a freezer bag for up to 6 months.

Prep it right
Plantains, especially green ones, can be diffi-cult to peel. Slice off the ends, cut the fruit into 3-inch (8-cm) sections and make a lengthwise slit in each section. Pry off the skin with your thumbnail or a blunt knife slipped under the skin. Soaking cut green plantain in ice water makes peeling easier, but you risk losing water-soluble nutrients that way. A harmless, milky liquid some-times seeps from the skin of a plantain. You can rinse plantains under water but be sure to pat them really dry. Discard all the strings that run the length of a plantain just under the skin.

Plantains require cooking. The easiest way is to bake them. Slit them lengthwise, dab with butter, sprinkle lightly with brown sugar and bake in a 375°F (190°C) oven for about 40 minutes or until tender. Always slit or puncture plantains with a fork before baking to prevent bursting. Plantains can also be steamed or boiled.

Culinary destinations

Plantains marry well with onions, shallots, ginger, garlic and hot peppers. Consider such fresh herbs as parsley, coriander and thyme. Brown sugar and spices such as cinnamon, cloves, allspice and nutmeg all work wonders.

Unripe plantains can be sliced thinly, deep-fried like potato chips and served with salsa. Or try brushing slices lightly with oil and cooking on the barbecue or grill. Dust with a little sugar and cinnamon before serving. Ripe plantains make a nice, sweet French fry (not unlike a sweet potato). Reduce fat by baking plantain sticks, tossed in a little oil and seasonings, in a 375°F (190°C) oven. Plantains are perfect in a curry and work well beside a roast. Try mashing with apples or squash. Parboiled slices of plantain are nice in a vegetable sauté with onions, ginger, tomatoes, peppers and thyme.

To your health

Bananas are often dubbed the "perfect food" but plantains may be even more perfect. Plantains contain 10 times more beta carotene than bananas with a 1-cup (154-g) serving of cooked plantain supplying 14 per cent of the Recommended Daily Intake (RDI) of vitamin A. Moreover, ounce for ounce, plantains contain more potassium, vitamin C and folate than bananas. Plantains are high in magnesium and vitamin B^6, and are a source of iron, too.

Plantains have long been regarded in the Caribbean as the ultimate remedy for tummy aches. In 1984, researchers in England gave the scientific nod to this age-old folk remedy. Their research verified that plantains can reduce the severity of ulcers and even heal them if used curatively. There's only one catch. Only green, unripe plantains do the trick.

Tip

When a recipe calls for ripe plantains, you can substitute unripe regular bananas.

Potatoes

Canadians eat more potatoes than any other vegetable. In fact, your average person eats a whopping 145 pounds (65.7 kg) of potatoes a year! Surprisingly, many people get a good portion of their vitamin C intake from this versatile tuber, which is dubbed the "Houdini of Vegetables."

Looks like/Tastes like

Knowing the different varietal names for potatoes isn't half as important as linking their shape with their culinary usefulness. In other words, long-shaped potatoes are perfect for baking, mashing, deep-frying and microwave cooking. There are two types of long potatoes, the **Russet** (a.k.a. **baking potato**), which has rough, brown skin, and the **Long White,** which has a light tan, thin skin. Both have a dry, mealy and fluffy texture. Round potatoes, on the other hand, are moist and not as starchy. Because they hold their shape in water, they're the right choice for boiling, microwave cooking and salads. But they don't make good bakers or mashers. Round potatoes come in **red** or **white**. Look out for a new variety, developed in Canada, called **Red Gold**. It's round with red skin, gold flesh, and is moist and waxy. Another Canadian invention is the **Yukon Gold**, an all-purpose potato (you can do anything with it) that has yellowish flesh and skin, with a medium-dry, firm texture that is deceivingly buttery. **New** potatoes are small, young potatoes that are newly harvested. They have very thin, flavourful skins and are ideal for boiling or steaming. Two exotic types of potatoes are purple potatoes (**Peruvian Purple, Purple Viking**, and so on) and fingerlings (**Banana, Apple, Rose Finn**, and so on). Purple potatoes are purple to almost black on the outside, and a deep blue-purple on the inside. Like Yukon Golds, they're all-purpose. **Fingerlings** have a sweet, crunchy flavour and a crisper texture than most potatoes. You can use them for anything, but they are best when cooked whole and not mashed.

Select it

Look for firm, dry potatoes that are free of blemishes, cuts, cracks or sprouted eyes. If you see a green tinge or cast on any potatoes, avoid them.

Try to buy potatoes of the same size, to ensure uniform cooking. The best buys are usually 5- to 10-pound (2- to 4-kg) bags of potatoes sold in big heavy paper bags, best for storage. However, you have to buy those potatoes sight unseen. Don't hesitate to ask the produce manager how fresh they are.

Store it right

Remember this motto: Not all taters like the fridge. Keep regular potatoes out of the fridge and new potatoes in the fridge. Temperature makes a big difference. The ideal temperature for regular potatoes is between

45°F and 50°F (7°C and 10°C); if they get too cold, potatoes get dark spots and develop an unappealing sweet taste. If they get too hot, they start to sprout, shrivel and lose nutrients. New potatoes, on the other hand, need cold temperatures to stop their starches from converting into sugars. And they're perishable. Store them in the fridge in a plastic bag and don't expect them to last more than a week. Regular potatoes can be stored for half a year, under the right conditions. But few people have those conditions, because the room temperature in most homes is just a little too hot for regular potatoes. So look for a cool spot (perhaps beside an outside wall, or on the porch or in the cellar) that is well ventilated and dry. Don't store potatoes under your sink, for they heat up every time you run the hot water. And keep your potatoes in darkness. Burlap or heavy paper bags keep out light. Transfer potatoes sold in plastic into paper bags. Think twice before you store onions with potatoes – they give off a gas that accelerates potato decay. But here's a friend: just a single apple tucked in between those potatoes can help stop sprouting.

Prep it right

Potatoes should be scrubbed well before cooking. If you see any greenish tinge on a potato, play it safe and throw it out – it could make you sick. Many people like to peel their potatoes, but the skin is full of fibre and potassium. Besides, the skin helps a potato keep its shape during cooking. If you must, peel the potato very lightly. Cut or peeled potatoes discolour when exposed to the air. Cook them immediately or reserve in water.

You can boil, steam, microwave, roast, bake and sauté potatoes. When cutting potatoes, keep the shapes uniform for even cooking. Cook potatoes in a minimum of water to prevent excess nutrient loss (many of a tater's vitamins are water-soluble). Boiling takes from 20 to 30 minutes and steaming takes from 30 to 40 minutes. Check for doneness with a fork. When baking whole potatoes in the oven or microwave, always prick with a fork first. And don't wrap those taters in aluminum foil (for baking or barbecuing) unless you want a steamed potato. Baking can be done in as few as 45 minutes in a 425°F (220°C) oven but you can extend that time by using a lower temperature oven, especially if you are cooking other foods in the oven at the same time. For best roasting results, boil or steam whole potatoes or chunks for 10 minutes first, then roast.

Tips

To lessen baking time by as much as half, place a metal skewer or oven nail through potatoes before cooking.

A food processor is death to mashed potatoes. Use an old-fashioned masher utensil to break up the potatoes and mix in the liquid ingredients with an electric mixer to fluff them up. It's best to use a ricer with Yukon Gold or red-skinned potatoes, which can become gummy and tacky if overworked with a masher.

Culinary destinations

Try baking a whole fish on a bed of thinly sliced potatoes and herbs. Or liven up a vichyssoise with carrots or fennel. Grate some raw potatoes and onions in the food processor, sauté like a huge pancake in a large frying pan with salt and nutmeg to make Swiss rosti potatoes. Add some store-bought tomato salsa, pesto or Greek tzatziki to your next batch of potato salad. Try goat cheese and olives in mashed potatoes made with extra virgin olive oil and roasted garlic. Make some potato biscuits with pancetta, Parmigiano-Reggiano and oregano, or buy a pizza crust and top it with thinly sliced potatoes mixed with olive oil, garlic, fresh rosemary and kosher salt.

Tips

Need a soup thickener? Use leftover mashed potatoes.

Thou shalt never throw out potato cooking water. Freeze it if you must. It's a perfect addition to stocks – especially vegetarian – and is excellent for bread-making, since yeast thrives in it.

To your health

Potatoes are an excellent source of potassium and fibre, especially if you eat the skin. A baked potato with skin contains 4 times more iron than a potato without skin. Likewise, a baked potato with skin has 4.8 g of fibre, while a baked potato without skin has only 2.3 g. There are 220 calories in a 7 ounce (200 g) baked potato. Potatoes are high in vitamin C. A baked potato with skin contains 26 mg of vitamin C, which is 43 per cent of the Recommended Daily Intake (RDI). Potatoes are also high in iron (if you eat the skin), thiamin, niacin and vitamin B^6, and are a source of folate.

As a primary food staple, potatoes are an important source of vitamin C. Soaked in vinegar, potato slices were once used as a scurvy remedy. Nowadays, the antioxidant powers of vitamin C help prevent free radicals from wreaking havoc on your health. A good source of fibre, potatoes can help keep you regular and prevent constipation. Due to their high quantities of potassium, potatoes may help prevent high blood pressure and stroke. Potato skins are rich in chlorogenic acid, a polyphenol, which has anti-cancer abilities. On the negative side, potatoes can contain high concentrations of a toxic alkaloid called solanine, signalled by a greenish tinge on a potato's skin. The tinge is actually chlorophyll and appears when potatoes are exposed to light or extreme temperatures. To be safe, do not eat potatoes with a greenish tinge – eating potatoes damaged in this way, especially in large quantities, can cause cramps, diarrhea and fatigue.

Radicchio

Think twice before you ignore those little crimson parcels full of taste called radicchio in the produce section. It may take you a while to warm up to this slightly bitter veggie, but once you do, you'll revel in salads made more beautiful by it – not to mention grilled vegetables, risottos, pastas . . .

Looks like/Tastes like

Radicchio resembles a small head of red cabbage, except the leaves have a lettuce-like texture. Usually the leaves are ruby-coloured and ivory-veined, they can range from purple to red, and there is a green variety. Radicchio is a member of the chicory family and tastes like it. It has a slightly bitter, peppery taste with a slight crunch. Radicchio tastes not unlike its cousin, Belgian endive, without the crunch.

Verona is the type of radicchio most commonly sold and cultivated in North America. Another lesser-known variety called Treviso is gaining popularity. Radicchio di Treviso originates from Northern Italy but will likely spread to North American specialty gardens quickly. Elongated and narrow, Treviso is shaped more like a Belgian endive than a round Verona radicchio.

Select it

Look for a firm, unblemished white core at the base of the radicchio head, free of holes and cracks. Radicchio can come in a tight or loose head – it doesn't matter, but make sure the leaves are plump, not dried out, with no signs of browning. Radicchio starts to brown from the outside in. If you see really small radicchio specimens, chances are they have been heavily trimmed to remove browned leaves. Very small heads of radicchio are likely less than fresh and should be avoided.

Store it right

Radicchio does not like to get wet. Wrap it in a paper towel and store in a perforated plastic or paper bag in the crisper. Stored properly, it lasts longer than most salad greens.

Prep it right

For salads, remove core at the base of the radicchio head with a sharp knife. Either break off leaves as needed or shred with a knife. Keep the core attached if you're grilling or braising radicchio – it stays intact, even when cut into wedges.

The easiest thing to do with radicchio is to tear, shred or slice it up into a salad. Its cup-shaped leaves can be used to serve up composed salads such as a rice salad or crab meat salad. But don't stop there. Radicchio is also wonderful stir-fried, grilled, braised or roasted. It also works well in a risotto or pasta sauce. Radicchio tastes best when well cooked and very tender, at which point its texture becomes almost creamy and the outer leaves become well browned, caramelized and piquant.

Culinary companions

In the greenery department, radicchio accents such sweet greens as Boston, bibb or looseleaf, while it pairs well with stronger-tasting greens such as Belgian endive or arugula. It can stand up to strong cheeses such as a robust Roquefort or a tangy goat cheese. Pancetta, bacon, ham or prosciutto combine nicely with radicchio, as do standard salad-dressing items such as olive oil, balsamic vinegar, red wine vinegar and Dijon mustard. Try it with lemon juice or zest, raisins and pine nuts.

Culinary destinations

Try it braised in a combination of chicken stock, red wine and raisins. Once it is thoroughly cooked (15 to 20 minutes), garnish with toasted pine nuts and freshly grated Parmigiano-Reggiano cheese. Radicchio turns into magic on a low-heat grill: just baste it with olive oil first and don't worry if the outside leaves turn very brown. Try shredding radicchio, sautéing it with garlic and hot pepper flakes, and tossing with pasta and freshly grated Parmigiano-Reggiano cheese.

To your health

One cup (40 g) of raw radicchio contains very few calories – only 9. It is a source of vitamins C and E, and folate.

Radicchio, along with other bitter greens, has long been considered a blood tonic by Europeans. Bitter-tasting foods stimulate the secretion of digestive juices. More recently, scientists have discovered anthocyanins in radicchio. These deep-coloured pigments belong to a broader group of phytochemical compounds called flavonoids. Anthocyanins have been shown in studies to have numerous health benefits, such as controlling cancer, heart disease and diabetes, improving circulation, reducing eye strain and even combatting the loss of memory and motor skills associated with aging.

Quick ways

Make a warm, Italian-style salad by tossing torn leaves of radicchio, Belgian endive and arugula. Sauté a few ounces of diced pancetta or bacon in extra virgin olive oil (and hot peppers, if you want), and then add a splash of red wine vinegar. Pour the hot dressing on the salad greens and serve immediately.

Radishes

I love to dip vegetables and nothing beats a radish. Not only do these firehouse-red orbs offer a pleasant peppery bite, but they're juicy and crisp, too.

Looks like/Tastes like

Red globes is the most common radish found in North America. These little red balls are sometimes called **button-red** radishes. They're 1 to 4 inches (2.5 to 10 cm) in diameter, have a solid, crisp flesh, are round or oval, and come in a variety of colours – red, white, purple or red-and-white.

French breakfast are elongated radishes that sport red shoulders and a white tip. They're a little milder than red globes and just as crisp.

White icicles average 6 inches (15 cm) in length. These tapered radishes are milder than red globes. Larger than white icicles, **California mammoth white** are oblong radishes averaging 8 inches (20 cm) in length. Their flesh is slightly pungent. Looking more like turnips than radishes, **Black Spanish** radishes have black skin that camouflages a shockingly white – and pungent – flesh. The texture is drier than other radishes. When cooked, Spanish black are milder, not unlike turnips. Whimsical **Easter egg** radishes come in a variety of pastel shades.

Native to Asia, **daikon** radishes are carrot-shaped and come in white, or green and white. (They're called *lo bok* in Chinese – daikon is the Japanese name.) Some of these radishes grow up to 18 inches (45 cm) long and weigh a mighty 3 pounds (1.25 kg). While the flesh is juicier and hotter than red globes, daikons are not as pungent as Black Spanish.

Chinese Misato Rose are round, Asian radishes, about 4 inches (10 cm) in diameter. Cream and green coloured on the outside, they have a beautiful rosy-pink interior.

Select it

The freshest radishes are sold with greens attached. Look for perky green leaves, firm, brightly coloured roots and a smooth, unblemished surface. Less fresh are those packaged in plastic – always inspect these carefully for mould. When choosing red globes, go for the smallest, as big ones may be pithy. Black Spanish should be heavy in the hand and free of cracks. A good daikon is evenly shaped, firm and glossy, with an almost translucent sheen.

Store it right

Ironically, you get longer refrigerator life from pre-bagged radishes than their fresher, greens-attached counterparts. For the latter, remove the tops before storing, for they draw nutrients and moisture from the roots. Keep radishes in a perforated plastic bag in the crisper. Red globes and daikons last for a week or 2, but Black Spanish last for months if they stay dry (wrapped in paper towel in a paper bag) in your fridge.

Prep it right

All a radish needs is trimmed stem and tip ends, plus a good scrubbing with a vegetable brush. Peeling is a matter of taste. Like beets, fresh radishes with their tops are two vegetables in one. You can eat radish greens raw or cooked. If they are fresh and perky, throw them in a salad as a substitute for arugula. You can also steam or sauté radish greens.

Culinary companions

Radishes work well with green onions, chives, mint, dill and thyme. Try them with sweet butter, sour cream, yogurt or mayonnaise. Increase their peppery bite with additions such as mustard, wasabi, horseradish or hot peppers. Asian or regular radishes combine well with soy sauce, Chinese vinegar, sesame oil, ginger, garlic and sesame seeds.

Culinary destinations

A simple snack of sliced raw radishes on a piece of homemade bread with fresh sweet butter is a culinary moment of bliss to any radish lover. Radishes also find their way on to Oktoberfest menus. In Italy and France, they dip radishes into extra virgin olive oil, sometimes with the addition of anchovies. Truly versatile, radishes can be dipped or dipped into. Mixed with sour cream, mayonnaise or yogurt with the addition of chives or green onions, they make for a dip with a bite. Toss some sliced radishes in your next linguine and pesto sauce, or marinate them with mushrooms and serve on couscous.

To your health

Radishes are low in calories with just 23 calories in 1 cup (116 g) of sliced raw radishes. Radishes are high in vitamin C and are a source of folate and potassium. Despite all that crunch, radishes are relatively low in dietary fibre.

Like all other cruciferous vegetables, radishes contain sulphurous compounds that have anti-cancer properties. A word of caution: If you are sensitive to aspirin, you may want to avoid radishes, for they contain salicyclates, which are compounds similar to the active ingredient in aspirin.

Quick ways

1. Thinly slice a bunch of radishes and chop 2 green onions. Heat some olive oil in a sauté pan, add radishes and green onions, and sauté until just tender. Season with salt to taste. Garnish with chives and serve.

2. Chop 9 radishes in a food processor. Add a minced garlic clove, ½ cup (125 mL) of mayonnaise, ½ cup (125 mL) of yogurt, the juice of half a lemon and 2 tablespoons (30 mL) of chopped chives and process. Season with salt and pepper. Makes 1 cup (250 mL) of vegetable dip.

Tip

Got some less-than-perky radishes in the fridge? Soak them in ice water for an hour or 2 and they will come back to life.

Rapini

Now here's a veggie that folks seem to have strong feelings about – they love it or hate it! The reason is simple: rapini is pungent and bitter. It may look like broccoli – even be related to broccoli – but that's where all similarities end.

Other names
No other green has more aliases. When it's not called rapini, it is called broccoli rape, broccoli rabe, or *broccoletti di rape, broccoli de rabe, brocoletto, rapa* and *raab*.

Looks like/Tastes like
Rapini looks like broccoli except with very slender stalks, more leaves and small clusters of tiny green buds, instead of one large head. It's medium to dark green in colour and sometimes you'll find it with sprouted buds, displaying pretty little yellow flowers.

Select it
Look for firm, crisp rapini with a strong green colour. Avoid bunches that are too tightly packed (with mushy interior leaves) or have yellowed leaves and stems. Rapini is best when all the flower buds are closed tight. The odd flower is okay, but not a bouquet!

Store it right
Before storing, remove any rubber bands or twist ties holding the bunch together. Store in the refrigerator, unwashed, in a perforated vegetable bag. For best results, use it within a day or 2 of purchase.

Prep it right
The entire plant is edible: stems, leaves and buds. The leaves tend to taste stronger than the rest of the plant. Thick stalks (more than ¼ inch/6 mm in diameter) benefit from peeling to remove the tough outer skin. You may want to slice the stalks lengthwise or cut them thinly on the diagonal to speed up cooking times. Or cook the stems first, and then add the leaves and buds.

Rapini is versatile: it can be sautéed, braised, steamed, boiled, stir-fried or cooked in the microwave. Quick cooking is the rule. All it needs is 2 to 6 minutes of cooking, depending on your taste. But beware – rapini can turn from a crisp, emerald green to a soggy, army green in a flash. Watch it carefully.

Culinary companions
Citrus, white wine vinegar, balsamic vinegar, garlic, hot peppers, anchovies, olive oil, butter, Parmigiano-Reggiano, scallions, shallots, onions and Italian sausage all work in harmony with rapini.

Culinary destinations
Try rapini in omelettes, quiches and frittatas. Toss it with pasta, olive oil, roasted garlic and slices of Italian sausage. Serve it *au gratin* or splash it with fresh lemon juice just

before serving. The pungent, earthy flavour of rapini marries well with eggs, pasta, risotto, polenta, potatoes and bean purée.

To your health
Rapini is an excellent source of vitamins A and C, and high in calcium, iron, potassium and magnesium. It is low in calories (and sodium, for that matter) and a source of fibre.

Another Cruciferous Club member, rapini belongs to the cabbage family and contains powerful phytochemicals such as indoles and sulforaphanes, which may protect heart, lung and intestinal health.

Tips
Keep the lid off when cooking rapini to prevent it from darkening. Although rapini pairs well with acidic ingredients such as balsamic vinegar or lemon juice, wait until the last minute to add these sour touches. Rapini turns a dull, olive-drab green if cooked or marinated in acids.

What do rapini and canola oil have in common? Canola oil is made from rapeseed, a close relative of rapini.

Rutabaga

When I was growing up, we ate lots of rutabaga, but we always called it turnip! In fact,
most Canadians don't know the difference
between these two separate vegetables. But
it's time we did. Canada is a major grower of
this fat root that loves cold climes. In fact,
rutabaga is dubbed "Canadian turnip" in other
parts of the world.

Other names
Rutabaga has quite a few aliases, including
yellow turnip, swede and neeps (the Scottish
nickname). The word "rutabaga" is derived
from the Swedish *rot bagga,* which roughly
means baggy root.

Looks like/Tastes like
Rutabagas look and taste like giant turnips,
but the flesh is yellow, compared to turnip's
white or opaque interior. The flavour is
sweeter and more assertive than turnips.
Rutabagas are tan or yellow, with a dark purple or reddish band at the top of their lumpy,
irregular, roundish shape. They range in size
from a ½ pound to 2 ½ pounds (250 g to 1 kg)
and are coated with a layer of wax.

Select it
Choose rutabagas that are firm and solid,
and never choose a soggy one. Pick ones that
are heavy for their size, which indicates a
moist rather than dry interior. Avoid wrinkles (indicating an old and woody vegetable), scars and bruises. Pass on any

rutabaga with mould on the waxed surface –
it should be shiny.

Store it right
Rutabagas store best in a cold, dry, dark
place rather than the refrigerator. Under the
right conditions, it will last up to 2 months.
If you don't have a cold place to store it, then
refrigerate it, unwrapped (unless it's cut) in a
warm part of the fridge away from walls and
the bottom shelf. Wrap cut rutabaga in plastic and refrigerate.

Prep it right
Most rutabagas are sold with a thick layer of
clear wax to prevent moisture loss and
lengthen storage times. Peel off the skin and
wax with a sharp paring knife. Rutabagas
can be difficult and awkward to peel. Just 1
or 2 minutes in the microwave oven at high
can help facilitate easier peeling. Cube, slice
or julienne.

   Rutabagas can be eaten raw or cooked.
The smaller the rutabaga the better when
eating it raw in salads or as vegetable sticks.
Rutabaga flesh is denser than turnips, and
takes longer to cook. Try it steamed, boiled,
roasted, baked, sautéed, stir-fried or mashed.
For best results when mashing, use a food
mill or ricer. A whole rutabaga (pricked
many times) can be cooked in a microwave
oven, simply wrapped in paper towel, for
14 to 17 minutes at high. You can substitute
rutabaga for any recipe calling for turnips.

Use leftover turnip purée or mash in your baking recipes. Substitute it for any recipe calling for pumpkin purée to make quick breads, muffins or cookies.

Many supermarkets now carry "convenience rutabaga" that has been peeled, sliced into sticks and prepackaged.

Culinary companions

Turnips and rutabagas pair with the same flavours. Salad partners include lemon juice, mayonnaise and vinegar, plus a range of fresh herbs such as parsley, chives, oregano, marjoram and thyme. Bacon, ham, prosciutto and pancetta all bring out the best in turnips, as do roasted meats and their juices. Walnuts and hazelnuts (plus their oils) combine well with turnips. Sharp flavours include horseradish and mustard. Chinese seasonings like soy sauce, ginger and sesame oil are complementary, as are Moroccan spices like saffron, fresh and ground coriander, cumin, cinnamon and nutmeg.

Culinary destinations

Grate equal amounts of rutabaga and carrots, and dress Asian-style with soy sauce, Chinese vinegar, ginger, honey, sesame oil and sesame seeds. Toss cooked cubes of rutabaga with yogurt or low-fat sour cream, and garnish with green onions. Coat slices or sticks of rutabaga in olive oil, season with herbs, salt and pepper, and roast in the oven. Turn to Moroccan recipes for novel ways to prepare rutabaga in stews served on couscous. Try rutabaga in a vegetable soup with leeks, garlic, carrots, turnip, tomatoes and rice.

To your health

Rutabagas contain more nutrients and calories than their cousin, the turnip. A 1-cup (240-g) serving of cooked rutabaga contains 93 calories. Rutabagas are an excellent source of vitamin C, with that single serving supplying 45 mg or 75 per cent of your daily needs. It is also high in folate and potassium, and a source of dietary fibre, calcium, iron, niacin and vitamin A. Although turnip roots contain no vitamin A, a 1-cup (250-g) serving of rutabaga supplies 13 per cent of the Recommended Daily Intake (RDI).

Rutabagas not only contain many nutrients, but are also members of the Cruciferous Club (cabbage family), which contain many powerful phytochemicals. Of note, rutabagas (especially raw) contain an exceptionally high rate of cancer-fighting glucosinolates, even in comparison with other cabbage cousins. Rutabagas are a source of folate, potassium and iron. The anemia-fighting iron is easily absorbed from rutabaga, due to the prevalence of the accompanying vitamin C. Meanwhile, both folate and potassium are associated with a reduced risk in heart disease.

Trivia

Turnips have been around since Roman times. The rutabaga, on the other hand, is a relative newcomer, surfacing in the 17th century. It's believed to be a hybrid of the turnip and kohlrabi. Rutabagas grow best in cold countries. Voilà! Canada is a major grower.

Salsify

Salsify was once in vogue during Victorian times but, like many root vegetables, it has experienced a real slump in popularity polls since the Second World War. Now some innovative farmers are bringing this root back to the market. Search, and ye shall find salsify!

Other names

The most popular alias for salsify is oyster plant. Other names include vegetable oyster, white salsify and oatroot.

Looks like/Tastes like

Salsify looks like a parsnip, with a thin, pale-tan skin and off-white flesh. It is covered with tiny rootlets and is from 6 to 12 inches (15 to 30 cm) long. Some salsifies are sold with their grass-like greens (called chards) attached. While salsify has been dubbed **oyster plant**, most people can't detect any oyster-like flavouring. It tastes more like a nutty artichoke. If it's eaten shortly after harvest, it is sweeter than stored salsify.

    Black salsify is not a variety of salsify, but another species that belongs to the same family. The proper name is **scorzonera**, but it's also called **viper grass**. Salsify and scorzonera are considered interchangeable by most cooks. The taste and texture are almost identical; however, scorzonera is sometimes described as having a faint, coconut taste. Scorzonera is a slightly longer root than salsify, with a black or dark brown skin and no rootlets. Plus, it's easier to peel than its cousin.

Select it

Look for salsify no longer than 8 inches (20 cm) long with a 1-inch (2.5-cm) wide diameter (scorzonera is longer). It should be firm – not as hard as a carrot, but nonetheless firm. Large, overly mature salsify taste tough and woody.

Store it right

If the salsify's greens are attached, be sure to cut them off before storing or they will rob the roots of nutrients and moisture. Store the roots as you would carrots, in a perforated plastic bag in the crisper. Salsify does not freeze well, raw or cooked.

Prep it right

Salsify discolours the moment you peel it and leaves a temporary, rust-brown stain on your hands. When peeling and slicing it, have a bowl of acidulated water (3 tablespoons/45 mL lemon juice or vinegar to 4 cups/1 L water) ready to receive the pieces. Alternatively, cook salsify with the skin on and peel after it is cool. Salsify breaks easily once cooked, so handle gently and don't overcook – it turns from succulent to mushy in an instant.

    You can eat salsify raw or cooked. Grate it raw and use in slaws. Or cook it first, let cool and serve cold in a vinaigrette or other sauce. Steaming keeps salsify intact better than boiling. Add it to stews and braises during the last 45 minutes of cooking. Simmer in stock, and then purée. Or braise with meats.

Culinary companions

Salsify merits a sauce, whether it is the Greek lemon sauce *avgolemono*, béchamel, vinaigrette or a cheese sauce. Complementary fresh herbs include chervil, parsley, basil, tarragon and thyme. Spices that work are nutmeg, black pepper, cinnamon and cayenne. Gruyère and Parmigiano-Reggiano are particularly well suited to salsify, as are nut oils such as walnut or hazelnut oil.

Culinary destinations

Salsify can be simply glazed like carrots with brown sugar, honey or maple syrup, or tossed in oil and roasted on their own or with an accompaniment of root vegetables. Thanks to its oyster connection, it works well in fish chowder, sautéed with scallops and cream or alongside a bread crumb stuffing for baked oysters. Try salsify in fritters, or braised in tomato sauce Provençal-style with garlic, basil and anchovies. Grated raw salsify shines in a creamy, mustardy vinaigrette and tastes heavenly in a creamed vegetable soup.

To your health

There are 91 calories in a 1-cup (135-g) serving of sliced, cooked salsify. It is high in vitamin B^6 and a source of dietary fibre, calcium, iron, magnesium, potassium, riboflavin and folate.

Like Jerusalem artichokes, salsify contains inulin, a type of carbohydrate that breaks down to fructose, a diabetic-friendly sugar. However, not everyone can digest inulin efficiently and it can cause flatulence in some people. Start off with salsify slowly to see how your body tolerates it. Once your body is used to it, the digestive disturbances are likely to wane and you can eat larger quantities of it.

Some women find that pre-menstrual symptoms are relieved when foods high in vitamin B^6 (like salsify) are consumed.

Salsify can cause a skin rash in some people. Wear gloves when peeling and slicing to prevent this.

Spinach

I always liked Popeye when I was a kid. Not only did that sailor man have nifty muscles, but he also liked the same veggie as I did! Spinach is quick and easy, available all year round, bursting with nutrients and absolutely delicious.

Looks like/Tastes like

There are four main types of spinach: savoy, semi-savoy, flat-leaf and baby. **Savoy** spinach has crinkly, dark-green curly leaves. It's often sold in pre-washed, 10-ounce (284-g) bags. **Flat-leaf** or **smooth-leaf** spinach has unwrinkled, spade-shaped leaves that are easier to clean than the curly types. **Semi-savoy** is a 50/50 mix of savoy and flat-leaf. **Baby** spinach leaves are of the flat-leaf variety and are usually no more than 3 inches (7.5 cm) long. These tender, sweet leaves are more expensive than their mature counterparts. Sold loose, not in bunches, baby spinach is most often tossed in salads, but can be cooked, albeit lightly.

Select it

Look for crisp, perky leaves with a vivid green colour and sweet smell. Avoid spinach that has yellowed, wilted or become soggy. Thick-stalked spinach (more than an ⅛ inch/3 mm in diameter) indicates overgrown spinach and is likely to disappoint in flavour. Wise spinach consumers choose spinach sold in bunches, rather than bags, which tend to camouflage the "real goods."

Store it right

If your spinach is bundled tightly, loosen it up. Tight rubber bands or twist ties can choke spinach, hastening spoilage. Store it unwashed and loosely wrapped in paper towel in a perforated plastic bag in your crisper.

Prep it right

Spinach usually needs a lot of washing. In fact, it may take you longer to wash it than cook it. Bunch spinach, especially savoy, requires thorough washing. Fill the sink with cold water, swish the leaves around, drain and repeat the process (sometimes several times) until no sand is left in the bottom of the sink. Packaged spinach is usually pre-washed but can benefit from a thorough rinse before you use it. Spinach stalks are edible, but most people prefer to trim them off, especially if they're making salads. Consider saving the stalks for soup or stocks. Flat-leaf spinach stalks are usually very narrow and tasty.

Spinach shrinks! Like all leafy greens, spinach has a high water content. One pound (500 g) of fresh spinach will reduce to about 1 cup (180 g) cooked. If you plan to use spinach in a cooked casserole, it's best to cook it down first, squeeze out excess water, and then use it. For a simple side dish, spinach can be sautéed in a little olive oil or butter. Pile as much spinach into the pan as you can, wait for it to wilt and reduce, move it over to the side of the pan with a spatula, and add the rest of the raw spinach leaves to the pan. You don't need any extra water or stock – the water left clinging to the leaves after washing provides ample moisture.

To your health

One cup (180 g) of cooked spinach contains an astounding 1,474 RE of vitamin A or 147 per cent of the Recommended Daily Intake (RDI). It is also an excellent source of folate (supplying more than a day's needs), iron, magnesium, potassium and riboflavin. That single serving contains 41 calories and 17 mg of vitamin C, or 28 per cent of the RDI. Spinach is also high in calcium, vitamin E and vitamin B^6, and is a source of thiamin.

The beta carotene and vitamin C found in spinach are two powerful antioxidants that can protect the body from damage caused by free radicals and may prevent degenerative disease, heart disease and cancer.

Although spinach is brimming with important minerals such as iron and calcium, our bodies can't absorb them well due to the high levels of oxalic acid also found in spinach. This chemical blocks their absorption. Only 5 per cent of the total calcium content in spinach is absorbed, and it's estimated that you need to eat 15 servings of spinach to absorb the same amount of calcium found in one glass of milk. Plus, people who have gout, kidney or bladder stones should avoid foods high in oxalic acids like spinach, because it can exacerbate these conditions.

Quick ways

1. Heat 2 tablespoons (30 mL) of extra virgin olive oil in a large sauté pan or wok, and toss in 3 whole cloves of peeled garlic. Sauté until the garlic turns golden and then add a large bunch of washed, chopped spinach leaves.

Sauté until just wilted. Season with salt and pepper and a squirt of lemon juice. Serve.
2. Steam a large bunch of fresh spinach leaves until wilted. Drain and cool. Squeeze out any extra moisture and chop coarsely. Mix with 1 cup (250 mL) of ricotta cheese and 2 tablespoons (30 mL) of chopped parsley. Season with salt, pepper, a pinch of onion salt and a pinch of nutmeg. Spoon 2 tablespoons (30 mL) of the spinach and ricotta mixture onto a flour tortilla and fold into a square. Repeat with 3 more tortillas. Sprinkle with shredded mozzarella cheese and bake on a nonstick baking pan in a 350°F (180°C) oven for 15 minutes or until the cheese on top is melted.

Tips

Frozen spinach has more nutrients than fresh spinach that's gotten old. Canned spinach has lower folate levels than fresh.

Spinach contains two important carotenoids: beta carotene and lutein. Studies show that these phytochemicals significantly reduce the risk of age-related macular degeneration. Two ½-cup (125-mL) servings of cooked spinach a week reduce your chances of macular degeneration by half!

Sprouts

You'd think that after tasting my first bean sprout, I'd never do it again! It was limp, over-cooked, smothered in monosodium glutamate and drenched in soy sauce. Chop suey from Toronto's Moon Glow Restaurant was a soggy, flaccid affair in the 1960s, but my family ate it with glee. Chances are those bean sprouts came out of a can.

Looks like/Tastes like

The biggest-selling sprouts in Canada are mung and soy bean sprouts, sold not only in Asian stores, but also in most supermarkets and green grocers. **Mung bean** sprouts have crisp white stems (2 to 4 inches /5 to 10 cm long), emerging from a yellow bean with its green coat sometimes still attached. **Soy bean** sprouts are larger, emerging from a bright yellow bean head about ¼ inch (6 mm) long. The stems are slightly thicker and longer than mung bean sprouts. They have a stronger, nutty, almost woody taste compared to the delicate taste of mung bean sprouts. Next, in terms of popularity, are **alfalfa** sprouts. They're usually sold in clear, plastic containers. They look like a mass of white hairs, with a profusion of seeds and tiny green leaves at the top. The flavour is mild and slightly nutty. The trendiest sprouts on the market today are **broccoli** sprouts. They look similar to alfalfa sprouts, but have a more pronounced, broccoli-like, slightly spicy flavour. Other popular seed

sprouts are **daikon radish** (peppery hot), **sunflower** (mild and nutty), **mustard** (mustardy), **onion** (light onion taste) and **clover** (sweet and mild). A variety of beans and grains are all sprouted, including **kidney beans**, **lentils**, **navy beans**, **yellow** and **green peas**, **buckwheat**, **wheat** and even the spice **fenugreek**.

Select it

Chinese bean sprouts are generally sold piled high in large plastic bags. Look for crisp (they should snap when bent) and bright white bean sprouts. Avoid any that are limp, brown, smelly or slimy. When choosing seed sprouts sold in clear, plastic containers, look for those with as little green growth as possible. The greener the seed sprouts, the older they are. Check for mould, too.

Store it right

Bean sprouts are more perishable than seed sprouts. Store bean sprouts in paper or perforated plastic bags in the refrigerator, but not in the freezer (sprouts cannot be frozen). Don't store anything on top of your fragile bean sprouts or they'll be crushed and deteriorate rapidly. They last only a day or 2.

Unlike bean sprouts, which do best in a dry environment, seed sprouts like a little moisture. If you've bought them in prime condition, they'll last a week or more in their container in the refrigerator. To extend shelf life, sprinkle them with a little water or mist with a plant sprayer every day.

Prep it right

One of the reasons sprouts are so popular is that they are so convenient. Very little preparation is involved. For Chinese sprouts, rinse them briefly in cold water, drain and spin dry in a salad spinner. Meticulous Chinese cooks always top and tail their sprouts. It's a tedious job but does create "silver sprouts" with no trace of bitterness. Commercial seed sprouts do not require rinsing. They are ready to eat.

Chinese sprouts are more versatile than seed sprouts. They can be eaten raw, tossed in soups, added to stuffings (such as spring rolls), blanched briefly and served cold, or quickly stir-fried. Seed sprouts can also be eaten raw or cooked. Put them in salads and sandwiches.

Culinary destinations

Toss your seed sprouts into any salad or use them as a garnish. Seed sprouts are an easy alternative to lettuce in sandwiches, tortilla wraps and pita pockets. Try them mixed with cream cheese to make a crunchy spread. Daikon radish sprouts are used in Japanese salads and rolled into sushi. Add Chinese bean sprouts to a mixed vegetable stir-fry or a stir-fry with pork or chicken. They are an essential ingredient in mu-shu pork and garnish most Thai and Vietnamese dishes. Put them in an Asian soup just before serving, or add them to a cold, noodle salad with sesame seeds.

To your health

From a nutritional standpoint, bean sprouts have much more to offer than seed sprouts. For instance, 1 cup (104 g) of raw mung bean sprouts contains more than ¼ of your day's

folate needs and 20 per cent of the Recommended Daily Intake (RDI) of vitamin C. You have to eat almost 5 cups (165 g) of alfalfa seed sprouts to yield the same results. On the calorie front, mung bean sprouts contain 31 per cup (104 g), soy bean sprouts contain 76 per cup (94 g), alfalfa contain 10 per cup (33 g), and radish seed sprouts contain 16 per cup (38 g). A 1-cup (94-g) serving of soy bean sprouts is an excellent source of protein and folate, and is a source of potassium and vitamin C. A 1-cup (38-g) serving of radish seed sprouts is high in folate and a source of vitamin C and niacin.

Food-safety concerns around sprouts have been raised in the past few years as outbreaks of *E. coli* and salmonella in alfalfa sprouts and daikon radish sprouts have occurred in Japan, the United States and Canada. It appears that seeds may have been contaminated by dead animals or feces in the fields.

Warning: Alfalfa sprouts contain an amino acid called l-canavanin that can provoke a flare-up of symptoms in people who have lupus.

Squash – Summer

Nothing is easier than preparing a whole variety of squash – green and golden zucchini, pattypan and crookneck – then sautéing in butter and fresh herbs.

Looks like/Tastes like

Zucchini (a.k.a. **Italian** squash and **courgette**) comes in several varieties: tried-and-true green, light green, variegated and yellow-gold. This long, straight, cylindrical squash is best young and small, no longer than 6 inches (15 cm).

Yellow crookneck (a.k.a. **gooseneck**) should have a fully developed s-shaped neck for best flavour. It has a buttery flavour and creamy texture. Look for yellow crookneck no larger than 4 to 5 inches (10 to 12.5 cm) long. **Yellow straightneck** are easily confused with yellow-gold zucchini. Look for a pale yellow colour unlike the deep yellow of zucchini. Sadly, the flavour is bland and watery in comparison to other summer squash.

Pattypan (a.k.a. **scallop**, **scallopini**, **custard** or **cymling**) look like little flying saucers with a scalloped edge. They are convex at the top and bottom, around 2 ½ inches (6 cm) in diameter and come in a variety of colours: white, green, yellow, plus yellow and green splashed together. These have a firmer texture than other squash and are juicy, meaty and sometimes even nutty.

Round zucchini are (surprise!) round and best when no wider than 6 inches (15 cm) in diameter. The colouring is green streaked with white and pale green. The squash are tender and rich tasting, but bruise easily and are best eaten as soon as possible. Varieties include the French **Ronde de Nice** and an American Southwestern variety called **Calabacitas**.

Vegetable marrow are mature summer squash, most popular in Britain. These pale green squash are large and long, with a bland, watery flavour requiring heavy seasoning to merit eating.

The long and skinny **cucuzza** squash has many an alias, be it **bottle gourd**, **calabash** and **tazamania bean**. Adding to the confusion, cucuzza (koo-KOOt-t'zah) is the Sicilian term for all squash. However, this pale green squash can grow up to 3 to 4 feet long (90 to 120 cm). It's often hanging from the rafters in Italian groceries. It has white pulpy flesh with many seeds in the centre and tastes like a zucchini-cucumber mix.

Select it

The smaller the summer squash, the better. Oversized versions, although cheap and plentiful especially at the height of summer, disappoint with a watery, tough and tasteless texture. (If you are gifted a 2-ton zucchini from someone's garden, stuff it for best results.) Look for firm summer squash with no blemishes or cuts. The skin should have a smooth, glossy sheen. (Some crookneck varieties have a slightly bumpy skin, which is fine.) If you find zucchini sold with its blossoms, buy them both to enjoy two vegetables in one – besides, if the blossom is there, it means that squash is young and tender.

Store it right
Summer squash can be stored in a plastic bag in the refrigerator for up to 5 days. Once cut, they deteriorate quickly. You can freeze summer squash for up to 6 months. Blanch slices (or whole pattypans) in boiling water for 2 minutes, and then plunge in ice water. Drain and pat dry with paper towels. Spread on baking sheets lined with parchment paper and flash-freeze until solid. Store in airtight freezer bags.

Prep it right
Summer squash have a tender, edible skin that does not require peeling. The only preparation required is trimming off the stem and blossom ends. Pattypan squash can be steamed whole or sliced into attractive rounds. Due to the high water content, marrow are best baked, with no added liquid.

Summer squash can be eaten raw or cooked. Cut it into sticks for a veggie snack or toss it into salads. You can grate summer squash and stuff it into a pita pocket for a novel sandwich. Summer squash needs only a light touch when cooking or it will turn to mush. Try it sautéed, stir-fried, braised, grilled, steamed or baked. Summer squash has a high water content. Take that into consideration when cooking it with other ingredients, such as in an omelette or pilaf.

Culinary destinations
Poach squash slices in chicken broth, drain and top with a knob of herb butter. Make "zucchini fettuccine" by peeling zucchini in long strips with a vegetable peeler – use them in your next lasagna or toss them with fresh vegetables for a mock pasta primavera.

Any summer squash is perfect for stuffing: consider onion, feta and dill, or spicy, seasoned ground lamb. Zucchini, crookneck and pattypan are all great as fritters or in Japanese tempura or Indian pakoras. They're the right ingredient for a ratatouille-type casserole with tomatoes, onions, eggplant and fresh herbs.

To your health
One cup (180 g) of sliced and cooked summer squash contains 36 calories, is high in folate and is a source of potassium, vitamin C and beta carotene. Beta carotene is stored in the vegetable's skin, so make sure you eat it. The flesh contains none of this antioxidant vitamin. Summer squash is a source of dietary fibre and has a high water content – more than 95 per cent.

Although summer squash is not as high in beta carotene as winter squash, it is still a good source of this important, cancer-fighting phytochemical. Turn to squash for a low-fat vegetable that offers fibre, preventing constipation and promoting regularity.

Quick ways
To stuff a zucchini, simply spoon out the flesh, leaving a ½ inch (1 cm) of flesh around the edges. Chop up the flesh and sauté with onions, celery, garlic and dill. Stuff the sautéed vegetables back into the zucchini, sprinkle with grated Gruyère and bake at 350°F (180°C) for 15 to 20 minutes or until golden brown.

Squash – Winter

I once visited the Ontario Food Terminal at Thanksgiving time and found myself transfixed by the winter squash displays. Thousands of these gorgeous parcels of Nature were arranged before me, splashed in a kaleidoscope of fall colours. There were crater-like Hubbards, cute little acorns and shapely butternuts. Winter squash is definitely a good-looker, full of marvellous cooking possibilities. Besides, it's inexpensive and quite versatile.

Looks like/Tastes like

If you've ever found yourself staring at a mound of winter squash in the store, trying to figure out who's who, you're not alone. Most consumers haven't ventured farther than the acorn or butternut. While squash aficionados will tell you differently, there's not that big a difference among varieties. Feel free to pick up a strange squash and use it in any squash recipe. Sooner or later you'll discover which one is right for you!

Acorn As the name implies, this squash is shaped like an acorn, with deeply furrowed skin tapering at one end. It's one of the smaller squashes to be found, accounting for some of its popularity. It also tastes great: the yellow-orange flesh bakes beautifully, becoming moist, rich and tender. You'll find it in many colours: dark green, tan, orange or even white (considered the tastiest). It's also known as **pepper squash**.

Butternut Butternut is many people's favourite. It is shaped like a bowling pin, with a bulbous end and a narrowing neck. Tan in colour, butternut weighs 2 to 4 pounds (1 to 2 kg). The skin is easier to peel than most squashes. It has a rich texture and an almost fruity, sweet flavour.

Buttercup This squash looks similar to the turban squash. It comes in green or orange with uneven, narrow stripes running lengthwise. It has a distinctive beanie cap opposite the stem end, which is the same colour as the stripes. Its orange flesh is fine-textured and creamy like a sweet potato or butternut squash.

Delicata Also known as **sweet dumpling** and **sweet potato** squash, delicata can really confuse a novice squash buyer. It comes in two different shapes: acorn-shaped or long and oval. The skin is pale yellow with dark green stripes running lengthwise. Look out for its unique, corn-like flavour.

Hubbard Here's the ugliest and the biggest of the bunch: the Hubbard. It looks like a prehistoric squash, weighing anywhere from 3 to 15 pounds (1.25 to 7 kg), with a bumpy, craggy skin that might be light green, blue green or dark green, depending on the variety. It has a mealy, yellow-orange flesh that's not as sweet as other winter squash.

Kabocha This variety originated in Japan and looks a bit like a buttercup squash, with a flattened turban shape. It has a green rind with light green streaks, encasing a very sweet flesh. The texture is delicate, almost fibreless, but drier than buttercup or pumpkin. In Japan, they grow it big, up to 7 pounds (3 kg), but North American varieties average in at 2 to 3 pounds (1 to 1.25 kg).

Pumpkin Many are surprised to learn that pumpkins are part of the winter squash family. Humungous Halloween-harvested pumpkins were never meant for the kitchen – look for smaller pumpkins (a.k.a. **sweet, sugar, cheese** or **pie** pumpkins) cultivated specifically for eating. Better still, purchase a **Calabaza** pumpkin (a.k.a. **West Indian** pumpkin, **Jamaican** pumpkin or **Cuban** squash). It delivers a sweet and moist, fine-textured flesh that is ravishingly orange. You're most likely to find it sold in big chunks (1 to 2 pounds/500 g to 1 kg) in specialty or Caribbean stores. It's perfect for pies, soups and stews.

Spaghetti This football-shaped, hard squash (a.k.a. **vegetable** spaghetti) is about a foot (30 cm) long and comes in pale to bright yellow, cream or tan. Unlike other squash, its cooked flesh turns into pale yellow, delicately flavoured, spaghetti-like strands that can be sauced, just like pasta, offering more vitamins and less calories and carbohydrates. Two new varieties are worth looking for. **Stripetti** is a cross between a spaghetti and delicata squash, and **Orangetti** is supposed to be sweeter and more moist than regular spaghetti squash with extra beta carotene, to boot! The larger the spaghetti squash, the thicker the strands. Small specimens have strands no thicker than angel hair pasta.

Turban Here is a beautiful orange squash with white and green markings that you can use as a table decoration one night and eat the next. The large, round turban-like base is topped with what looks like another squash growing out of the middle. Its thick, sweet orange to yellow flesh is creamy, moist and reminiscent of hazelnuts.

Select it

Look for hard squash. If you can press your nail into the skin or scrape some of the skin off, it's immature. The stem should be hard, too, not spongy or skimpy. The rind should be dry and free of cracks, soft spots or bruises. A cream, tan or orange skin should have no green tinge to it (deep green splashes or stripes are fine). Choose a squash that seems heavy for its size and remember that bright colour is no indication of sweetness. Look for a dull, matte surface. If it's glossy, it may be waxed. The best butternut have a small bulb end and thick neck. Choose the largest spaghetti squash you can find to get thicker strands and more flavour.

Store it right

Squash lasts longest when it's stored out of the fridge in a cool, well-ventilated, dry spot. Butternut, Hubbard and Stripetti, if stored properly, can last from 2 to 3 months. Others last less well, lasting 2 weeks at the most. Once cut, a squash deteriorates quickly. Wrap it in plastic, store in the fridge and eat as soon as possible. Despite a squash's Mr. Tough Guy appearance, it needs careful handling.

Prep it right

Cutting a squash can be no easy feat, especially if you are dealing with a large, heavy one. You can soften the rind by placing the entire squash in the microwave. Cook at high for 2 to 5 minutes, depending on the size – pierce the skin with a knife in a few spots to release steam. To cut, use a large chef's knife or cleaver and give the squash a good whack. Then tap the knife with a blunt object like a rolling pin or mallet until it cuts right through. Or, once the knife is halfway through, lift it (and attached squash) up and gently hammer it against the cutting board until the knife breaks through the surface.

Peeling a squash is a challenge that's best avoided. Try baking, roasting, steaming or even microwaving squash with its skin on. It's easily removed, once cooled, or you can simply eat it and reap the fibre.

The microwave makes quick work of squash. You can cook it whole, unpeeled. First, pierce it several places with a sharp knife. Cook a small squash (1 ½ pounds/ 750 g) at high for 8 to 12 minutes (turning once, at half-time) or until it is tender when pierced with a knife. Let stand for at least 5 minutes before serving.

You can bake squash whole (remember to pierce it first) but it cooks much faster if split in two. Turn the cut side face down in a glass baking dish filled with about ½ inch (1 cm) of water to keep it moist. Bake in a 375°F (180°C) oven for 45 minutes to an hour, or until tender.

Many winter squash develop a more moist, creamy texture when they are steamed rather than baked. Cut the squash into wedges with skin attached and steam. Once cooked, any squash (except spaghetti) can be mashed or whirled in the blender to create a purée. For best results, drain the purée in a strainer for 15 minutes before storing in the fridge. Squash purée can be refrigerated for up to 3 days and frozen for up to 6 months.

Culinary destinations
Roast or microwave acorn, butternut or delicata halves and stuff them with rice and herbs or a traditional bread stuffing topped with grated cheese. Or use squash halves as edible serving bowls to present chili con carne or a vegetable sauté. Roast any squash (except spaghetti) in cubes tossed in olive oil, garlic, hot pepper flakes and rosemary. Purée opportunities are limitless: mix a pure squash purée with applesauce and cinnamon, with goat cheese and thyme, or with orange zest, fresh ginger and butter. Toss spaghetti squash strands with olive oil, garlic and Parmigiano-Reggiano or top it with tomato sauce. Cooled spaghetti squash strands make a novel pasta salad.

To your health
All winter squash contain many of the same nutrients, but in varying amounts. For instance, a 3-½-ounce (100-g) serving of cooked butternut squash contains 70 per cent of the Recommended Daily Intake (RDI) for vitamin A, while the same serving of Hubbard contains 60 per cent, pumpkin 10 per cent and acorn, just 4 per cent. Acorn squash, on the other hand, contains 4.4 g of fibre in the same-sized serving while spaghetti squash contains only 1.1. Butternut contains the most vitamin C, with 25 per cent of the RDI in the same-sized serving and spaghetti squash contains the least, at 5 per cent. All squash are a source of folate and potassium. Calorie content per serving ranges from 20 to 56 calories.

Winter squash, especially butternut and Hubbard, are a superior source of beta carotene. Numerous epidemiological studies have shown that people with a diet rich in beta carotene are less prone to heart disease, stroke, cataracts and some cancers. Meanwhile, winter squash is a good source of dietary fibre, which prevents constipation, ensures regularity and protects against diseases of the bowel such as diverticulitis and colon cancer.

Quick ways

Make squash rings by cutting an acorn
or delicata squash crosswise into 1-inch
(2.5-cm) thick slices. Brush with olive oil
and sprinkle with thyme or oregano, or
both. Bake at 375°F (190°C) for 20 to 30 minutes or until tender. Sprinkle with freshly
grated Parmigiano-Reggiano as soon as it
comes out of the oven.

Tip

*Store leftover squash purée in your freezer
and save it for a rainy day. You can use it in
any recipe calling for pumpkin, such as
bread, muffins, pie, flan or custard. In fact,
many bakers opt for squash instead of
pumpkin for a brighter orange colour.*

Sweet Potatoes

There's nothing like the smell of sweet pota-
toes baking in a hot oven. It's a culinary per-
fume that carries with it memories of falling
leaves, brisk windy days and Thanksgiving
celebrations. But since these sweet bundles
of nutrition are available year round, there's
no reason to limit your consumption to the
fall.

Other names

Sweet potatoes are often called yams in
both Canada and the United States. However, true yams are not botanically related
to sweet potatoes. If you see something
labelled a "yam" in North America, there's
a 99.9 per cent chance that it is a sweet
potato.

Looks like/Tastes like

Sweet potatoes are shaped like long potatoes,
but are not botanically related to them.
While potatoes have blunt ends, sweet potatoes are more pointy. Skin colours cover a
range, depending on variety: yellow, orange,
copper, light pink and red. All sweet potatoes
have coloured flesh, from yellow-orange to
red-orange.

Select it

Choose firm, well-shaped sweet potatoes
with a smooth skin, free of blemishes and
cuts.

Store it right

Don't make the mistake of refrigerating your
sweet potatoes. They start to decay as soon
as the temperature starts to drop below 10°C
(50°F). Keep sweet potatoes at room temperature, in a dry, dark place where they'll keep
for up to 10 days. Handle them gently; sweet
potatoes bruise easily.

Prep it right

Sweet potatoes can be cooked in their skins,
which fall off easily after cooking. Or peel
off their skins with a vegetable peeler when
they're raw.

Sweet potatoes are never eaten raw and
always cooked, both in savoury and sweet
preparations. Bake, microwave, steam, boil
or grill them. Sweet potatoes can be substi-
tuted for most recipes calling for regular
potatoes. They make a sweet French fry
and, when thinly sliced, work beautifully in
Japanese tempura. Toss them into soups or
stews. Try grating them into pies, puddings
and muffins.

Tips

Whenever possible, cook sweet potatoes
whole in their jackets. Most of the nutri-
ents are found next to the skin.

If you rub a sweet potato with a little but-
ter or olive oil before baking, the skin will
come off more easily when cooked.

Culinary companions

Orange juice and orange zest go with sweet potatoes, along with orange-flavoured liqueurs such as Grand Marnier and Cointreau. Sweet additions include brown sugar and maple syrup. Nutmeg, cumin, ginger, cloves, allspice, cinnamon and curry powder are compatible spices and fresh herbs such as coriander, parsley and chives liven up sweet potatoes. Try them with apples or pears, raisins, currants and hot peppers.

Culinary destinations

Make a sweet potato chowder with leeks, jalapeños, mushrooms, tomatoes, parsley, cumin and fresh coriander. Split open a baked sweet potato and treat it to a dollop of spicy salsa or a dab of butter followed by a drizzle of maple syrup. Pan-fried sweet potato, corn and chive pancakes taste delicious with yogurt or sour cream. Equally tasty are sweet potatoes matchsticks in a mixed vegetable stir-fry. Toss sweet potatoes into a chili with Italian sausage and kidney beans, or add them to your next risotto with wild mushrooms, thyme and Parmigiano-Reggiano. Sweet potato pie with pecans is heavenly.

To your health

A medium, cooked sweet potato (without skin) contains 158 calories and is a source of dietary fibre. That serving contains more than double the Recommended Daily Intake (RDI) for vitamin A and 41 per cent of the RDI for vitamin C. Sweet potato is also high in vitamin B^6 and is a source of vitamin E, folate, potassium and iron. When you eat the skin, you'll get double the fibre, potassium and folate than that found in the flesh on its own.

Sweet potatoes are a formidable source of antioxidant vitamins, especially beta carotene, which may help prevent heart disease, cataracts, strokes and certain cancers.

Swiss Chard

Everything about Swiss chard is pretty straight-forward – except its name. It grows like a charm, delivers a sweet mild taste and is easy to cook with. But that darn name has everyone scratching their heads! Nobody really knows how the Swiss connection started, since this vegetable originated in the Mediterranean.

Other names
The most frequently used alias is chard. Other less common names are silver beet, rhubarb chard, sea kale beet and spinach beet.

Looks like/Tastes like
Swiss chard has long, flat, celery-like stalks that can be wide or narrow, depending on the variety. The large leafy greens can be a foot (30 cm) long or more! They're flat or frilled with white or red veins, depending on the variety. It looks a bit like bok choy.

The most common variety of Swiss chard, **White King**, has snow-white stalks and deep green leaves. **Ruby** varieties have red stalks and veins. A new variety, called **Bright Lights,** has brilliant multi-coloured leaves and stems.

Select it
Look for crisp stalks and perky leaves for delicious Swiss chard. The stalks should be heavy, not light (those are dry and fibrous), and the leaves shouldn't be yellow, torn or wilted.

Store it right
Store Swiss chard in the refrigerator crisper in a perforated plastic bag. It lasts only a few days, so eat as soon as possible.

Prep it right
Always separate the leaves and stems of Swiss chard before cooking it. They can be used in the same preparation but the stems require longer cooking than the leaves.

If the stems seem tough or stringy, peel them lightly. You can cut the stem crosswise, on the diagonal, or into long, lengthwise strips. The leaves can be cooked whole (for stuffing or wrapping), chopped coarsely, or stacked up, rolled and sliced into thin ribbons.

Use Swiss chard leaves just like spinach. Sauté in extra virgin olive oil and spritz with lemon juice – to serve hot or cold. Put it in omelettes, soups, frittatas, quiches, ravioli or casseroles. Small, young leaves can be tossed into salads. The stems can be steamed (without the leaves) and served with butter and herbs, or braised with wine.

Culinary destinations
Try Swiss chard with golden raisins, pine nuts and Parmigiano-Reggiano cheese as a vegetable sauté or pasta sauce (see recipe, page 229). Teamed with mushrooms, Swiss chard is superb in a frittata or omelette. Complementary herbs include basil, parsley, fresh coriander, oregano, sage and rosemary.

Serve grilled fish, roast chicken or eggs Benedict on a bed of steamed Swiss chard. Try it in a Chinese stir-fry with some ginger, garlic and sesame oil. Or stir it up with chicken strips and black bean sauce. Swiss chard works well in most Italian creations, be they gnocchi, ravioli or pasta sauces. Parboil large whole leaves, plunge in cold water and use them as vegetable wrappers filled with coleslaw or noodle salad.

To your health

A ½-cup (88-g) serving of cooked Swiss chard contains only 18 calories, no fat and is a good source of fibre. Swiss chard is an excellent source of beta carotene – almost all of it is found in the leaves, unless the stalks are pigmented. It's also high in potassium, with 480 mg of potassium in that same-sized serving, and is a source of vitamin C. Although Swiss chard contains both calcium and iron, the absorption of these minerals is hampered by oxalic acid (just like spinach).

Turn to Swiss chard for antioxidants (beta carotene, vitamin C and a small amount of vitamin E). These powerful phytochemicals may help reduce your risk of cancer, heart disease, stroke and cataracts. However, people with gout, kidney stones or rheumatism should not go overboard with Swiss chard, due to the prevalence of oxalic acid.

Quick ways

Take 4 cups (144 g) of whole Swiss chard leaves and steam until wilted. Cool, squeeze out extra moisture then chop finely. Heat some olive oil in a large pan and sauté some chopped onions and minced garlic. Toss in some chopped parsley (a little oregano and rosemary are nice, too) and 3 chopped tomatoes. Cook for a few minutes. Add the Swiss chard and ½ cup ricotta cheese. Cook until heated through and serve on hot pasta.

Taro

You can't judge a book – or a vegetable – by its cover and taro is a case in point. This clumsy, earthy-brown tuber is a stranger to most Canadians. It's the kind of veggie that looks more like a prehistoric remnant than a modern cooking ingredient. But if you're a fan of Cantonese food, chances are you've tasted taro either as the airy, dim sum dumpling called woo kok *or as the crispy weave of an edible food basket called bird's nest.*

Other names

Taro is often confused with malanga (a.k.a. tannia), which looks similar to taro but has a pronounced, musty taste, not appreciated by everyone. In the Caribbean, taro is called dasheen or eddo. Popular in Japanese cooking, taro has also been dubbed the Japanese country potato. The Cantonese name for taro is *woo tau*.

Looks like/Tastes like

Taro is a starchy, potato-like tuber belonging to the arum family. It's an important staple for many parts of the world and more than 100 varieties exist. There are two main types of taro to watch out for. The first type, sometimes called **Tahitian** taro, is large (½ pound to 2 pounds/250 g to 1 kg) and barrel-shaped, about the size of a rutabaga. It has a shaggy, brown, bark-like skin with concentric, ring-like markings. The crisp flesh is white, cream or violet-grey, speckled with tiny brown or red dots. The other type of taro is much smaller – about the size of a small to medium potato – weighing in from 2 to 6 ounces (50 to 170 g). It also has a brown, bark-like, hairy skin with ring markings around an elongated, kidney bean shape. This type is prized for the small, egg-sized cormels that sprout at the tip.

Taro is crisp when raw but has a dry texture once cooked. It tastes like a potato with hints of artichoke and chestnut. It's slightly sweet and nutty. Cooked taro leaves are used in Caribbean and some Asian cuisines. In the Caribbean, these big, spade-shaped leaves are called callaloo and they taste like spinach or Swiss chard.

Select it

Look for firm taro with no signs of shrivelling or mould. Choose the large variety when you want a dry, nutty texture for soups or stews. The small ones can be cooked whole and have a moist texture. You'll find taro in Asian, Latin American and Caribbean food stores.

Store it right

Don't refrigerate taro. Store it in a well-ventilated, dry, cool place (try a hanging basket). Unlike most root vegetables, it's quite perishable and can be stored only a few days. Use it before it turns soft.

Prep it right

Remove the taro's skin and under layer with a sharp paring knife. Taro exudes a sticky juice that can cause serious skin irritations, so wear gloves when paring or cook it with the skin on and then remove it. Keep taro in cold water right after peeling to stop discolouring.

Always cook taro and taro leaves. Taro can be boiled, steamed, braised, stir-fried, deep-fried and roasted. Taro is often puréed or mashed, and then formed into fritters or dumplings that are pan-fried or deep-fried. Try it thinly sliced or shredded, then deep-fried. Taro soaks up a lot of liquid during cooking and absorbs flavours, making it perfect for soups and stews. Taro leaves can be boiled, steamed or braised, or added to soups and stews.

Culinary destinations

Shred some taro, form into loose pancakes and deep-fry. Or use it instead of potatoes in potato latkes. Prepare it like French fries or slice into thin strips, toss with oil and herbs, and then roast. Taro tastes wonderful combined with beef in a Chinese stir-fry or in a Brazilian soup with hot sausages, tomatoes, onion, garlic and fresh coriander.

To your health

Taro is loaded with important nutrients. A 3-½-ounce (100-g) serving contains 142 calories and is an excellent source of dietary fibre (5 g per serving). It is also a source of vitamins C and E, potassium, magnesium and folate. Tahitian taro is even more nutritious with fewer calories: a 3-½-ounce (100-g) serving has only 44 calories, but is an excellent source of vitamin C, supplying 63 per cent of the Recommended Daily Intake (RDI). One serving of Tahitian taro is also high in magnesium, potassium and beta carotene, and is a source of calcium, iron and riboflavin.

The sticky juice that taro exudes when it is cut can cause serious skin irritations. Taro and taro leaves should never be eaten raw, for they contain a highly carcinogenic substance called calcium oxalate that is destroyed by cooking.

Trivia

Taro is boiled, mashed and fermented, then served as *poi* in Hawaii and Polynesia. Tourists to these countries are often less than enthusiastic about this bland and sour national dish with a texture like mush.

Tomatillo

The tomatillo is the one that got left behind. Cultivated since ancient Aztec times, it was ignored while all those other New World vegetables (like corn or peppers) were embraced by the rest of the world. Today, its roots remain grounded in Mexico, creeping north only to California and Texas.

Other names
Pronounce tomatillo "toe-ma-TEA-o." For such an obscure fruit, the tomatillo has a lot of names: husk tomato, Mexican green tomato, jamberry, jamberberry, Chinese lantern, *tomate verde* and *tomate de Cascara.*

Looks like/Tastes like
The tomatillo is enclosed in a papery husk that ranges in colour from pale green to grocery-bag brown. The edible fruit inside looks like a green cherry tomato. It can be as small as an inch (2.5 cm) in diameter or the size of a large plum. It's eaten when it's green but does ripen to yellow, sometimes with a purplish tinge.

Tomatillo tastes like an unripe, very tangy tomato. It has a slightly gelatinous texture and lemony, almost herbal overtones. The flavour is quite acidic when raw, but intensifies and mellows with cooking.

Select it
The condition of a tomatillo's husk tells volumes about the hidden fruit. Look for husks that are light brown, fresh looking and not shrivelled or dried up. A tomatillo should fit snugly in its husk – give it a little squeeze to see how good the fit is.

You want to eat a tomatillo that is green. Yellow (riper) tomatillos lack the flavour and tanginess of the green ones.

Store it right
Tomatillos store remarkably well. Unlike tomatoes, tomatillos shouldn't be stored at room temperature – you don't want them to ripen. Remove the husks and store in a sealed plastic bag. If they're in good condition, they'll store up to a month.

You can freeze tomatillos whole. The easiest way is to dehusk them, put them on a cookie sheet, freeze until solid and then transfer them to a freezer bag. Or poach them first, in just enough water to cover. Bring to a boil and simmer lightly for 5 minutes or until they are soft but not broken. Store the cooled tomatillos and cooking liquid in 1-cup (250-mL) capacity freezer-safe containers for a fresh alternative to canned tomatillos.

Prep it right
When you remove the papery husk, you'll discover that the tomatillo is covered by a sticky, harmless substance. Rinse thoroughly before using. Use them raw or cooked.

Tomatillos can be chopped or sliced raw to be used in dips and no-cook sauces. But more commonly, tomatillos are cooked. They can be poached, steamed and sautéed. To roast tomatillos, put them in a 450°F (230°C) oven, still in their husks, and cook until soft (10 to 15 minutes). Check regularly to prevent them from bursting. Tomatillos are rarely served on their own, but as a sauce, used to complement other foods. They offer a citrusy edge to soups, casseroles, eggs, chicken, and so on.

Culinary companions
Among fresh herbs, fresh coriander is the number-one companion. Parsley, basil, mint and chives work well, too. Hot peppers, red onions, garlic and lime juice are standard seasonings in many tomatillo preparations. Roasted cumin, thyme and ginger are good, too. Bell peppers, cucumbers, tomatoes and jicama are often paired with tomatillos, as are cheese, eggs and pumpkin seeds.

Culinary destinations
Think of Mexican, Tex-Mex or Southwestern cuisines when cooking with tomatillos. They are the famous ingredient in salsa verde, but are also found in chilled soups, chicken enchiladas, huevos rancheros, relishes and beef dishes. Try scrambling some eggs with fresh hot peppers, Monterey Jack cheese, avocados and tomatillos. Or make a papaya and tomatillo salsa. Even guacamole tastes better with the addition of tomatillos.

To your health
There are only 42 calories in a 1-cup (132-g) serving of chopped raw tomatillos. Tomatillos are a source of vitamin C, dietary fibre, potassium and niacin.

Quick ways
To make a quick salsa verde, poach a ½ pound (250 g) of tomatillos in water to cover until soft and tender. Set aside to cool. Meanwhile, finely chop 1 (or more) fresh hot pepper, ½ red onion, 1 clove garlic and a handful of fresh coriander. Mix everything together in a medium bowl. Squirt with lemon or lime juice and sprinkle with roasted cumin and salt to taste. Use this as a dip for corn chips, a filling for an omelette, or a sauce for burritos or enchiladas.

Trivia
The tomatillo belongs to the physalis species of plants and is closely related to the cape gooseberry and the ground cherry. Even wider familial ties link it to the nightshade family, which includes tomatoes, potatoes and eggplants, to name a few.

Tomatoes

The French first dubbed this veggie "love apple," but in fact, the whole world is in love with the tomato. The average Canadian eats more than 68 pounds (31 kg) a year – that amounts to 174 average-sized tomatoes!

Looks like/Tastes like

There are more than 300 varieties of tomatoes, ranging from tiny currant tomatoes (less than an ounce/28 g) to the king of tomatoes – the beefsteak – which can weigh up to 2 ½ pounds (1.1 kg).

Slicing or **globe** tomatoes are the ubiquitous round and classic tomato that tastes best in season, grown locally. Generally, there are three to four slicing tomatoes to a pound. Imported **cluster** tomatoes (sold with the vine still attached) can be expensive but better tasting than other imported tomatoes that have been gassed with ethylene to ripen during transport. Slicing tomatoes are best raw but can be cooked.

Plum tomatoes (a.k.a. **Italian**, **paste** or **Roma**) are oval-shaped and 3 to 4 inches (8 to 10 cm) long. They are smaller than slicing tomatoes and bigger than cherry. Plum tomatoes have thick and meaty walls with less juice and more flavour than slicing tomatoes. They are the perfect choice for making paste (as the name implies) and all general tomato cooking needs. The seeds are smaller, less bitter and not always necessary to remove.

Cherry and **pear** (a.k.a. **Tear Drop**) tomatoes are bite-sized tomatoes that can be very sweet and juicy. These tend to taste better than slicing tomatoes during the winter.

Beefsteak tomatoes are the largest of all. These huge and juicy tomatoes are best for slicing into salads or sandwiches and rarely appear in the winter months.

Yellow and **green** tomatoes can come in any of the above types. Yellow tomatoes are less acidic and more mild than their red cousins. Green tomatoes are generally unripe tomatoes, but there are some new varieties that are green when ripe.

Select it

Look for firm but not rock-hard tomatoes. A good tomato is heavy for its size, noticeably fragrant and richly coloured for its variety. Don't buy bruised or cracked tomatoes.

Store it right

Don't refrigerate tomatoes. Cold temperatures interfere with the ripening process and zap flavour. Keep tomatoes at room temperature and resist the urge to line them up on the windowsill. In direct sunlight, tomatoes overheat and deteriorate. Speed up the ripening process as you would any piece of fruit (yes, it's a fruit) by placing in a brown paper bag with an apple or banana. You can store ripe tomatoes in the fridge, if you must, but it's better to eat or cook with them immediately.

To freeze tomatoes, wash, dry thoroughly and pack in a freezer bag. You can freeze whole tomatoes for up to 6 months. A frozen tomato is easy to peel – simply run it under hot water, then slip off the skin with a sharp knife. To remove seeds, cut the partially frozen tomato in half and scrape the seeds out with your finger or a small spoon. Use previously frozen tomatoes for cooking only.

Prep it right

Most of a tomato's nutrients are stored in the skin and the jelly-like substance that encases the seeds. Although many recipes for cooked tomatoes call for peeled and seeded tomatoes, it's really a matter of taste. Seeds can cause bitterness and the skins can shrivel and become tough and unpalatable. That said, many cooked tomatoes taste delicious (and are more nutritious) with their skin and seeds included.

To peel a fresh tomato, take a sharp knife and slash an "x" at the base. Drop the tomato into boiling water and remove when the skin starts to curl off the tomato (30 to 60 seconds). Remove with a slotted spoon, submerge in cold water and drain. When the tomato is cool enough to handle, slip off the skin.

Or try the microwave method. Microwave at high for 15 seconds. Let stand for 1 minute and the skin should be loose enough to peel off easily.

To remove the seeds, cut a fresh tomato in half crosswise, then gently squeeze it into a sieve over a bowl to catch seeds as juice runs into the bowl.

Tomatoes react adversely – creating a bitter aftertaste – if they come in contact with metal bowls and cookware that are aluminum or not stainless steel. Copper is the worst culprit, as the reaction can be toxic! Use stainless steel, enamel ware, glass, Pyrex or china when working with tomatoes. Before you put tomato sauce or paste in a plastic storage container, spray it with a liberal coating of cooking spray to avoid staining.

While ripe, seasonal tomatoes taste great raw, eaten out of hand or sliced into a salad. Out-of-season tomatoes may need a little help. Try sprinkling with a little sugar or marinating in salt, lemon juice, sugar and oil for 15 minutes before serving raw.

Tomatoes can be roasted, broiled, baked, grilled (try cherry tomatoes on a skewer), braised and sautéed.

Tip
Try cooking stuffed tomatoes in muffin trays. They are guaranteed to stay intact!

Culinary companions

Any fresh herb works with tomatoes, but basil is tops. Mediterranean flavours include garlic, olive oil, hot pepper flakes, capers, olives, balsamic vinegar and Parmigiano-Reggiano cheese. Just about any cheese works with tomatoes, from Swiss to ricotta to goat cheese. Indian and Middle Eastern dishes pair tomatoes with cumin, fresh and ground coriander, fennel, ginger, cinnamon and more. Tomatoes are one of the most compatible ingredients you'll ever encounter. Just ask any child who loves ketchup!

Culinary destinations

Try roasted tomato and garlic soup; a salad of fresh tomato slices, bocconcini, basil and olive oil; sliced tomatoes and caramelized onions on focaccia; stuffed tomatoes with barley and mushrooms; fried green tomatoes; tomato jam preserve; fresh (no-cook) tomato sauce for pasta; yellow tomato salsa with fresh coriander; or put some fresh tomato juice in your next homemade vinaigrette. The possibilities are endless!

To your health

A single tomato is not exactly bursting with nutrients, but most of us never stop at one tomato. Accumulatively (especially in sauces and pastes) tomatoes offer excellent amounts of vitamin C, beta carotene, potassium, folate and vitamin E. Two fresh plum tomatoes contain only 26 calories and supply 23 mg of vitamin C or 39 per cent of the Recommended Daily Intake (RDI). Ounce for ounce, smaller tomatoes have more vitamin C than larger, according to one study. Most of a tomato's vitamin C is concentrated in the jelly-like substance that encases the seeds.

Tomatoes – especially processed or cooked tomatoes – are high in lycopene, a plant pigment that is considered to be a more powerful antioxidant than its cousin, beta carotene. Studies have shown that lycopene is effective in reducing the risks of many types of cancer, including prostate, colon, rectal and stomach. Meanwhile, tomatoes contain two other cancer-fighting phytochemicals: P-courmaric and chlorogenic acid.

On the negative side, many people are allergic to tomatoes. Plus, tomatoes contain a substance that can cause acid reflux, leading to indigestion and heartburn.

Quick ways

Here's a quick pasta supper for two in the summertime. Slice 8 plum tomatoes into quarters. Toss in a bowl with 2 tablespoons (30 mL) of extra virgin olive oil, one teaspoon chopped garlic and 2 tablespoons each of chopped fresh basil and mint. Cook under the broiler until tender. Sprinkle with lots of freshly grated Parmigiano-Reggiano and ground black pepper. Serve on hot pasta.

Trivia

Botanically speaking, the tomato is actually a fruit – a berry to be exact. Legally speaking, however, it is a vegetable. More than a century ago, a U.S. Supreme Court declared that the tomato was legally a vegetable.

Turnips

I never liked turnip until I tasted it in Marrakesh. Bathed in cinnamon and saffron, tender to the bite, served on a bed of fluffy couscous . . . the turnip of Morocco was a far cry from the despicable mush of my childhood nightmares. But nowadays it is easier to love turnips than ever before. New varieties come in a pallet of pastel colours. Plus, sweet and tender baby turnips are increasingly available, too.

Other names
Turnips are constantly confused with their cousin, rutabaga. Both belong to the cabbage family.

Looks like/Tastes like
Turnips are usually spherical in shape, looking not unlike a toy top. A turnip can be as small as a golf ball or as large as a baseball. (They used to be grown to huge sizes – up to 50 pounds/23 kg – but that unappetizing trend has stopped). Turnips are usually white, or creamy white, but there are new, golden-yellow and red-skinned varieties. White turnips are often splashed with purple, pink or green at the top. Raw turnips have a crisp texture, and a sweet, slightly peppery taste. The flavour sweetens with cooking. Young fresh turnips are sometimes sold in bunches, with greens attached.

Select it
For the sweetest, most tender turnips, choose the smallest you can find. If the greens are attached, make sure they are perky, have good green colour and are not wilted, yellowed or slimy. Pick turnips that are heavy for their size. A light one might be spongy inside. The flesh should be smooth, taut and unblemished. Wrinkled turnips are woody and old.

Store it right
If turnips are sold in a bunch, remove the rubber band before storing and cut off the greens, which should be stored separately. Store in plastic bags. The turnip roots will last up to a week; the greens no more than a day or 2.

Prep it right
Turnips are easier to peel than rutabagas. In fact, very small turnips need not be peeled, just scrubbed well. Peel with a vegetable peeler, as you would an apple. Turnip can be sliced, cubed, julienned, balled or "turned" out. To turn out, first cut turnip into sticks (about 3 inches by 1 inch by 1 inch/8 cm by 2.5 cm by 2.5 cm), and then pare off the corners so that it has rounded edges instead.

You can eat turnip raw or cooked. Small, tender turnips can be grated or julienned and dressed as salad fare. Whole tiny ones can be dunked in a dip. To cook, try steaming, boiling, sautéing, stir-frying, roasting and deep-frying turnip. Cook it in stews and soups, too. For best results when mashing, use a food mill or ricer, rather than a masher. The greens (especially young ones) can be eaten raw as a bitter salad green. Their flavour mellows with cooking. Steam or sauté them.

To enhance the flavour of turnip, toss in a little sugar (or brown sugar, honey, maple syrup) during cooking.

Culinary companions
Turnips and rutabagas pair with the same flavours. Salad partners include lemon juice, mayonnaise and vinegar plus a range of fresh herbs such as parsley, chives, oregano, marjoram and thyme. Bacon, ham, prosciutto and pancetta all bring out the best in turnips, as do roasted meats and their juices. Walnuts and hazelnuts (plus their oils) combine well with turnips. Sharp flavours include horseradish, mustard and wasabi. Chinese seasonings such as soy sauce, ginger and sesame oil are complementary, as are Moroccan spices such as saffron, fresh or ground coriander, cumin, cinnamon and nutmeg.

Culinary destinations
Shred or grate turnips to combine (or replace) cabbage in slaws and sauerkrauts. Cut them into wedges, marinate with herbs, lemon juice and olive oil, and then grill or roast them in the oven. Glaze turnips with brown sugar, maple syrup, marmalade, apricot jam, port, sherry or sweet Madiera. Toss them into a soup with apples or pears. Mash turnips with potatoes and roasted garlic, or team them up with other root vegetables in a gratin with cream, nutmeg and Gruyère cheese. Sauté turnip greens in garlic and extra virgin olive oil or steam until tender, and then dress Japanese style (see Tokyo Beet Greens on page 240).

To your health
Although turnip roots are not quite as nutritional as rutabagas, they do have one up on their cousin: edible leaves. Turnip greens offer a striking array of vitamins and minerals. A half-cup (72-g) serving of boiled turnip greens contains a measly 14 calories, but is jam-packed with 396 RE (retinol equivalent, the unit of measurement for vitamin A) of vitamin A, supplying 39 per cent of the Recommended Daily Intake (RDI). Turnip greens are also an excellent source of folate (38 per cent of RDI), high in vitamin C, and a source of calcium, iron and dietary fibre. Turnip roots are not as well endowed. One cup (230 g) cooked turnip contains 48 calories and is high in vitamin C. Unlike rutabagas, turnips contain no beta carotene. They are, however, high in dietary fibre and a source of potassium and folate.

As members of the Cruciferous Club (cabbage family), turnips contain powerful phytochemicals that help to prevent cancer. Moreover, epidemiological studies reveal that populations eating a diet high in leafy greens (including turnip greens) have lower rates of cancer, particularly lung cancer.

Turnip greens rank high in bioavailable calcium. Just 2 servings (144 g) of turnip greens supply the same amount of bioavailable calcium as that contained in a glass of milk. Turnips contain potassium and folate, two nutrients that enhance heart health.

Watercress

Looks like/Tastes like

Watercress is just one among many different types of cress, all members of the mustard family. Watercress is well known, yet the others will remain in obscurity until they become commercially cultivated. Many home gardeners, however, reap the joys of cress. Names abound: **garden cress, broadleaf cress, cressida, land cress, winter cress, upland cress** and **curly cress**. All have a peppery tang like their cousin, watercress.

Watercress has dime-sized, dark green glossy leaves and leggy stems. It's often sold with its stems soaking in water in the salad greens section of your grocery. It has a spicy, mustardy bite that can vary in intensity from bunch to bunch.

Select it

Look for perky, crisp leaves with good green colour. Opt for a bunch that has more leaves than stems. Smaller plants tend to be less peppery. Avoid yellowed, wilted, soggy or smelly specimens.

Store it right

Watercress wasn't really made to be stored. If you can't eat it as soon as possible, remove the rubber band or twist tie holding the bunch together (all that togetherness promotes rotting). Wrap watercress loosely in a paper towel and store in a perforated plastic bag in your crisper.

Prep it right

It's all edible, although not everyone is crazy about the stalks, which can be tough. If you're cooking watercress, cook the stalks first before the tender leaves. Watercress needs a thorough rinse or 2 in cold water. Blot dry with paper towels or give it a whirl in your salad spinner.

Most people eat watercress raw in salads, sandwiches (an English teatime classic) or as a garnish. But watercress can be cooked. Once heated, watercress develops a milder flavour. Sauté it lightly until just wilted or toss it into a stir-fry during the last minutes of cooking. Watercress makes a wonderful soup, whether it's a rich version with leeks, potatoes and cream, or a light, clear Asian soup.

Culinary companions

Citrus and watercress go hand in hand in many salads. Complementary greens include Belgian endive, radicchio and romaine. Pecan, walnuts and pistachios accent the nutty taste of watercress. Leeks, onions, shallots and green onions all combine well with watercress, as do such Oriental seasonings as ginger, sesame oil and oyster sauce.

Culinary destinations

Next time you're grilling, present the results on a bed of watercress. You can toss watercress into just about any salad and it will offer a nice, peppery bite. Try it in a cold Chinese noodle salad or in an endive, pear and walnut salad. Season your next ground-turkey burger or bread stuffing with it. Chop up some watercress and scramble with eggs. Or use it instead of lettuce in a sandwich.

To your health

One cup (34 g) of raw, chopped watercress contains a measly 4 calories yet is high in vitamin A and a source of vitamin C.

Watercress is a member of the cruciferous family, a group of cabbage-related vegetables containing powerful phytochemicals that may help reduce the risk of cancer and heart disease. In the meantime, watercress contains an arsenal of antioxidants (vitamins C and E and beta carotene) offering protection from free radicals (unstable molecules found in the body that can harm cells). Fresh watercress juice is a traditional remedy for skin problems, be they acne or eczema.

Quick ways

1. Emerald Rice: heat some oil in a wok or large frying pan. Add some grated ginger, 2 chopped green onions, 2 cups (500 mL) of chopped watercress, ½ cup (125 mL) of chopped fresh coriander and 2 cups (500 mL) of chilled, cooked rice. Break the rice up with the spatula as you stir-fry. Drizzle in a well-beaten egg, if you wish. Cook until the rice is heated through, season with salt and pepper to taste and serve.

2. Watercress Dressing: place the following in a blender or food processor: 1 cup (250 mL) of plain yogurt, 1 cup (250 mL) of chopped watercress, 1 chopped green onion, 1 chopped garlic clove and the juice of half a lemon. Season with salt and pepper and pour over your next salad or steamed vegetables.

Yams

Most North Americans think they've eaten a yam before, but their lips have probably never touched one! A true yam is very different from a sweet potato both in appearance and taste. But ever since African slaves in the Deep South confused the American sweet potato with a yam, this tuber-confusion has persisted.

Other names
The name yam comes from the African word *name* or *gname*.

Looks like/Tastes like
Yams are white-fleshed, long starch tubers with a rough scaly skin quite dissimilar to the smooth skin and orange flesh of sweet potatoes. Yams contain no beta carotene, in comparison to the beta-carotene-rich sweet potato.

Sweet potatoes grow in the United States, but no true yams do. Yams grow in the Caribbean, Africa and Asia.

There are more than 600 varieties of yams growing across the world's tropical and sub-tropical lands. As a result, yams come in a multitude of shapes, colours and sizes. A yam can weigh up to 200 pounds (91 kg) and can be several feet long, but most yams sold in North America are a smaller, more manageable size. Some are round, or shaped like sweet potatoes or cylindrical logs. Some look like horseradish and one variety is described as looking like a bear claw. The skin may be brown, black-brown or rusty tan with a scaly or shaggy texture. The flesh is commonly white, but can also be ivory, pale yellow or even light purple.

Select it
Look for yams in Asian, Latin American and Caribbean stores. Choose small, firm yams that are heavy in the hand. Scrape the skin deeply with a fingernail. The flesh should be juicy and slippery, not dry. Avoid withered yams or those with cracks, soft spots or sunken bruises.

Store it right
Yams last up to a week in a dry, well-ventilated, cool place. Don't refrigerate them, and you don't need to wrap them in plastic. Once cut, a yam exudes a sticky juice that forms a dry, airtight seal around the cut area, preventing spoilage.

Prep it right
First, wear gloves. That sticky juice that yams exude irritates the skin of most people. Due to the stickiness, you may need to rinse under running water as you prep yam. Use a paring knife to slice off the skin and under layer. Cut into manageable chunks, and then remove the skin. Yam discolours when cut, so put peeled and cut yam into a bowl of acidulated water (3 tablespoons/45 mL of lemon juice or vinegar in 4 cups/1 L of water).

Yam are never eaten raw, only cooked. You can boil, steam, bake, sauté or fry yams. Try them in soups and stews.

Culinary destinations

Yams have a bland flavour that cries out for larger flavours. Think of garlic, lime, sour oranges, fresh coriander, mint, hot peppers, horseradish and very flavourful sauces. Serve gently simmered cubes of yam with a spicy salsa or a flavourful mayonnaise. Deep-fry yam French fries or chips, and sprinkle with cayenne pepper and salt. Try braised yam in a rich garlic sauce with onions and Seville oranges. A traditional Cuban stew combines yam with sweet and hot peppers, garlic, onions, vinegar, bay leaves and oregano.

To your health

A serving of 1 cup (136 g) of cooked yam contains 158 calories. Just a single serving is an excellent source of dietary fibre (5.3 g) and potassium (911 mg) – twice the amount of potassium found in a medium banana. Yams are also a good source of vitamin C, supplying 27 per cent of the Recommended Daily Intake (RDI) in a single serving. Yams are high in vitamin B^6 and a source of folate, iron and magnesium.

Never eat raw yam. It contains a carcinogenic compound called dioscorine, which is destroyed by heat when cooked.

Yams contain phytoestrogens that may reduce discomforts associated with menopause. In fact, the hormones used to develop oral contraceptives were first extracted from yams.

Yams are one of the best food sources for potassium and a good vegetable source for iron. Dietary potassium can help regulate blood pressure and iron helps treat and prevent anemia.

Trivia

In Africa, yams are sliced, sun-dried and ground into a flour used to make pudding.

Recipes

Arugula, Strawberries and Goat Cheese Salad

If you can put tomatoes in a salad, why not strawberries? Technically, they're both fruits. This salad is good to entertain with, especially if you design each plate creatively. Give this salad a liberal grinding of black pepper and the strawberries will dance on your tongue with flavour.

Serves 4

1	small red onion	1
	Olive oil for basting	
1 lb	arugula leaves, washed and torn	500 g
2 tbsp	extra virgin olive oil	25 mL
2 tsp	balsamic vinegar	10 mL
12	strawberries, washed and cored	12
¼ cup	crumbled goat cheese	50 mL
	Freshly ground black pepper	

❥ Cut the red onion in half, peel off the skin and cut each half into small wedges with the root portion attached (this way it won't fall apart on the grill). Baste with a light coating of olive oil and grill until tender and charred.

❥ Place the arugula leaves in a salad bowl and drizzle on the oil and vinegar. Toss.

❥ Arrange one quarter of the leaves on each salad plate. Arrange 3 sliced strawberries, 1 spoonful of crumbled goat cheese and one quarter of the grilled red onion on each plate. Season with freshly ground black pepper and serve.

Tips

As an alternative to grilling the red onions, sauté them – sliced thinly – in a little olive oil.

Remember to wash the arugula leaves very well. This green sometimes needs 2 or 3 rinses in a sink full of water before all the sand disappears.

Baby Carrots and Sugar Snap Peas

This is an easy and pretty dish. If you've never tried nutmeg on your vegetables before you are in for a treat.

Serves 4

1	small cooking onion	1
½ lb	sugar snap peas	250 g
2 tbsp	vegetable oil	25 mL
2	quarter-size slices of fresh ginger	2
½ lb	baby carrots, sliced in half lengthwise	250 g
	Water or chicken stock	
20	fresh mint leaves	20
¼ tsp	nutmeg	1 mL
	Salt	

❧ Peel the cooking onion. Cut in quarters then cut each quarter in half, cross-wise, and loosen up the onion pieces. Trim and de-string the sugar snap peas.

❧ Heat the oil in a wok or large frying pan. Add the ginger and cooking onion and stir-fry until the onion softens. Add the baby carrots and sugar snap peas; stir-fry. Add a few tablespoons of water or chicken stock if needed. Stir until tender, about 6 to 8 minutes, adding small amounts of liquid if the pan becomes dry. Add the mint leaves and stir to mix.

❧ Transfer to a serving dish, sprinkle with nutmeg and season with salt.

Beets with a Bite

When the sweet taste of beets meets the spicy bite of horseradish, it's a match made in heaven. Beets and horseradish are an age-old Jewish combination, especially at Passover. Here's my easy rendition.

Serves 4

1	bunch beets (3 large or 4 medium)	1
1	clove garlic, crushed	1
¼ tsp	salt	1 mL
4 tsp	chopped shallots	20 mL
4 tsp	extra virgin olive oil	20 mL
2 tsp	bottled horseradish sauce	10 mL
1-½ tsp	red wine vinegar	7 mL

❧   Wash and trim the beets so that 2 inches (5 cm) of stem remain attached, along with the tap root. Cook in boiling water until tender (45 to 60 minutes). Rinse under cold water and drain.

❧   In a small bowl, mix the garlic and salt. Add the shallots, oil, horseradish sauce and vinegar, and whisk to mix.

❧   Use a sharp knife to slip the skins off the beets, trim the ends and slice crosswise into rounds. Drizzle with the dressing and serve.

Tip
These beets taste best if you dress them when they are warm. Serve right away, or let them marinate in the fridge for up to a day.

Braised Napa Cabbage

When Chinese napa cabbage is slowly braised, it's transformed into a silken mass of deliciousness. This easy dish requires the biggest frying pan or wok you can find. Don't let the mountain of cabbage worry you when you start cooking – It will reduce to a quarter of its original size.

Serves 4

2 lb	Chinese napa cabbage	1 kg
2 tbsp	vegetable oil	25 mL
2	green onions, chopped	2
1	garlic, chopped	1
1-inch	fresh ginger, peeled and grated	2.5 cm
¼ cup	chicken or vegetable stock	50 mL
½ lb	fresh mushrooms, sliced	250 g
¼ tsp	salt	1 mL
½ tsp	sugar	2 mL
1 tsp	sesame oil	5 mL

❧ Trim the stalk end of the cabbage and slice the whole cabbage into thirds, crosswise. Cut each third into quarters lengthwise, so that the leaves are cut into approximately 4- by 3-inch (8- by 10-cm) pieces. Break up the leaves and set aside.

❧ In a large wok or frying pan at medium high, heat the oil and stir-fry the green onions, garlic and ginger for 1 minute. Add the cabbage and stock, cover and steam for 2 minutes. Using a spatula, gently turn the cabbage so that the top leaves are at the bottom. Replace cover and steam for 2 minutes. Repeat, turning the leaves every 2 minutes and reducing the heat if required, until the cabbage has steamed for a total of 10 minutes. Remove the cover, add the mushrooms, reduce the heat to medium low and cook, uncovered, for 10 minutes, stirring occasionally. Add the salt, sugar and sesame oil. Mix thoroughly and serve.

Tip
Any type of mushroom will be tasty in this dish, but why not choose something different from the familiar button? Try, for example, cremini or shiitake mushrooms.

Brussels Sprout Salad

You can serve this salad warm or chilled. Try not to eat all the pistachios as you shell them!

Serves 4

4 cups	Brussels sprouts, trimmed and cut in half	1 L
1	pink or red grapefruit, peeled, seeds removed and sectioned	1
¼	red onion, sliced thinly	¼

Vinaigrette

1	clove garlic, crushed	1
½ tsp	salt	2 mL
⅓ cup	extra virgin olive oil	75 mL
2 tbsp	lemon juice	25 mL
2 tbsp	maple syrup	25 mL
¼ cup	shelled salted pistachios, chopped coarsely	50 mL

❧ Steam the Brussels sprouts for 3 to 5 minutes or until just tender and emerald green. Drain and pat dry with a paper towel.

❧ In a small bowl, whisk all of the vinaigrette seasonings together.

❧ In a large bowl, toss the Brussels sprouts, grapefruit and red onions with the vinaigrette. Arrange on a plate and garnish with chopped pistachios.

Buttery Chayote

I first tasted chayote in Grenada. In the Caribbean, it is served stuffed with crab or dished up in stews. It has a lovely, delicate taste, not unlike its squash cousins. This simple sauté lets chayote's flavour shine amid butter and herbs. Serve it alongside roast pork or grilled fish.

Serves 4

3	chayotes, peeled and pitted	3
2 tbsp	butter	25 mL
½ cup	chopped shallots	125 mL
2 tsp	chopped fresh rosemary	10 mL
1 tbsp	chopped parsley	15 mL
2 tbsp	cooking sherry	25 mL
	Salt	

❧ Cut the chayote into ¼-inch (6-mm) thick slices and set aside in a bowl of water. Heat the butter in a sauté pan at medium. Once melted, add the shallots and sauté for 2 minutes or until tender. Add the drained chayote slices to the pan along with the rosemary and parsley. Sauté for 2 minutes, and then add the sherry. Continue to sauté for 15 to 20 minutes at medium low. (If the pan gets too dry, add a spoonful or two of water.) When the chayote is tender, add salt to taste and serve.

Tip
Sliced chayote is as slippery as soap. As soon as you start to peel it, it oozes a transparent, harmless sticky liquid. That liquid dries like a thin surface of glue on your hands and it's not always easy to wash off, so wear gloves while you're handling it. Here's a Filipino trick I learned: first, slice the chayote lengthwise (beware – there is a thin, white flat seed in the middle) and rub the two exposed surfaces together. This little rub makes the sticky stuff come out en masse. Rinse both halves well under water, and now the task of peeling will be less sticky. Once the chayote is peeled, slice thinly and discard the white seed in the middle. Immerse sliced chayote in a bowl of water and drain when you're ready to cook with them.

Cauliflower in Curry Vinaigrette

Here's an easy way to dress up some freshly steamed cauliflower. You can serve this dish hot or cold.

Serves 4

1	head cauliflower	1
2 tbsp	chopped flat-leaf parsley	25 mL

Vinaigrette

3 tbsp	extra virgin olive oil	45 mL
1 tbsp	lemon juice	15 mL
1	clove garlic, crushed	1
1 tsp	curry powder	5 mL
1 tsp	Dijon mustard	5 mL
¼ tsp	salt	1 mL
½ tsp	sugar	2 mL
	Freshly ground black pepper	

- ❧ Cut the cauliflower into florets. Steam until tender but still crisp.
- ❧ Meanwhile, whisk all the vinaigrette ingredients in a small bowl or shake in a small jar.
- ❧ In a mixing bowl, sprinkle the cauliflower (it should still be piping hot) with parsley, toss with the vinaigrette and season with freshly ground black pepper.

Tip
This vinaigrette also works wonders with steamed yellow wax beans, zucchini or corn niblets.

GET FRESH!

Cucumber Raita

There's nothing like a cool cucumber raita to douse the fires of a hot Indian meal. But don't stop there. Raita can also double as a dip or roll it up with some smoked salmon to make a fancy, wrap sandwich.

Makes one cup

½	seedless, English cucumber, grated	½
	Salt	
½ cup	yogurt	125 mL
1 tbsp	fresh mint, shredded	15 mL
	Pinch cayenne	
	Pinch ground cumin	

❧ Put the grated cucumber in a sieve with a bowl underneath. Sprinkle liberally with salt, mix and leave to drain for 20 minutes. Squeeze out any extra juices with the back of a spoon or your hands.

❧ In a medium bowl, mix the cucumber, yogurt, mint, cayenne and cumin. Season with salt, if desired.

East-West Slaw

This colourful coleslaw surprises with a peppery finish, thanks to the presence of daikon radish. To smooth out the radish's rough edges, I've dressed this salad with an Indonesian-style peanut sauce. If you're in a rush, substitute the peanut sauce with a store-bought one.

Serves 4

Peanut Sauce
Makes 3/4 cup (200 mL)

1 tbsp	canola oil	15 mL
¼ cup	minced shallots	50 mL
1 tbsp	chopped garlic	15 mL
½ tsp	hot pepper flakes	2 mL *
2 tbsp	soy sauce	25 mL
1 tbsp	lime juice	15 mL
3 tbsp	chunky peanut butter	45 mL
3 tbsp	chicken stock or water	45 mL
¼ cup	coconut milk	50 mL
1 cup	grated daikon radish	250 mL
2 cups	grated carrots	500 mL
4 cups	shredded red cabbage	1 L
½ tsp	salt	2 mL
1 tsp	rice vinegar	5 mL
	Fresh coriander and chopped peanuts	

❦   To make the peanut sauce, in a frying pan at medium heat, heat the oil and sauté the shallots, garlic and hot pepper flakes for 3 minutes. Whisk in the soy sauce, lime juice, peanut butter, chicken stock or water, and coconut milk; simmer for 2 minutes. Transfer to a bowl and allow to cool.

❦   In a large bowl, mix together the daikon, carrots and cabbage. Add the salt and rice vinegar and toss. Add the peanut sauce and toss until thoroughly mixed. Garnish with fresh coriander and chopped peanuts and serve.

* More if you like it hot!

Fish Baked on Fennel

This is an easy, low-fat entrée that highlights the delicious chemistry between fish and fennel. You can use any type of white fish fillet in this recipe, and I particularly like it with tilapia. Serve it with Lemony Baby Artichoke Risotto (page 226) or plain white rice.

Serves 4

1	fennel bulb	1
	Juice of half a lemon	
1	onion, thinly sliced	1
3	medium carrots, sliced into matchsticks	3
4	cloves garlic, peeled	4
1 tbsp	extra virgin olive oil	15 mL
1 lb	(4 pieces) white fish fillets, such as tilapia, orange roughy, sole	500 g
	Salt, freshly ground black pepper	
½ cup	plain yogurt	125 mL
½ cup	white wine	125 mL
1 tsp	Dijon mustard	5 mL
3 tbsp	chopped flat-leaf parsley	45 mL

❧ Wash and trim the fennel bulb. Chop the fronds coarsely and reserve. Cut the fennel bulb into thin slices and set aside in a bowl of acidulated water (3 table-spoons/ 45 mL lemon juice or vinegar to 4 cups/ 1L of water) to stop browning. In a separate bowl, mix the drained fennel with onions, carrots and garlic, and toss with olive oil. Place vegetables in a 13- by 9-inch (3.5-L) baking dish and bake uncovered in a 350°F (180°C) oven for about 30 minutes or until the fennel is just tender. Toss vegetables once, halfway through cooking.

❧ Meanwhile, wash and pat dry the fillets. Season with salt and pepper. In a small bowl, whisk together the yogurt, wine and mustard. Arrange the fillets over the fennel and carrots, pour over the wine mixture, and sprinkle with fennel fronds and parsley.

❧ Bake, uncovered, another 10 to 20 minutes, or until the fish flakes (cooking time depends on how thick the fillets are).

❧ Be sure to serve each fillet with a whole garlic clove.

Tip
The wine is optional. You can substitute it with stock or clam juice.

Green Beans with Thai Roasted Chili Paste

Roasting brings out deeper, more complex flavours from hot peppers and it also mellows them a bit. This recipe, which lasts for a week in your refrigerator, makes enough paste for several stir-fries.

Serves 4

The paste

10	small, fresh hot peppers such as Thai or Serrano peppers	10*
2 tbsp	garlic, minced	25 mL
¼ cup	red onion, minced	50 mL
	Cooking spray	
2 tbsp	fish sauce	25 mL
2 tbsp	brown sugar	25 mL
1 tbsp	vegetable oil	15 mL
2 tbsp	vegetable oil	25 mL
1 lb	green beans, trimmed	500 g
2	garlic cloves, chopped	2
¼ cup	chicken or vegetable stock	50 mL
½ tsp	salt	2 mL
1–2 tsp	Thai roasted chili paste	5–10 mL

❧   Trim the stem ends off the peppers. Put the whole peppers, garlic and red onion in a piece of aluminum foil that has been sprayed with cooking spray. Fold into a flat package, securing corners and edges. Place the package directly on a medium-high burner and cook 4 minutes on each side. It's cooked when it is deep brown and very fragrant. Open up the package carefully, allowing contents to cool. Transfer to a blender. Add fish sauce, brown sugar and oil and blend into a smooth paste.

❧   Heat two tablespoons of oil in a wok or large frying pan at medium high. Add garlic and stir-fry a few seconds, then add the green beans. Stir until the wok or pan gets dry, then add the salt, stock and chili paste. Turn the heat to medium and cook, covered, stirring occassionally, for about 6 to 8 minutes or until the beans are tender. Serve.

Tip
The paste will crackle and smell wonderful while cooking. It helps to take the package off the burner and open it up very carefully once or twice to make sure it's not burning and to also stir up the contents for more even cooking.

* You'll find these at Asian, Latin American or specialty foodstores.

Jicama and Snow Pea Toss

Serves 2

1 tbsp	canola oil	15 mL
2	green onions, chopped	2
2 cups	jicama matchsticks	500 mL
1 ½ cups	snow peas	350 mL
¼ tsp	salt	1 mL
	Pinch white pepper	
½ tsp	sugar	2 mL
½ tsp	sesame oil (optional)	2 mL

❥ Heat a wok or frying pan to high and add the oil. Stir-fry green onions for 30 seconds. Add the jicama, snow peas, salt, pepper and sugar, and stir-fry at medium high for 3 to 5 minutes or until the snow peas are tender. Drizzle with sesame oil and serve.

Tips

To prepare the jicama, cut it in half, peel off the skin and remove the layer of fibre directly under the skin, too. Slice the jicama into ¼-inch (6-mm) thick slices. Pile the slices on top of each other and cut into matchsticks, about ¼ inch (6 mm) wide. Reserve the julienned jicama in a bowl of water.

To prepare the snow peas, remove the small stem end and pull it like a thread along the back of the snow pea. Leave the snow pea whole.

It's best to use a Teflon-coated or stainless steel pan for this dish, as the jicama turns grey in a carbon or cast-iron pan.

Lemony Baby Artichoke Risotto

Celebrate artichoke season (spring and fall) with this dish. I like to use baby arti-
chokes – which are a catch if you can find them – since you don't have to remove
their chokes. But feel free to substitute globe artichokes, instead. You'll need
about three large ones.

Serves 4

12	baby artichokes (or 3 globe artichokes)	12
1	lemon	1
2 ½ cups	chicken stock	625 mL
1 cup	white wine	250 mL
1 tbsp	butter	15 mL
1 tbsp	extra virgin olive oil	15 mL
2	cloves garlic, chopped	2
1 cup	arborio rice	250 mL
3 tbsp	chopped flat-leaf parsley	45 mL
3	green onions, chopped	3
	Zest of half a lemon	
⅓–¼ cup	freshly grated Parmigiano-Reggiano	75–50 mL
	Freshly ground black pepper	
½ tsp	salt	2 mL

❧ Clean and trim artichokes. Slice baby artichokes into quarters or globe artichokes into eighths. (Have a large bowl of water containing the juice of one lemon at
your side. Artichokes brown quickly when cut, so work quickly and immerse sliced
artichokes in acidulated water as soon as possible.)

❧ In a medium saucepan add stock and wine and bring to a boil. Reduce the
heat to low.

❧ In a large, heavy-bottomed saucepan melt the butter and olive oil at medium
low heat. Add the garlic and drained artichokes and sauté for 3 to 5 minutes or until
tender. Add the rice, parsley, green onions and lemon zest. Stir to coat and sauté until
a white dot appears in the middle of most of the grains of rice (about 2 to 3 minutes). Set your timer to 20 minutes and add a ladle full of the the hot stock and wine
mixture, stirring all the while. Once the liquid is absorbed, add another ladle full.
Stand by your rice until the liquid is all gone or your timer goes off, which should
happen at about the same time – the timer's there to pace you.

❧ Once all the liquid has been absorbed, stir in the Parmigiano-Reggiano and
black pepper, and season with salt.

❧ Serve immediately.

Little Leek Bundles

Leeks get no respect in most kitchens. Usually they're relegated to soups and casseroles but they never get starring roles. Try dressing them up the French way and everyone will ask for an encore.

Serves 4

3	large leeks	3
½ cup	chicken stock	125 mL
½ cup	half-and-half cream	125 mL
1 tsp	dried tarragon	5 mL
¼–½ cup	grated Gruyère	50–125 mL
	Freshly ground black pepper	

❧ Trim the leeks very carefully, slicing off just the roots so as to leave as much of the tough end as possible, and cutting off the dark green ends. (The result should be pieces from 5 to 8 inches/12.5 to 20 cm long, depending on the size of the leeks.) Cut each leek into quarters, lengthwise. Wash very carefully, fanning the leek from the root end out.

❧ Tie a piece of kitchen string around each leek bundle. Arrange in an 11- by 7-inch (2-L) baking dish. The leeks should fit snugly inside the dish.

❧ In a small bowl, mix together the stock, cream and tarragon. Pour over the leeks. Bake, uncovered, in a 350°F (180°C) oven for 45 minutes or until the leeks are tender. Remove from the oven, snip off and discard the strings, sprinkle with Gruyère and place under the broiler for about 3 minutes or until golden brown and bubbling. Serve with freshly ground black pepper.

Tip

These little bundles look so attractive tied up that you may be reluctant to untie them before serving. Try substituting chives for the kitchen string for a pretty, edible string, perfect for entertaining.

Okra in a Tomato Curry Sauce

This easy dish serves up crisp pods of okra bathed in a spicy, alluring sauce. Serve it on a bed of rice with grilled fish or meat. Or go vegetarian with a sidecar of cucumber raita and warmed pita bread. If you can't find black mustard seeds, use yellow. In a pinch, you can even use mustard powder!

Serves 4

2 tbsp	canola oil	25 mL
2 tsp	black mustard seeds	10 mL
1 tsp	cumin seeds	5 mL
1 cup	thinly sliced onions	250 mL
2 tsp	grated fresh ginger	10 mL
1 tbsp	chopped garlic	15 mL
1	jalapeño pepper, minced	1 *
2 cups	chopped fresh or canned tomatoes	500 mL
1–2 tsp	sugar	5–10 mL
3 tbsp	lemon or lime juice	45 mL
1 tsp	curry powder	5 mL
1 lb	okra	500 g
	Salt and pepper	
	Fresh coriander	

❧ Heat a large frying pan to medium high and add the oil. Toss in black mustard and cumin seeds, stirring constantly to prevent burning. Once the seeds start to pop (in a minute or so) reduce heat to medium low and add the onions, ginger, garlic and jalapeño. Cook until the onions turn golden brown, stirring occasionally, about 10 to 15 minutes.

❧ Add the tomatoes, sugar, lemon or lime juice and curry powder. Bring to a boil and add the okra. Braise the okra in the curry mixture, with the lid off, for about 10 to 12 minutes or until the okra is slightly floppy and can be pierced with a fork.

❧ Season with salt and pepper. Transfer to a serving dish and garnish with coriander.

* You can substitute 1/4 to 1/2 tsp (1 to 2 mL) cayenne powder or hot pepper flakes to taste for the jalapeño if you prefer.

Orecchiette with Swiss Chard and Goat Cheese

In Italy, "small ear" pasta (pronounced oh-reh-K' YEH-teh) is served with turnip tops and anchovies. My variation is sweeter with Swiss chard, but if you prefer it slightly bitter, go traditional with turnip tops or try escarole or rapini.

Serves 4

¼ cup	golden raisins	50 mL
3 tbsp	pine nuts	45 mL
1 tbsp	extra virgin olive oil	15 mL
3	cloves garlic, chopped	3
1	onion, chopped	1
1 lb	Swiss chard, stems and leaves separated, chopped	500 g
½ cup	chicken stock	125 mL
½ cup	white wine	125 mL
4 oz	goat cheese, crumbled	113 g
1 lb	orecchiette	500 g
	Freshly grated Parmigiano-Reggiano	
	Salt	
	Freshly ground black pepper	

❤ Soak raisins in hot water for 10 minutes, drain and set aside. Toast pine nuts in a dry frying pan on medium-high heat for 3 to 5 minutes or until golden, and set aside. Heat oil in a nonstick frying pan and sauté garlic and onions until fragrant. Add Swiss chard stems and sauté for a few minutes. Add leaves, stock and wine. Cook until the chard is fully wilted. Sprinkle goat cheese and raisins on top and stir until dissolved and fully mixed. Keep warm.

❤ Meanwhile, cook orecchiette in boiling salted water until al dente. Drain, and return to the pot or place in a warmed serving bowl. Add Swiss chard sauce and toss. Sprinkle with Parmigiano-Reggiano cheese. Season with salt and pepper, and serve garnished with toasted pine nuts.

Tip
Ruby Red chard tastes the same as regular Swiss chard, but it bleeds pink juice and doesn't give the right colour to this dish.

Parsnip Kebabs

These are fun as appetizers, or as a side dish at a summer barbecue. Kids happen to like these, too, especially if they're involved in making them.

Serves 3, or 6 as a side dish

3	parsnips, peeled	3
1	apple, peeled, cored and cut into 1-½-inch (4-cm) cubes	1
¼	red onion, cut into ½-inch (1-cm) thick slices	¼
10	cherry tomatoes	10
3	mushrooms, thickly sliced	3
2 tbsp	extra virgin olive oil	25 mL

Dip

½ cup	yogurt	125 mL
1 tbsp	mango chutney	15 mL
¼ tsp	cumin powder	1 mL
	Salt	
	Freshly ground black pepper	

- Soak 6 wooden skewers in water for 1 hour.
- Steam parsnips for 3 minutes, or until tender. Remove from steamer and, once cool, cut into 1-½-inch (4-cm) pieces. Thread the fruits and vegetables on to a skewer, alternating the colours so it looks appealing, taking care to distribute the pieces evenly. Repeat with the remaining skewers. Baste the kebabs with olive oil.
- Heat a grill pan or a barbecue to medium high. Grill the kebabs, turning and basting regularly until well browned and tender (about 15 minutes).
- While the kebabs cook, mix the dip ingredients in a small bowl and season with salt and pepper to taste.
- Serve hot off the grill with dip.

Pesto Potatoes Gratin

Here's a rich and creamy, Italian version of scalloped potatoes. Just a dollop of pesto and some grated Asiago bring these taters to new heights. Try it with a roast chicken dinner or prepare it a day ahead and use it for entertaining.

Serves 6

2	cloves garlic	2
4	large Yukon Gold potatoes, washed, peeled and halved	1 kg
2	bay leaves	2
1 tbsp	extra virgin olive oil	15 mL
⅔ cup	sliced shallots	150 mL
1 cup	grated Asiago cheese	250 mL
1 cup	half-and-half cream	250 mL
1 tbsp	basil pesto	15 mL
½ tsp	salt	2 mL
	Freshly ground black pepper	

❦ With the broad side of a large knife, smash unpeeled garlic cloves, and remove skin. Put the garlic, potatoes and bay leaves in a pot filled with water. Bring to a boil, covered, and then simmer until just tender (about 10 to 15 minutes). Drain, discard bay leaves and garlic, and rinse with cold water. Cut potatoes into slices ⅛-inch (3-mm) thick.

❦ Meanwhile, heat oil in a sauté pan and fry the shallots at medium low until golden and crisp. Drain on a paper towel.

❦ Arrange the potato slices in a greased 13- by 9-inch (3.5-L) baking dish. Sprinkle the shallots on top, tucking some under a few of the potato slices. Sprinkle on an even layer of cheese. In a measuring cup, mix together the cream, pesto and salt, and pour over the potatoes.

❦ Bake, uncovered, in a 350°F (180°C) oven for 30 minutes. Place under the broiler for 3 minutes to brown the top. Season with freshly ground black pepper just before serving.

Tip
To reduce fat, substitute 2 per cent evaporated milk for the cream.

Portoburgers

This is the kind of veggie burger that even carnivores can sink their teeth into – it's meaty, juicy and full of flavour. I like to serve Portoburgers on big slices of focaccia to make them even more special.

Serves 2

1	head radicchio	1
½	red onion	½
	Extra virgin olive oil	
2	large portobello mushrooms, stems removed	2
2	slices Swiss cheese	2
	Two hamburger buns or focaccia	
	Tahini sauce (see page 238)	

❧ Don't trim the core off the radicchio or onion – it holds things together while grilling. If you have a mesh tray for grilling vegetables, slice radicchio and onions into wedges and baste with olive oil. If not, cut the radicchio in half, and baste it and the onion half with olive oil.

❧ At high heat, grill the radicchio, then the onions, then the mushrooms, adding each new ingredient at 5-minute intervals and turning each at least once halfway through cooking. Remove the radicchio and onions and set aside. Put the cheese on the mushrooms and grill 2 more minutes. Place the buns (or focaccia) on the grill. When the bread is grilled and the cheese melted on the mushrooms, remove and assemble each sandwich, slicing the radicchio and onion if necessary. Drizzle the veggies liberally with tahini sauce and serve.

Tip

Try topping your portoburger with roasted red pepper, grilled eggplant strips, a dab of tapenade or a slathering of home-made mayonnaise. Your jaw's the limit!

Rapini Sautéed with Tangerines

The bitter bite of rapini is tempered by the sweet addition of tangerines in this dish. To round out the flavour, I've added garlic and anchovies. Due to the latter ingredient, think twice before you add any salt to this.

Serves 4

1	big bunch rapini	1
2 tbsp	extra virgin olive oil	25 mL
2	cloves garlic, minced	2
4	anchovy fillets, minced	4
2	seedless tangerines, peeled and sectioned	2

❧ Wash the rapini well and trim the ends. Cut into pieces approximately 2 inches (5 cm) long. Steam for 3 to 5 minutes at a rapid boil until tender. Drain, rinse with cold water and drain again.

❧ Heat a sauté pan to medium high, add oil and garlic, and sauté until the garlic turns golden. Add the anchovies. Sauté, mixing garlic and anchovies together. Add drained rapini and tangerine sections, and sauté until heated through. Serve.

Tip
Mandarins, tangerines or oranges work just as well in this dish.

Roasted Sweet Potato Slivers

This dish was inspired on a Thanksgiving weekend several years ago when I was torn between making sweet potatoes or pumpkin pie. There was no time for both, so the sweet potatoes won . . . but the spicing is distinctly like pumpkin.

Serves 4 to 6

2 lb	(4 medium) sweet potatoes, peeled, cut into slices ¼-inch (6-mm) thick	1 kg
1	Spanish onion, thinly sliced	1
3 tbsp	canola oil	45 mL
½ tsp	cinnamon	2 mL
½ tsp	ground ginger	2 mL
¼ tsp	ground nutmeg	1 mL
2 tbsp	maple syrup	25 mL
	Salt	
	Freshly ground black pepper	

❧ In a large bowl, toss together the potato and onion slices, oil, cinnamon, ginger, nutmeg and maple syrup until evenly coated.

❧ Spread the potato mixture in a single layer over 2 oiled baking sheets. Season with salt and freshly ground black pepper to taste. Bake at 400°F (200°C) for 30 minutes or until golden brown. Halfway through, turn them over with a spatula. Serve.

Tips

These potatoes are a crowd pleaser. That's why this recipe is so large. Cut it in half if you're serving only 2 or 3 people for dinner.

Using parchment paper instead of an oiled baking sheet is easier, but it results in potatoes that are not quite as crunchy and crisp.

Spaghettini with Salmon and Asparagus in Black Bean Sauce

Here's an East-West dish of pasta tossed with Chinese-style steamed fish. I find that rainbow trout works just as well as salmon in this recipe.

Serves 4

1 lb	salmon fillet, washed and patted dry	500 g
1 inch	fresh ginger, peeled and cut into matchsticks	2.5 cm
1	green onion, trimmed, sliced into thin, lengthwise strips	1
1 tsp	cooking sherry	5 mL
2 tsp	sesame oil	10 mL
3 tbsp	black bean and garlic sauce	45 mL
1 lb	spaghettini	500 g
	Salt	
2	carrots, sliced into 3-inch (8-cm) long matchsticks	2
1	bunch asparagus, ends snapped, cut on diagonal in 3-inch (8-cm) long pieces	1
1 tbsp	olive oil	15 mL
	Fresh coriander, coarsely chopped	

❦   In a shallow heat-proof bowl, place the fish and scatter ginger and green onions on top. In a separate, small bowl, mix together the sherry, 1 teaspoon (5 mL) of sesame oil and 2 tablespoons (30 mL) of black bean and garlic sauce, and pour over the fish. In a steamer, steam fish for 8 to 10 minutes or until done.

❦   Meanwhile, in a large pot of rapidly boiling salted water, cook the spaghettini for 6 minutes. Add the carrots and asparagus and cook another 2 minutes or until the noodles and veggies are *al dente*. Drain and return to pot. Toss with olive oil, 1 teaspoon (5 mL) sesame oil and 1 tablespoon (15 mL) black bean and garlic sauce. Remove the skin from the fish and use a fork to break up the fish into bite-size pieces. Toss the salmon pieces and cooking juices with the pasta. Serve in individual bowls, garnished with fresh coriander.

Tips
Try sake, scotch or white wine as a substitute for the cooking sherry in this recipe.

You can use a bamboo steamer to steam the fish, or put the dish on a cake rack in the bottom of a covered wok filled with water until it touches the rack.

Sukhothai Squash Soup

Sukhothai is an ancient Thai city littered with decaying pagodas and half-standing temples. While this is not a Thai recipe, the name stuck when I came up with this combination. Don't let the Thai curry paste stop you from trying this. You can substitute curry powder in a pinch.

Serves 4

1	butternut squash	1
1 tbsp	vegetable oil	15 mL
1	medium red onion, thinly sliced	1
1 tbsp	grated fresh ginger	15 mL
2 tsp	Thai red curry paste	10 mL
4 cups	chicken stock	1 L
2	ripe pears, peeled and chopped	2
1 tsp	salt	5 mL
2 tsp	brown sugar	10 mL
14 oz	low-fat or regular coconut milk	398 mL
	Fresh coriander, chopped	

❧ Cut the squash in half, scoop out the seeds and place cut-side down on an oiled baking sheet. Bake at 375°F (190°C) until tender (about 50 minutes.). Once it is cool enough to handle, scoop out the flesh and set aside.

❧ Heat a large soup pot to medium, add the oil and sauté the red onion until tender. Add the ginger and curry paste, and sauté 1 minute, stirring constantly. Add the squash, stock, pears, salt and sugar, bring to a boil and simmer for 15 minutes. In a blender or food processor, purée in batches. Return to soup pot, bring to a simmer and stir in the coconut milk. Cook until thoroughly heated. Serve garnished with coriander.

Tip
You can bake the squash ahead of time, and keep it wrapped in the fridge until you're ready to use it.

Sweet Onion and Gorgonzola Pizza

When your taste buds discover this savoury meeting of sharp, blue cheese with candy-sweet onions, you won't miss the tomato sauce in this pizza. It's a rich mouthful best enjoyed in small amounts. Serve it as an appetizer or as a light lunch with a salad.

Makes 1 large or 2 small (8-inch/20-cm) pizzas

1 tbsp	extra virgin olive oil	15 mL
2	large sweet onions	2
	(Vidalia, Sweet 1015 or Walla-Walla), thinly sliced	
¼ cup	balsamic vinegar	50 mL
¼ cup	sugar	50 mL
¼ tsp	salt	1 mL
	Extra virgin olive oil	
1 large	Pizza crust (or 2 small)	1 large
4 tsp	fresh sage, chopped	20 mL
2 tbsp	pine nuts	25 mL
8 oz	gorgonzola cheese, crumbled	225 g

❧   Heat the oil in a large sauté pan at medium high and sauté onions for 10 to 12 minutes, until the onions start to turn golden. Add the vinegar and sugar, reduce heat to medium and cook for about 20 minutes, stirring occasionally, until most of the liquid is absorbed. Remove from heat, stir in salt and let cool.

❧   On a baking sheet, brush the pizza crust lightly with oil and spread the onions, sage, pine nuts and cheese evenly on top. Bake at 400°F (200°C) for 7 to 10 minutes, until the cheese is bubbling and the crust is golden. Serve immediately.

Tip
If you want to make 2 small pizzas, try using flour tortillas or pita bread.

Tahini Sauce

This rich sauce is the finishing touch on Portoburgers (see page 232), but it also adds a nutty, slightly spicy taste to grilled eggplant, zucchini, sweet peppers, fennel, tomatoes or green beans. You can even use it as a salad dressing.

Makes 1 cup

½ cup	tahini paste	125 mL
3 tbsp	lemon juice	45 mL
¼–⅓ cup	water	50-80 mL
2	cloves garlic, crushed	2
½ tsp	salt	2 mL
¼ tsp	paprika	1 mL
	Cayenne pepper to taste	

❧ Put the tahini paste in a small bowl and use a fork or small whisk to blend in the lemon juice gradually. Blend in a spoonful of water and repeat until mixture is the desired consistency. Add the garlic, salt, paprika and cayenne pepper.

Tip
This sauce can be doubled and stored in your fridge in an air-tight container for several weeks.

Three Butters

All you need is these three butters in your fridge to cast a little magic over any steamed vegetable. Try them on green beans, wilted spinach or fresh corn on the cob. They add a little elegance and lots of flavour, and last in the fridge for several weeks.

Makes 3 logs

Southwest Butter

¼ cup	unsalted butter, at room temperature (half a stick)	50 mL
1 tbsp	chopped fresh coriander	15 mL
½	fresh hot pepper, minced	½
2 tsp	lime juice	10 mL
	Salt	

Roasted Garlic Butter

¼ cup	unsalted butter, at room temperature (half a stick)	50 mL
4	cloves roasted garlic (see page 154)	4
10	leaves fresh basil, chopped	10
	Salt and pepper	

Lemony Herb Butter

¼ cup	unsalted butter, at room temperature (half a stick)	50 mL
2 tbsp	flat-leaf parsley, chopped	30 mL
½ tsp	lemon zest	2 mL
1	green onion, finely chopped	1
	Salt and pepper	

❧ Each butter is made the same way: in a small bowl, mix together all the ingredients with a fork. Put the butter on a piece of plastic wrap and roll into a log. Refrigerate until hard.

Tip

Southwest Butter is particularly good on fresh corn. Roasted Garlic Butter is wonderful on potatoes, broccoli, mushrooms and wax beans. Try Lemony Herb Butter on zucchini, spinach, okra or cauliflower.

Tokyo Beet Greens

The Japanese often steam their greens until they are wilted, dress them in soy sauce and sesame seeds, and enjoy them chilled or at room temperature. This recipe is designed for the tops of a beet bunch. It's quick and simple, and produces a lovely, dainty dish of greens.

Serves 2

1	bunch beet greens, washed well, stems removed	1
1 tbsp	soy sauce	15 mL
1 tsp	rice vinegar	5 mL
¼ tsp	sugar	1 mL
½ tsp	sesame oil	2 mL
	Toasted sesame seeds	

❧ Slice leaves lengthwise, into thirds. Steam until wilted. Drain well in a colander, pressing down with the back of a spoon to squeeze out any extra moisture. Set aside on a small serving plate.

❧ In a small bowl, mix together soy sauce, rice vinegar, sugar and sesame oil. Drizzle over the greens and sprinkle with toasted sesame seeds. Serve at room temperature or chilled.

Tip
Use the greens cut from a fresh bunch of beets. Or try spinach, Swiss chard or mustard greens. These greens come in larger bunches than the ones that come with beets, so double the recipe.

Tricolour Pepper Pasta

*While you can serve this pasta hot off the stove, I suggest trying it at room tempera-
ture. All it needs is a 10-minute rest and – funnily enough – the flavours intensify as
the temperature cools. Try it as an entrée with a green salad, or bring it along to a
potluck. With all this colour, it can't help but be a pretty dish.*

Serves 4

2 tbsp	extra virgin olive oil	25 mL
1	Vidalia or Spanish onion, thinly sliced	1
2	cloves garlic, chopped	2
1	yellow sweet pepper, thinly sliced	1
1	red sweet pepper, thinly sliced	1
1	orange sweet pepper, thinly sliced	1
1 tbsp	balsamic vinegar	15 mL
1 tsp	salt	5 mL
½ cup	chicken stock or white wine	125 mL
¼ cup	fresh basil, chopped	50 mL
¼ cup	fresh mint, chopped	50 mL
¾ lb	fusilli pasta	375 g
¼–½ cup	freshly ground Parmigiano-Reggiano	50–125 mL
	Zest of one lemon	
20	black olives, pitted and chopped coarsely	20
	Freshly ground black pepper	

❧ In a large frying pan, heat oil at medium and add onions, garlic and peppers.
Reduce heat to medium low and sauté for about 15 to 20 minutes or until the peppers and onions are very soft. Add the balsamic vinegar and salt, and sauté another
minute. Add the chicken stock, basil and mint, and sauté until heated through.

❧ Meanwhile, bring a large pot of salted water to boil. Cook the pasta until
al dente. Drain.

❧ In a large bowl, toss the pasta with the pepper mixture. Mix in the cheese,
lemon zest, olives and freshly ground pepper to taste. Let sit for 10 minutes before
serving.

Tips
*Be sure to use fusilli, or any twisty, curly pasta that can trap all
the different elements of this sauce in one bite.*

If you don't have any fresh mint, just double up the basil.

Vegetable Curry

*This rich, yogurt-infused dish goes well on a mound of rice. Wrap any leftovers in a
tortilla the next day for an instant roti!*

Serves 4 as a main dish, 8 as a side

2 tbsp	canola oil	25 mL
2 tsp	cumin seeds	10 mL
1	large onion, chopped	1
3	cloves garlic, chopped	3
1 inch	ginger, peeled and grated	2.5 cm
1–2	dried hot red pepper, crumbled	1–2
2 cups	diced potatoes (3 medium)	500 mL
2 cups	diced carrots (3 large)	500 mL
2 cups	chicken or vegetable stock	500 mL
3 cups	cauliflower florets	750 mL
1 tbsp	ground coriander	15 mL
1 tsp	turmeric	5 mL
¼ tsp	cardamom	1 mL
1 cup	yogurt	250 mL
	Salt	
¼ cup	roasted blanched almonds	50 mL
	Chopped fresh coriander	

❧   In a large pot, heat oil at medium high. Toss in the cumin seeds and sauté for
1 minute. Add the onion, garlic, ginger and hot pepper, reduce heat to medium low
and sauté until onions are tender.

❧   Add the potatoes and carrots, increase heat to medium and sauté for 2 minutes. Add 1 cup (250 mL) of the stock and bring to a boil. Reduce heat and simmer
gently, covered, for 10 minutes. Mix in cauliflower, coriander, turmeric and cardamom and simmer, covered, for another 5 to 10 minutes or until all the vegetables
are tender.

❧   In a medium bowl, mix yogurt with remaining stock and add to the vegetables. Cook another few minutes at low heat (to prevent the yogurt from curdling)
until everything is heated through. Season with salt to taste. Transfer to serving dish
and garnish with roasted almonds and fresh coriander.

Tip
*You can use ½ tsp (2 mL) of cayenne pepper or hot pepper
flakes instead of whole dried pepper. Use more, if you like it
hot!*

Watercress, Grapefruit and Avocado Salad

I've given this classic salad an Asian twist with a dressing of honey, soy sauce and sesame oil. It's a scrumptious combination bursting with nutrients: vitamins E and C, folate and fibre.

Serves 4

Dressing

1 tbsp	orange juice	15 mL
2 tbsp	canola oil	25 mL
1 tsp	sesame oil	5 mL
¼ tsp	freshly grated ginger	1 mL
2 tsp	honey	10 mL
½ tsp	soy sauce	2 mL
	Pinch white pepper	

1	bunch watercress, thick stalks removed	1
1	head Boston lettuce, torn	1
1	avocado, peeled and sliced	1
1	grapefruit, peeled and segmented	1
1	green onion, chopped	1
¼ cup	chopped fresh coriander	50 mL
2 tbsp	toasted sesame seeds	25 mL

- Whisk together the dressing ingredients in a small bowl.
- In a large salad bowl, combine the watercress, lettuce, avocado, grapefruit, green onion and coriander. Toss with the dressing. Garnish with sesame seeds and serve immediately.

Tips

Be sure to dry salad greens thoroughly after washing them or you'll get a soggy salad with a washed-out dressing.

Toast sesame seeds in a dry frying pan at medium-high heat, stirring regularly, for 5 minutes or until golden-brown.

Apricot Galette

I'm a bit of a coward when it comes to making pastry from scratch. So here's a simple recipe that involves frozen puff pastry, fresh apricots and a smattering of pistachios. It's easy to make and can be served hot from the oven, or cold at a picnic or summer buffet.

Serves 6 to 8

1 lb	frozen puff pastry, defrosted	500 g
1 lb	apricots	500 g
2 tbsp	lemon juice	25 mL
2 tbsp	chopped salted pistachios	25 mL
¼ cup	sugar	50 mL
1 tbsp	unsalted butter, cold	15 mL

❧ Roll the pastry out on a lightly floured piece of parchment paper until it is about ⅛-inch (3-mm) thick. Using a plate or cardboard stencil, cut out 2 circles, 6 inches (15 cm) in diameter. Remove the leftover pastry and cut the parchment paper around the pastry circles so that you can lift each one with its parchment paper lining and transfer to a baking sheet.

❧ Blanch the apricots in boiling water for 45 to 60 seconds. Use a slotted spoon to transfer them to a bowl of ice water. Once they are cool, use a sharp knife to slip the peels off. Sprinkle lemon juice over the apricots and cut in half, slice and sprinkle with lemon juice again.

❧ Leaving a ¾-inch (2-cm) margin on the outside, arrange the apricots on the pastry rounds in a pinwheel pattern. Sprinkle each galette with 1 tablespoon (15 mL) of pistachios. Brush the margin lightly with water. Sprinkle with 2 tablespoons (25 mL) of sugar over each galette. Dot each one with ½ tablespoon (8 mL) of butter.

❧ Bake in the lower third of a 375°F (180°C) oven for 45 to 50 minutes or until the pastry is golden and crisp.

Tip
This recipe is equally tasty with peaches or nectarines.

Baked Apples with Brie

When I entertain, I like to bake a round of brie with apples and walnuts stuffed beneath the pastry shell. Here's the same concept, with a bit of a twist: baked stuffed apples topped with chunks of melted brie. You'll love how the aroma of the apples fills your house while they're baking.

Serves 4

½ cup	black raisins	125 mL
¼ cup	walnuts, chopped	50 mL
¼ cup	brown sugar	50 mL
½ tsp	cinnamon	2 mL
4	apples	4
1 tbsp	butter	15 mL
1 cup	apple juice	250 mL
4 oz	brie	112 g

- In a small bowl, mix together the raisins, walnuts, sugar and cinnamon.
- To prepare the apples, slice off the top and dig out the interior, using a spoon or a melon baller to create a shell ¾ inches (2 cm) thick. Gently peel the skin off the top half of the apple shell. Then stuff each one with a quarter of the raisin mixture. Dot apples with butter and place them in a small baking dish. Pour apple juice over apples.
- Bake at 375°F (190°C) for 45 minutes, basting every 15 minutes. Remove from oven and top each apple with a 1-ounce (28-g) piece of brie. Return to oven and bake another 15 minutes or until the cheese is oozing. Serve hot.

Tip
The best apples to use for this recipe are Golden Delicious, Idared or Northern Spy.

Cold Cantaloupe Soup

This cold soup offers a refreshing start to a summer meal. It's a sweet soup gar-nished with savoury ingredients that's perfect for entertaining or just staying cool when the weather's got you wilted.

Serves 4

1 ½ lb	(1 medium) cantaloupe	750 g
½ cup	orange juice	125 mL
3 tbsp	fresh lime juice	45 mL
1 tsp	sugar	5 mL
	Pinch salt	
¼ cup	plain yogurt	50 mL
2 oz	prosciutto, sliced thinly	56 g

❤ Slice the cantaloupe into wedges, cut off the rind and chop into 1-inch pieces. Put the cantaloupe, orange juice, lime juice, sugar and salt in a food processor and whirl until smooth.

❤ Serve the soup in bowls with a tablespoon of yogurt on top, sprinkled with prosciutto threads.

Tips
The sugar is optional. If you have a perfectly ripe cantaloupe it will supply enough sweetness on its own.

Pernod gives this soup some anise-flavoured zip. Try adding just 1 tablespoon (15 mL) to the recipe.

Kiwi Jade Chutney

Kiwi – with its sweet and sour flavours – makes a fine chutney. Serve it with grilled chicken, roasted pork tenderloin or even pork chops. Try some with Indian curries, too.

Makes 2-1/2 cups (625 mL)

1 cup	black raisins	250 mL
1 tbsp	canola oil	15 mL
1	onion, chopped	1
1 inch	fresh ginger, peeled and minced	2.5 cm
1	clove garlic, chopped	1
1	stick cinnamon	1
2	whole dried peppers	2
6	firm kiwi, peeled and diced	6
½ tsp	ground nutmeg	2 mL
¼ tsp	ground cardamom	1 mL
1 tsp	curry powder	5 mL
¼ cup	brown sugar	50 mL
¼ cup	rice (or white) vinegar	50 mL
½ tsp	salt	2 mL
	Freshly ground black pepper	

❧ Soak raisins for 1 hour in water. Drain and reserve ¼ cup (50 mL) of the water. In a medium saucepan, heat oil and sauté the onions, ginger, garlic, cinnamon and dried peppers for 3 minutes. Add the remaining ingredients, including the raisin water, bring to a boil and simmer for 5 minutes. Cool and remove cinnamon stick. This chutney will keep stored in a sterile glass jar in the fridge for up to a week.

Tips

Briefly cooking this chutney prevents the kiwi from disintegrating.

Substitute 1 teaspoon (5 mL) of ground cinnamon if you don't have a stick of cinnamon handy. Just add it to the pan when you add the other spices.

Mango Salsa

This salsa offers up a quartet of flavours: sweet, sour, salty and hot. It's a cinch to make and, like most salsas, the flavours intensify if you let it sit in the fridge for a few hours before serving. Mango salsa is the perfect counterpoint to grilled poultry or fish, Tex-Mex dishes or even curry served on rice. Be sure to use fully ripe mangoes.

Serves 4

2	ripe mangoes, peeled and diced into ½-inch (1-cm) cubes	2
½ cup	sliced red onion	125 mL
1	garlic clove, crushed	1
¼ cup	fresh coriander, chopped	50 mL
	Juice of 1-½ limes	
2	sweet red peppers, roasted	2
1	large dried hot pepper, dry-roasted	1
	Salt	

❧ In a non-metallic mixing bowl, add the mangoes, red onion, garlic, fresh coriander and lime juice. Dice red peppers and add to mixture. Chop dried hot pepper and add. Salt to taste. Refrigerate for at least 1 hour before serving.

Tips

If you don't have time to roast a sweet red pepper, bottled roasted pepper works fine, too. Or, you can substitute 2 roasted peppers with 1 fresh sweet red pepper.

Dry-roasting a hot pepper brings out richer flavours. Plus, it's simple to do. Either roast it in a dry frying pan at medium heat for a few minutes or until it turns dark brown, or roast it in your toaster oven. It's easy to burn a dried hot pepper, so watch it carefully.

You can use fresh peaches or papaya instead of mango.

GET FRESH!

Savoury Nectarine and Chicken Stir-Fry

Not everyone can take the culinary leap from fruit as a sweet to fruit as a savoury entrée. But if you're adventurous and enjoy fruit salsas on grilled chicken, you're likely to enjoy this novel stir-fry. Serve it over steamed white rice for a simple, one-wok meal.

Serves 2

Marinade

2 tbsp	soy sauce	25 mL
1 tbsp	sherry *or* Chinese cooking wine	15 mL
2 tsp	corn starch	10 mL
½ lb	chicken breast, sliced into ¼-inch (6-mm) strips	225 g
2 tbsp	canola oil	25 mL
1 inch	ginger, peeled and minced	2.5 cm
2	cloves garlic, chopped	2
2	green onions, chopped	2
4	nectarines	4
1	sweet red pepper, sliced thinly	1
1	jalapeño, minced	1
3 tbsp	orange juice	45 mL
1 tbsp	soy sauce	15 mL
½ tsp	sesame oil	2 mL

❧ Mix together the marinade ingredients and marinate the chicken for at least 10 minutes.

❧ In a wok or large frying pan at high, heat 1 tablespoon (15 mL) of oil. Add the ginger, garlic and green onions, and stir-fry for about 30 seconds. Add the marinated chicken and stir-fry until it is no longer pink. Remove from wok and set aside. Rinse out wok well.

❧ Cut the nectarines into halves and then slices. In the wok at high, heat the remaining oil, and add the red and jalapeño peppers; stir-fry until soft. Add the chicken mixture and nectarines, and stir-fry until heated through. Add the orange juice, soy sauce and sesame oil and stir-fry for 1 more minute. Serve.

Strawberry, Kiwi and Banana Smoothie

Here's nutrition in a glass. Chock full of antioxidants and calcium, this smoothie makes a good breakfast-on-the-run for any busy person. Kids happen to like it, too – but don't tell them it's good for them!

Makes 4 cups (1 L)

4	strawberries, hulled and sliced	4
1	banana, peeled and sliced	1
1	kiwi, peeled and sliced	1
1 cup	silken tofu *or* plain yogurt	250 mL
¼ tsp	vanilla	1 mL
2 tbsp	honey	25 mL
1 cup	orange juice	250 mL
6	ice cubes	6

❥ Put all the ingredients in a blender except the ice cubes. Blend until smooth. Add the ice and blend again.

Tips

If you use tofu, this makes a thick shake. Feel free to thin it with water.

You can substitute blueberries or raspberries for the strawberries.

You can freeze the smoothie and serve it as a frozen dessert.

Papaya and Orange Salad

Lime is a papaya's best friend. Here's a recipe that teams these two buddies in a yummy, fruity green salad. If you can't find any mesclun greens, Boston lettuce can be used instead.

Serves 4

Dressing

3 tbsp	canola oil	45 mL
3 tbsp	lime juice	45 mL
½ tsp	sugar	2 mL
¼ tsp	salt	1 mL
¼ tsp	hot pepper flakes	1 mL
2 tbsp	chopped fresh chives	25 mL
2 tbsp	chopped fresh coriander	25 mL
½–¾ lb	papaya	225–340 g
1	navel orange	1
½ lb	mesclun salad greens	225 g
½	English cucumber, sliced	½
½	red onion, sliced	½

❧ In a small bowl, whisk together dressing ingredients. Add more hot pepper flakes if you like it hot!

❧ Cut the papaya in half, lengthwise, scoop out the seeds and peel. Cut into slices ¼-inch (6-mm) thick. Peel the orange, making sure to remove all of the white pith. Break the orange in half, then slice each half into ¼-inch (6-mm) thick half moons.

❧ Toss the salad greens with half of the salad dressing. Arrange the greens on 4 individual salad plates, and arrange the cucumbers, red onions, papaya and orange slices on top. Drizzle the remaining dressing on the papaya and orange slices. Serve.

Poached Rosemary Pears

Here's a beautiful dish that shows off a pear's voluptuous curves. Drizzle them with chocolate sauce or nestle them up against some vanilla ice cream.

Serves 4

1¼ cup	sugar	300 mL
2 tsp	chopped fresh rosemary	10 mL
	Zest of one lemon	
	One quarter-size slice of fresh ginger	
1 tbsp	balsamic vinegar	15 mL
4	firm cooking pears	4

❧   In a large measuring cup or bowl, add enough water to the sugar to make 4 cups (1 L). Transfer to a medium saucepan and bring to a boil, stirring occasionally. Reduce to a simmer and stir gently until all the sugar dissolves. Add rosemary, lemon zest, ginger and balsamic vinegar and let simmer.

❧   Peel each pear, leaving the stem on, and slip it into the simmering liquid. Poach pears gently, turning them occasionally, for 20 minutes or until a knife slides easily in and out of a pear.

❧   Remove pears carefully from liquid and let cool. Simmer the liquid until half remains and reserve. When the pears are cool enough to handle, slice about ¼ inch (6 mm) from the bottom of each one so it can stand up straight.

❧   Arrange pears in a shallow bowl, pour over the liquid and chill before serving. Serve, garnished with a curled lemon peel slice or sprig of fresh rosemary.

Tips

This dish can be made a day ahead, and stored in the refrigerator.

The best pears for poaching are Bartlett, Anjou or Bosc.

Watermelon Granita

Here's an easy way to dress up a watermelon and eat it with panache. Serve this dish in chilled parfait glasses garnished with a sprig of fresh mint, delicate shreds of crystallized ginger or fresh, plump berries. It also tastes fine on vanilla ice cream.

Serves 6

3 lbs	watermelon, preferably seedless	1.5 kg
1 inch	fresh ginger	2.5 cm
¼ cup	lime juice	50 mL
½ cup	extra fine sugar	125 mL

❧ Trim the rind off the watermelon and slice into chunks. Purée in a blender or food processor, and pour into a sieve placed over a large bowl to remove any seeds.

❧ Peel the ginger and grate it finely. Put the grated ginger in a small sieve placed over a bowl and use a spoon to press down on the grated ginger. Add 1 teaspoon (5 mL) of ginger juice to the watermelon purée, along with the lime juice and sugar. Mix until the sugar is dissolved.

❧ Pour the mixture into a large shallow container appropriate for freezing. Freeze, uncovered, until the surface starts to solidify (which can take around an hour). Run a fork along the surface to create a coarse, crystallized texture. Repeat every 20 minutes until the watermelon is completely frozen. Store in a closed container in the freezer.

❧ To serve, scrape the granita into parfait glasses and serve immediately.

Tips

This recipe can take up to 4 hours to freeze. If you don't have time to scrape it several times, freeze it in ice cube trays. Before serving, use the food processor to create a sorbet texture rather than a granular granita.

You can spike this granita with 2 tablespoons (25 mL) of vodka, if desired!

Index